NAVIGATING THE *SHOCK* OF PARENTHOOD

Warty Truths And Modern Practicalities

-From A Mom With Twins

Kathleen A. Cawley, PA-C

Hi Judy!
Thanks for reading my book.
I hope you enjoy the feminist tones!
Take Care
Kathleen

NAVIGATING THE SHOCK OF PARENTHOOD
Warty Truths And Modern Practicalities
-From A Mom With Twins

Copyright © 2022 by Kathleen A. Cawley, PA-C

ISBNs:
979-8-9871068-0-8 (print)
979-8-9871068-1-5 (eBook)

Library of Congress Control Number: 2022919531

Published by: Twin Willow Press
California, USA

Book formatting by Kimberly Martin of Jera Publishing
Cover Design by John Edgar Harris

Although I am a physician assistant, I am not your physician assistant. Reading this book does not create a patient provider relationship between us. This book is not intended as a substitute for the medical advice of physicians. The reader should consult a physician in matters relating to their health and their children's health particularly with respect to any symptoms that may require diagnosis or medical attention.

While the author has made every effort to provide accurate telephone numbers, internet addresses, and other contact information at the time of publication, the author does not assume responsibility for errors or changes that may occur after publication. Further, the author does not have control over nor assume responsibility for the content of third party websites mentioned in this book. References to trademarks in no way indicates any relationship with or endorsement by the trademark owner.

What I Am Grateful For

I'm grateful for my husband who is an active, involved, devoted, and loving Dad. And for how he gets me to lighten up, and just go with the flow when I wind up getting too rigid with the kids. And for how well he does "goofy" and "playing the boob" with the kids. And for how he gets them all riled up and happy and screaming just before bed.

I'm grateful for my Mom who comes over regularly and showers my kids with love and attention. For being able to see my kids through her eyes as she enjoys watching them grow into themselves. For her endless patience with and forgiveness of my often impatient and irritating self. For getting to watch my kids joyfully scream "Grandma!" every time she comes over.

I'm grateful for two happy, vivacious, spirited kids whose giggles are contagious and who name their "pet" flies and keep spiders in Tupperware. For these kids, who have forced me to grow in unexpected ways, and who show me the world through fresh and innocent eyes.

Invictus
By William Ernest Henley

Out of the night that covers me,
  Black as the pit from pole to pole,
I thank whatever gods may be
  For my unconquerable soul.

In the fell clutch of circumstance
  I have not winced nor cried aloud.
Under the bludgeoning's of chance
  My head is bloody, but unbowed.

Beyond this place of wrath and tears
  Looms but the Horror of the shade,
And yet the menace of the years
  Finds, and shall find, me unafraid.

It matters not how strait the gate,
  How charged with punishments the scroll,
I am the master of my fate:
  I am the captain of my soul.

William Ernest Henley, 1875.

....Yeah, riiiight! That's all well and good until the kids show up!
Then "the menace of the years" finds me afraid, very afraid!
And "master of my fate!?" ha, ha, ha! hee, hee, hee...so funny!
But, "Wrath and tears?" Yeah, I get that part.

Kathleen Cawley, 2022.

Contents

Foreword

Parenthood arrived late and hard for me. Married at 39, we soon discovered my husband had prostate cancer. It was advanced for his age. After the desperate banking of sperm, we got him through major surgery, and dodged the proverbial bullet. He was cured.

We both wanted children, but we had frozen sperm and old eggs. Over the next five years, I went through six rounds of intrauterine insemination (IUI), two breast biopsies, four surgeries to revise a uterine septum, three hysterosalpingograms (HSGs) (Hate those!), two miscarriages, five rounds of invitro fertilization (IVF), three egg donors, and a stroke. It was kind of a rough time. Then I had a very scary, high risk, medically complicated, misery inducing twin pregnancy at the age of forty-five.

I'm a physician assistant. I cared for families and children for most of twenty years. People trusted me with their health, their worries, their sorrows, their hopes and joys. But none of it, not the medical insight, not the shared intimacies of patients, not maturity nor the trials of life prepared me for pregnancy or parenthood. These two life experiences force great change and growth upon all of us. And that can be quite hard.

The trick with new parenthood is that we are not in this crazy adventure alone. Many parents have gone before, and they become one of the greatest communities you will ever have the honor of knowing. They will bring you laughter and perspective, blunt truths, and poop stories.

When my twins were young, and I was just a newbie parent, I relied heavily on the advice forum from a parents-of-twins group. I sought and received help and support almost daily. I was given so much shared wisdom and perspective. This was the community of parents helping parents.

As the years moved inexorably forward, I slowly found that I was now the one offering help to new and sleepless parents. To the shared wisdom of others, I added my own experience, and the diverse and varied insights of my relentless research. Typically, parenting books are about parent*ing*. The topic of parent*hood* is neglected. And, the really challenging parts of parent*hood* don't wind up in books at all. Well, I'm going to discuss as many of those silent stressors as I can. I'll throw in a bit of parenting insight just to round out the support. Hopefully, this will give you a bit of an edge in the wild and wacky game of parenthood.

Thoughts on Navigating *Covid* Parenting

If you've ever written a book while simultaneously raising kids….tee, hee, hee what a silly thing to do! But, *if* you have been so silly, *then* you'll know that time proceeds rapidly along at its own pace while you attempt to birth a book. Really. Stars will live and die. The earth will spin wildly around the sun an egregious number of times. Your babies will sprout hair from newly smelly arm pits. And, a coronavirus pandemic will blossom on earth stealing away the lives of people you love, and rendering new meaning to everything you've written over the last millennium.

As a medical professional, I knew what was coming when Covid hit. Some of it anyway. You learn about pandemics in medical school, and you learn about the inevitability of the one that's coming. But theory and lived experience are not the same thing.

Coronavirus came around when I was full-time parenting and full-time writing. I had been considering going back into patient care, but Covid prevented that. Health issues make me too high risk. So, I put my *almost* birthed book down, and didn't pick it up again for a year and a half. Not even once did I crack the book files. All my days and all my time became consumed by family care and childcare and homeschooling and helping us all mentally and physically make it through. When I finally had time to again reach for this book that I'd worked sooo hard to gestate over sooo many years, I found myself mentally exhausted. So, let's have some up-front talk about Covid and parenthood. How do we find our way through this scary, exhausting, relentless new world?

The first thing we need to acknowledge is that the burdens of the pandemic have fallen very heavily and very squarely on the shoulders of women. For many, the completely untenable burden of the first and second shift, work and motherhood, has been buried further under the third shift of teacher/ mental health worker/ risk assessor/ family survival expert. As usual, there is no extra compensation for this new and enormous burden. In fact, a pay cut or economic disaster may come along with your new duties. It's a lot to take.

You may feel a bit lost. Perhaps disillusioned. Perhaps re-evaluating your life and your priorities. Well, you're not alone. Many of us have caregiver burn-out. Many of us have anxiety burn out. Many of us have worked so hard to make life bearable for our families that we've forgotten what we ourselves need. Many of us have frazzled our brains with constant risk assessment and reassessment. Many of us are disillusioned by the failed promise of "hard work = success = happiness." Many of us feel directionless and perhaps purposeless. Or maybe we are just confused about what to do now or what to do next.

As a middle-aged woman who's been out here awhile, I can tell you that sometimes life is like this. Messy, uncomfortable, confusing, anxiety provoking, even scream inducing. Me, I like a good plan. A long term plan with steps. Right now, I ain't got no plan for nuttin' and it all feels kinda painfully uncertain.

Then, there's our kids. There they are, all needy and questioning, right in the middle of this morass of stress and strain and world-on-its-headness. It may help to remember that many kids can be quite resilient. If *you* can model adaptability, it can be a chance for them to gain great strengths. And despite the fact that Covid has divided some families, many of us have some likeminded friends and relatives that we can be grateful for. Kids need to hear us speak about these things, and so do we.

Even more important can be teaching your kids that this is a phase in life. That it will change with time. What it will change into is unknown, but then we never really know what the future holds for any of us. When we are young, we don't have the life experience of good and bad times, of waiting out or working through the tough parts. Just verbalizing this to kids may help them to see a brighter future as a possibility. (Psssst, a brighter future is possible for you too!)

Be aware, however, that some vulnerable children may spiral down and need real help. If a child was struggling with mental health issues before Covid restrictions hit, then they may move deeper into depression or anxiety. Professional help for these kids is hard to find right now, but I encourage you to seek it out if your child is in need.

Getting outdoors can be hard for some urban families, but it's often enormously helpful to everyone's mental and physical health. Even if you have high risk family and need to mask, I encourage you to take advantage of outdoor space as much as you can. Regardless of your kids ages, regardless of whether you identify as "outdoorsy" or not, the change of scenery and freedom of movement can let our stressed and contained souls breathe a bit.

It can also help to adjust expectations and embrace the certainty of uncertainty. It's likely that we will be juggling Covid risks for years to come. Hopefully, that juggle will become easier and less fraught with fear. But, if you have vulnerable family members you are trying to protect, then the constant evaluating and reassessing of risks is likely to continue for a while.

We all have Covid stories and challenges, and many parents are also juggling enormous work pressures. Unfortunately, this may be the new normal for a while. And, unfortunately, moms are probably the people most burdened with the weight of all these new decisions. Because the mental load just wasn't big enough before!

Nevertheless, we are not alone. You are not alone. Not in navigating Covid. Not in navigating parenthood. So, let's shine some light on things and see if we can't make life a bit easier.

PART I

GROWING INTO
PARENTHOOD

1

THE INTRODUCTION or...YIKES! THERE'S A BABY IN MY HOUSE!

We CAN BE KNOCKED COMPLETELY off our feet by the radical change that a baby brings to our world. We are each of us hit by a very personal, very individual, and very emotional whirlwind that can shake the teeth right out of you. This massive life change arrives suddenly, real and solid, in the wiggly form of a dependent little being. Reality has landed in your home and taken up residence. *You* are now responsible for the care and feeding of wild beasts! And this is just the beginning.

There is a whole world of issues and concerns that likely never occurred to you in your pre-parenthood existence. Like, projectile pooping. Myth or reality? Hmmm? You may also find it's not always clear what to do with the bizarre behaviors that will descend upon your life. For example, "Why is my toddler licking the sidewalk?" and "Should I stop him?" Answer: Probably, but considering he's already had half the playground bark in his mouth, it might not really matter all that much!

Then suddenly there's all this childcare, pre-school, soccer camp, music class, kindergarten stuff to figure out. You'll be relying heavily on that "child development and parenting" course you had in school. "Wait," you say, "*What* class?" You mean, you got 12 *years* of American History, but zero instruction on parenting? Math out the wazoo, but nothing on child development? The history of English kings, Egyptian pharaohs, and the Industrial Revolution, but nothing on pregnancy, childbirth, or parenthood? Yeah, it's like that for all of us. Most of us are just winging it without any real guidance on how to raise a teeny tiny human beastie.

You realize there's a lot that you're responsible for these days. You *must* develop all the strengths, and resolve all the weaknesses of each of your children. You *must* nurture resilience, self-esteem, internal motivation, emotional intelligence, science, technology, engineering, mathematics, music, art, language, self-actualization, psychological well-being, tap dancing, and gourmet eating skills. Oh, and coding. Don't forget coding. You must do it while looking hip, sexy, and not at all tired. You must do it while working too many hours outside the home for not enough money. Or perhaps, you will do it as a stay-at-home mom. Working nonstop, without breaks, or pay, or adult contact, and maybe going a bit crazy at home. This home you've been told should be organized, clean, and stylish. A home in which everything is precisely folded and sparsely furnished, containing only "items that bring you joy."

Okay parents, you have no guidebook, limited experience, no sleep, maybe a clueless partner, and expectations are a bit crazy. Your wild little animals are screeching, and don't seem to understand rational, logical thought. So, how are you doing? Struggling a little bit maybe? Yeah, it's okay. We all do. These little critters do not come with instructions. I keep looking in the old hospital papers, but nooooo nothing there. No secret manual on smart wild beasts! As grown-ups we went off into the world and got ourselves jobs and professions. We know our way in the work world and thought we knew what we were doing with our partners. (Until we had kids and everything changed!) But short creatures with partially developed brains, wild plans, endless energy, puppy dog eyes, and a keen taste for trouble? I don't think that was covered in my many years of schooling. And, dag nab it, just when it seems to be careening along in the right general direction, the kiddos *change* and it all goes wacko...again! Sigh.

Most of us go into all this thinking we're ready when, in fact, we're quite blind. I certainly was. But I'm not blind now! I'm 57 and my twins are 12 years old. I've learned a thing or two that just might ease your way, and open your eyes to a new perspective on the crazy life of new parenthood. Child development experts can offer very helpful information in the early years of parenting. I'll guide you to some of the best of these experts. But, there's a lot that gets left out in your average burp and breastfeed, diaper and potty training advice book. What about your *own* emotional transition to parenthood? What about relationship issues that arise when we change from partners to *partners-who-parent*? How will our cultural structure affect a million parenthood decisions? Where are the many forces and pressures you're struggling with coming from? Frankly, there's a great deal that insight can do to make your life as a parent a better one.

I have found that experienced parents, who have lived the life and walked the walk and wrangled the gaggle of toddlers, can bring you life-saving and often side-splitting insights. As you grow into parenthood, you'll gather these pearls of wisdom into your life like the precious gifts they are. This book is full of these pearls from hundreds of parents who are parenting in today's stress filled world. I've gathered them up, and I'm bringing them to you. Knowledge is power. I hope that with the knowledge you pull from this book, you will gain the power to shape your life, your children's lives, and your family life into something rewarding, rich with meaning, actually fun, and a little less wacko.

2

GROWING PAINS FOR GROWN UPS

NOW THE DISCLAIMER. THE BEGINNING of this book may sound a bit dark. But, that's just because I'm going to talk about things no one tells parents-to-be. Just hang in there. I love being a Mom. I adore my kids. And parenting *can* be truly wonderful. However, the whole truth is more interesting, and considerably more helpful, than the cheery clichés.

The dark truths about parenthood are rarely discussed with "outsiders." There's an unspoken agreement that if you aren't a parent you won't get the realities. If you *do* see the dark side, well, we'd probably stop having kids, and human beings would die off! You see, there is a great deal of *loss* involved in having kids. To be sure there is much that we gain, but I'll come to that later. No one talks about the other stuff, so let's give it voice.

For many, the first loss hits when trying to get pregnant. The test goes positive, and we dance with glee. Then we lose the baby in a miscarriage. When I lost my first pregnancy, I told many of my closest friends and family. I needed the support. It hurt. A lot. But what really amazed me was to learn that 9 out of 10 of my closest women friends and family members had gone through their own miscarriages...and never told a soul! Only when I opened up to them did they feel free to share their stories. There's all this dark secret pain and loss left unspoken by couples trying to conceive. In fact, many studies have shown that 15-25% of known pregnancies will end in a miscarriage.

When we lose a pregnancy we also lose a bit of our illusion of having control over our world and our bodies. We couldn't stop the miscarriage. We might not get pregnant again. We have these terribly powerful desires to bring a life into this world only to discover we may be helpless to fulfill them.

Many couples also go through some form of fertility treatment, which can compound the feelings of loss. Time and again that little pink line fails to appear. Time and again you fail to conceive. Maybe your eggs aren't good. Maybe it's the sperm. Maybe it's your uterus or someone's scarred tubes. Maybe no one knows why. Maybe the miscarriages start to line up. That's a lot of heart break and loss for something that started with such hope and anticipation. Some couples turn to donor eggs or sperm in their determination to create a family. A tremendous gift this donation of eggs and sperm. An amazing gift of life. And yet, to accept someone else's genetic gift you must first give up on your own genetic footprint. It's lost from this world forever.

So, your unconscious sense of your body as young and perfect... poof...gone. Your sense of control over your life and body and destiny... poof...gone. Maybe your genetic history ...poof ...gone. And with each personal loss, comes individual growth and change. Always a wee bit painful that "growth and change" stuff. It tends to come with much confusion and angst. Then suddenly you're pregnant, and it looks like it's gonna stick this time. Depending on how much loss you've had getting to this point, you may feel light and joyous or utterly terrified.

Many women have nice, pleasant pregnancies. But not all of us do. In fact, some women struggle and yes, *suffer*, through what they had hoped would be a time of *joy*. Frankly, mine was the pits! Ah well. "Life is what happens while you're making other plans." And thus, for some of us, the loss of the long-treasured pregnancy of our imagination...happy, relaxed, and full of contented nesting. Poof...gone.

Have you pictured how your baby will be born? Home? Hospital? Birth center? Doctor, mid-wife, or doula? Who will be there with you for this life changing and joyous occasion? I very much hope you get to choose these things, and that events unfold as you envision them. But don't blame yourself if things don't go as planned. There's a lot you don't really have control over in this growing and birthing of babies thing.

As for me, by the time my "birth experience" arrived, I was so miserable that I just wanted the babies *out* and the suffering to end. We had arranged and planned for a C-section that turned into an emergency when my blood pressure dropped through the floor, and the babies' heart rates shot up. For me the lights were going out, everything was going black, and the room was erupting in controlled pandemonium. I was on the verge of losing consciousness. The world was literally dark.

I heard the anesthesia attending lean into the resident saying, "Push ten of neo."[1]

The resident replied, "It's in."

The attending, "Push another ten."

The resident, "Already on its way."

As the medication brought my blood pressure back up, the lights came back on for me. I heard a baby cry. My doctor said something about "cord wrapped around her neck" then another baby cried. My husband later explained that when the twin's heart rates showed stress, my OB just flew into overdrive. That wonderful woman pulled both babies out in record time. Fortunately, those anesthesiologists also pulled *me* out of my downward spiraling blood pressure!

Still in the operating room, they brought the babies to me. Frankly, my reaction was, "Yeah, okay. I see 'em." There were no trumpets or choirs or anything that felt remotely glorious or even triumphant. I was too drained from months of confining and claustrophobic pregnancy, and the seeming chaos of delivery. Kevin, on the other hand, was as high as a kite! He paced between holding my hand and peeking at the

---

[1] They were referring to a medication used to increase blood pressure in someone whose blood pressure has dropped dangerously low.

babies. Joy suffused his face. He was already infatuated with the babies. However, I was physically and emotionally exhausted. I *didn't* want to see the babies. I *didn't* want to hold them. I just wanted a chance to recover. To feel well again.

It's okay to feel these things. Really. It's okay to feel these things! Pregnancy and delivery can be hard, hard going for some women. Don't feel bad if you're not oozing love at this point. You will connect to your baby(s). Sometimes it's at delivery. Sometimes a few hours later. Sometimes days or weeks later. It's okay. Your body just spent nine months feeding and growing that cuddly little parasite. It's okay if you need a break before you're mentally and emotionally ready to throw yourself into the endless giving that is America's bizarre ideal of motherhood. You may find, however, that your partner has already fallen in love with the baby for you.

That's what I could see on Kevin's face even in the delivery room. Love and joy and wonder.

I very much wanted Kevin to have those first minutes of his babies' lives. So, I sent him off to follow our twins to the nursery. And yet, this was a problem. You see, some women can experience uncontrollable shaking and shivering after a delivery, especially a C-section. A friend had warned us about this. Did we listen? No. I'd sent my mother and husband to the nursery. So, here's some advice. Make sure someone stays with a new mom after the delivery or C-section! Being alone, perhaps paralyzed by a spinal or epidural, while shaking uncontrollably can be quite scary.

This pregnancy and delivery stuff is *not* all glory and grace. If you're reading this while pregnant, don't start worrying. Many, many women have nice normal pregnancies and deliveries. On the other hand, if you're pregnant and not "lovin" the experience, well sister, you're not alone. There are also many women who do *not* have the glowing, rarified experience of pregnancy and childbirth that is so casually promised to all. It doesn't mean you did anything wrong if your personal experience is not so wonderful. There are some things you simply can't control.

Remember, that our culture's current breezy attitudes towards pregnancy and childbirth are partially due to the struggles women have had breaking into the world of work. For many years, we have had to minimize the difficulties some women have with pregnancy in order to counter derisive and dismissive attitudes that would be used to exclude women from jobs, education, and careers. The movement to insist that women can work through pregnancy and motherhood has been vital in facilitating greater freedom. The backlash to this, however, is the creation of the "It's all an easy breezy walk in the park" myth of pregnancy and childbirth. Some women have even spoken of feeling guilty when they didn't have an easy time of it. At this point, we need to recognize the intrinsic value of childbirth to society. If we truly appreciate the value of childbearing, then perhaps we can build societal systems and attitudes that are supportive of the full range of pregnancy experiences.

Part of that more supportive attitude can start with partners, family, and community. Many cultures around the world offer special care to pregnant women and new mothers. Frankly, I don't think there's anything more feminist than valuing this uniquely female contribution to our world. If you're struggling with pregnancy or childbirth, please know that down through the ages, an easy-breezy childbirth was considered a blessing not a given. Not a standard to be met.

Meanwhile, hang in there. You will feel *tons* better once those kiddos are born and you get your body back from the wild throes of jacked up hormones. You will feel better again. I promise.

You will not, however, get your old life back. That is gone forever. Yes, your new life will be loaded with riches. Still, you might mourn that old life more than you thought. Recognizing this loss, will help you understand part of what's going on for mom and dad in the first few years of parenthood. Before the arrival of baby, you spent your life learning the skills of adult independence. Professional skills. Relationship skills. Adult-child-of-older-parents skills. Financial skills. Home care and budgeting skills. You've probably been cruising along with a fine sense of mastery over your life. But a baby sets up a whole new learning curve.

They show up as blindingly cute little lumps that don't sleep, pee and poop constantly, and often fuss. They are utterly completely helpless, and utterly completely innocent. You will discover they have their own personalities from day one. Within *one year* they will progress from wiggly half-blind lumps to walking, understanding speech, and starting to talk! They change and grow and develop at an absolutely phenomenal rate. Do you think those adult life skills you acquired will prepare you for parenting? No. They will not. It's a whole new skill set. And just when you master the skills of the newborn stage...they change! Now *you* have a whole new set of skills to learn too! Holy mackeroly! You used to feel confident, accomplished, maybe even capable. Now you discover you haven't got a clue!

You will not be working late, and you will be stressed to the max about the need to do so. You will not be stopping at the gym on the way home from work, nor enjoying a quick bike ride on those long summer evenings. You will not be sleeping in any kind of normal pattern. You will be waking up waaay too early. You will not have time for hobbies, reading, classes, or extra responsibility at work. You will not have the time or energy for your partner. (More on that later!) Instead, you will be doing a *ton* of laundry. Your house will be a mess. You'll find yourself worrying about how much lead is in balsamic vinegar? How much arsenic is in rice? Mercury in tuna? Fire retardants in sofas? You will feel confused, and a bit stunned by what has happened to your life. You'll start to wonder just exactly who is this person inhabiting your body?!

Perhaps you're familiar with the concept of "developmental stages." Babies, toddlers, and kids go through stages as they grow. Sometimes this process is, shall we say, *rocky*. It's hard having to figure out *everything* in life. What they don't tell you is that parents are also going through developmental stages of their own each time their child changes. You will be continually faced with new challenges. Continually acquiring new skills. Continually juggling new priorities that are clashing with old ones. And continually confronting emotional baggage from your past. Parenthood is gonna keep you on your toes. In the first year you will rarely feel a sense of mastery over anything. My twins were five years old before I occasionally started to feel like I'd gotten a small grip on parenting. And usually, right when you're feeling all slick and supermomish, something comes along and firmly puts you back into the rank and file of the clueless.

So, "why?" you ask, would anyone have kids?? Well, here's the thing. On the one hand, you'll be wondering how you could have made such an insane mistake. Yet, at the same time you'll find you don't *really* want to give them back. The love you will feel (not always) will be intense. I remember the moment I realized I would step in front of a train to save them. I'd do anything to keep them safe from harm. Really, truly anything. They are amazing little beings and watching them grow into themselves is such an astounding privilege. You will see the whole world anew though fresh innocent eyes. Ladybugs, ants, dirt, and water that falls from the sky will all be new. They trust you absolutely and you'll strive with all you've got to be worthy of that trust.

Loss is a part of growth. Parenthood is a time of exponential growth for adults. It comes with some loss and some pain. But it also opens new doors to the world. It stretches us to be more. And it brings these new little people deep into our hearts. Many new parents are wholly unaware of how hard the first year can be. But now you know. And with that conscious awareness, you can step back a bit when the going gets tough, and realize that this too shall pass. That it's just growing pains for grown-ups. That as you accumulate growth and skills you'll feel better. It will be better. And remember, no guts, no glory.

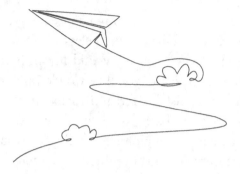

3

TRIALS AND TRAVAILS
OF THE FIRST YEARS

OKAY, I'VE REVEALED SOME OF the "unspeakable" taboo truths about the "dark side" of parenthood (cue Darth Vader breathing). Have you decided to give up on the whole "having baby" project? I suspect not. The desire to have children is often blindingly strong. I certainly would have given these concerns little heed when I was trying to have kids. Now that you have a bit of insight, let's explore how to prepare for this challenging transition.

Protecting Relationships While Feeling Overwhelmed

One book I recommend is *Baby-proofing Your Marriage: How to Laugh More and Argue Less as Your Family Grows* by Cockrell, O'Neill, and Stone. It discusses many of the most irksome issues that develop between partners who are now co-parenting a fragile butterfly. The book is written with input from both the male and female perspective on many issues. After reading it, my husband said he was relieved to know that the struggles *we* were having were so common. Ours were normal struggles and conflicts. If other people had worked them out, then so could we.

Babies do put a huge strain on a marriage or partnership. With multiples, the stress is logarithmically increased. Your life will be savagely altered by the needs and demands of parenting. At times, you will be exhausted and hurting.

You may well find yourself taking out your frustrations on your spouse. Their failings may be magnified by your own frustrations with how life is unfolding in these days of personal loss, massive sleep deprivation, life shaking responsibility, and deep heart stopping joy. Sigh. The first year of parenthood can be emotionally very confusing. You're supposed to be content and happy, joyous and fulfilled. But the truth for many is much more complex. You're giving up a lot from your old life, and the demands of the new one are truly daunting. There are going to be some negative emotions popping up. It's important to know that it's okay to have mixed feelings about the whole motherhood – fatherhood deal you just bought into.

Personally, I was angry and kinda bitchy for much of the first year. Okay, a lot bitchy. Then I realized that my anger was a sign that I'd sacrificed too much of myself in this act of continual giving.[2] Maybe with a singleton one can find a bit more balance in the first year or maybe not. Certainly, with twins or the arrival of your second child, I think you need to realize that you'll wind up sublimating most of your own needs for theirs. Even with involved spouses, the demands of the first year are truly *huge*.

That's why communication with your partner is very, very important. It can be quite difficult, but you must have these conversations. In all likelihood, you will both feel as if you have no more to give, and that the other person is not doing enough in the new much larger work load of family life. It is certainly true that today's fathers step up to the challenges of family life in ways that past generations could evade. It's also true that many new dads find that three or four months into family life, there is less equal sharing than they had expected. Here is where I'll give you some tools and thoughts to help you start this conversation. Bear in

---

[2] *The Dance of Anger*, by Harriet Lerner, is a useful if slightly dated book on this topic.

mind that this process has the potential to pull you together as a couple and deepen the love in your life *or* to drive a wedge of resentment and distance between you. We all love our children. That said, let's discuss some of the conflicts a child's presence generates in today's families.

For the record: I have been a full-time stay-at-home parent. A full-time outside working parent. And a full-time stay-at-home while also a part-time outside the home working parent. I have been a full time stay-at-home-parent and full time mid-life career changing professional. Whew!

Important topics to discuss *with your partner.*

1. Child care work is an especially difficult and draining type of work that is distinct from other forms of family and life work. (Yes, it has rewards…yada, yada, yada.)

2. House work that is done *while supervising* or teaching children is really a form of extra hard childcare work.

3. House or home care work that allows the adult to work alone *without supervising* children *is* work. It is also a refreshing break from child care. For example: mowing the lawn, home/car repair or maintenance that is done without simultaneously supervising children, grocery shopping alone, paying bills alone. There is a huge difference between painting the fence by yourself with earbuds in and your favorite tunes blasting as opposed to painting a fence with 2-year-old and 5-year-old "helpers." The first is actually a nice bit of alone time.

4. By dinner time, an out-of-the-house working parent and a stay-at-home working parent are tired. However, the outside worker is "kid-fresh" after a day of adult interaction. The stay at home worker is "kid-fried" after a day of unrelenting, unbroken service and little adult interaction. These are the facts like them or not.

5. Primary working parents feel the burden of financially supporting the family in a deeply stressful way. They are also balancing powerful and conflicting demands between work and home.

6. Primary at home parents make a huge personal *financial sacrifice* when they stop full-time paid work to "lean in" and meet the

family's needs. Years away from work (or reduced hours, or taking a position with less overtime expectations) results in lower pay that is not "caught up" if they do return to work. This has a huge impact on Social Security benefits as well as the building of other retirement benefits. There is a very real risk of poverty in retirement for these, often female, parents. A stay-at-home parent brings years of unpaid labor to the table of family life.

7. Personally, I believe that, when possible, a family with a stay-at-home parent should take out a separate retirement account in that parent's name and fund it with automatic deposits from the family income check. The same way the working parent's retirement is funded. This will not make up for any employer matching of retirement deposits, but it's a start. It will not make up for lost Social Security benefits either. That will have to come with legislation that gives child rearing monetary value in the Social Security system. At the very least, $20 a paycheck can become a symbolic and concrete recognition of the contributions and sacrifice made by the stay-at-home parent.

8. Many women (not all) feel that with the arrival of a baby, the woman often becomes the sole family-care-*professional* and that their husband has become the family-*day-laborer*."

9. Many women (not all) want their partner to step up to the role of a family care *co-professional and not become a passive day laborer*. Without a co-professional partner, most women are unable to lighten the family burdens enough to maintain an adult life. This can lead to significant emotional pain.

10. Some women (not all) have a hard time *sharing control* over family life.

11. Some men (not all) have a hard time knowing how to *be* a professional co-parent.

12. If you want to have a co-professional parent, you have to cede some control over things. Let go of perfectionism. Embrace different approaches to tasks. Leave the field of play and don't hover.

13. If you want to become a co-professional parent, then act like a professional. Look for what needs to happen. Learn, discuss, track, plan, research, be present and involved in an on-going way. Expect the job to be constantly changing. Stay on your toes. No kicking back and relying on your co-worker to babysit you. No waiting for The Boss to spoon feed you instructions.
14. Being a wage earner *and* a professional co-parent is hard, yet it offers *tremendous* rewards. Love, intimacy, connection, purpose, pride, joy…all the things that make life worth living.
15. Being a stay-at-home parent *and* ceding some authority to a co-parent is hard, yet it gives you the space to breathe, lets you release resentment, and draws you closer to your partner. Most importantly, it allows you to acknowledge parts of your identity that are not related to motherhood.

These issues are further challenged by the fact that many families in our culture consist primarily of parents and kids. Our grandparents, aunties, and uncles are often far away and only intermittently connected. If you haven't discussed the implications of these issues before the birth of your children, then do it now. It's never too late.

It's Not Your Mamma's World

A lack of family and community support is taken for granted in our culture. It is our normal. Parents figure it all out, and make it all work. And yet, it's not the norm in many parts of the world where extensive networks of family and friends help to care for and raise children. Furthermore, in many other westernized countries a tight web of family services eases the financial and labor burdens of our smaller modern family. These same services also make it easier for both parents to work outside the home. Once your baby actually arrives you'll begin to discover the high cost of childcare in our country. Yet ironically, we truly don't pay childcare workers nearly enough. (And we give tax breaks to the rich?! Hmm, not sure about those priorities.) Often this issue becomes a huge barrier to keeping both parents working before the kids hit school age. Getting by on one income is, of course, far from easy for many families. Often it is simply impossible.

At some point in the first year these difficulties will hit home. You might feel inadequate. Why are you unable to handle the kids alone? Are you a wimp? Didn't your parents do it without help? How are you going to make this work financially and professionally? Well, you're not a wimp. The pace of life was quite different for our parents. Expectations were vastly different. Three square meals and send 'em out to play was considered good parenting. And you *could* send them out to play because the neighborhood was full of other kids who had been sent out to play. Only a minority of middle class women worked outside the home. Working class families also tried to keep mothers with young children at home. That left many women in the neighborhood and able to help each other out. E-mail didn't exist. Nor did cell phones, and no one had a social media platform to maintain. Television consisted of three channels, plus PBS. In addition, no one had to worry about bisphenol-a, phthalates, and other endocrine disrupters. There was no such thing as "concerted cultivation." People didn't worry that a lack of "kindergarten readiness" would set their child up for a failed school career and dead-end jobs. In my day, we didn't attend pre-school. From a young age I ran free with older siblings. How we all managed to obtain college degrees without rigorous pre-school intervention remains a deep mystery. In the past, parents were responsible for providing love and care. The kids were in charge of growing up. I have no idea what my mom did with her days, but she certainly wasn't entertaining her kids nor carting us around to different activities or play dates.

Now, however, we are responsible for formulating our children's self-esteem, their emotional intelligence, their capacity for commitment, and internal motivation. There is always the next, latest, greatest psychological litmus test of your child's future success that parents are charged with "developing." So, cut yourself, and your partner, some slack. Our world is complicated, crazy paced, battered by too much information, filled with new responsibilities, loaded with ridiculous expectations, and greatly lacking in support for families.

Thinking About Childcare and Work

In your first year of parenthood, you may find yourself in a continuous struggle to work out how to care for your children. I'm not talking about how to feed infants or how to potty-train. That's a different chapter. I'm talking about how to arrange adult care of young kids. There is no longer a "right" formula for how to do this. Nor is there any consensus of what's "best" for the kids. Nor are there standard easily accessed family services to tap into. So, this becomes one more thing you have to figure out on your own.

1. Will mom or dad stay home with the kids? For one year? Three years? Until they are in middle school?
2. How will you keep a stay-at-home-parent (SAHP) sane?
3. Will they get any child-free time?
4. Are there grandparents who can help? Do you want them to help?
5. Will you pay a nanny for a few hours per week to get the SAHP a break?
6. Can you find and retain a part-time nanny or will you lose them to a fulltime job offer?
7. Perhaps both parents will go back to work fulltime. Can you find a nanny you trust?
8. Will you send your kids to an in-home daycare?
9. Can you afford to have two kids in daycare at the same time?
10. How do you find the daycare? (Look for recommendations from local mother's clubs, city/county listings, word of mouth, playground referrals.)
11. Are your kids doing okay in their childcare?

All of these questions and more will come back again and again during your child's early years. They are quite challenging, and require a huge investment of time and energy.

Pay attention to this next bit, Daddy-o. As a co-professional parent, modern moms may expect you to pro-actively participate in researching and investigating childcare. Failure to "own" this parenting task may result in deeply harbored resentment from Mommy-o. You must discuss this together.

Once you do have childcare set up, you may find it isn't actually working! Sigh. It can be exhausting and frustrating. It's very important to remember that *what* you, your kids, and your partner need in life will change over time. Whatever you set up now isn't written in stone. You can change how you set up your life. Then, you can change it again.

You may find yourself restructuring your family life several times over in the early years of parenthood. If it's not working, don't be afraid to change it. There is no "right" formula. You may find that what you thought would work *just doesn't.*

I had planned on returning to work between 3 to 6 months after delivery. Unfortunately, I wound up with severe postpartum carpal tunnel syndrome, and ultimately with surgical repair on both wrists. As a result, I didn't get back to any kind of outside work until the kids were a year old. During that first year of work, I changed jobs three times before I found something stable with workable hours. Part way through, our wonderful nanny had to leave, so we tried to find a new one. After extensive searching we had to let go three subpar nannies. We then gave up on that plan and spent weeks researching childcare options. Eventually, we found a great daycare. Perhaps your first few years of parenthood will have a more straightforward trajectory. But chances are good that you and your partner will find yourself juggling the unexpected and veering wildly off plan. This is to be expected. Open your mind to the new possibilities and go with the flow.

Things to Consider When Both Parents Work

When you have two parents working and multiple young kids, life is just crazy. You're waking up extra early to get ready before the kids are stirring. Then you're running around doing everything for your dependent little beings. You've got diapering, dressing, bottles, sunscreen, packing the daycare bag, more diapers, lovies, blankies, lunches, snacks, more bottles, and then clothing changes for everyone after the babies spit up on your work clothes. Then you're racing to get them to daycare so you can get to the office on time. Which leads us to the car seat issue. If Daddy-o is dropping off the kids, then he either needs to remove the car seats and leave them at daycare for the pick-up person to use or he has to do the pick-up himself. If you have two young kids, then you may wind up needing to own four car seats to equip two cars. Otherwise, you could be taking two car seats in and out of the car every morning and evening. Frankly, that's a giant pain in the rear!

In our family, my work day was just too unpredictable. That meant my husband was doing both drop-off and pick-up. This made it impossible for him to put in the "extra" hours at work that were expected of him. The conflict between family needs and work demands put enormous pressure on both of us. In many families it becomes a source of parental discord. Once you do get home from work, the mad dash continues. The kids are tired and want attention while parents are running around trying to pull together a dinner for toddlers and adults. Next, you give baths, change a zillion diapers, put PJs on, read stories, change diapers again, sing songs, tell stories and put the kids to bed. Then...you do dishes, laundry, try to prep for the next day, look at the crumb strewn floor, decide to ignore it and collapse. Lights out for grown-ups in our house was 8:30 or 9 p.m. Chances were strong that our "not so good sleeper" would wake us up at least once during the night.

When it's a particularly bad night, one of your kids might wake up at 2 am...sick. Throwing up on the rug, running a high fever, and inconsolable by anything except a cartoon. Their sibling would, of course, be awakened by the commotion and also start crying. It's misery all around. Meanwhile, you're wondering, "Who's going to miss work tomorrow? Him or me? Who missed last time? Who has the most pressing need to be at work?" You know that by the time the virus goes through both kids there will be a week of missed work at a minimum. And then you and hubby are gonna get the bug too. Nowadays, you may also have to deal with Covid testing, quarantining, and risk assessments! Whoa!

A year into this craziness, I decided it just wasn't working for us. I sat down and did some calculations. My job did not offer much in sick leave or vacation time. Like many women returning to work with kids, I had compromised on salary and benefits in the hope of more reasonable hours. Unfortunately, men are rarely expected to make this sacrifice. That is a problem in our culture. When calculating the cost of working, you need to include more than just childcare hours. Add in commuting costs of gas, the expense of an extra car, lost days of pay when staying home with sick kids, and extra costs paid to nanny services for taking care of sick kids. Don't forget you still pay for daycare when your kids are home sick with you or a back-up nanny. Consider increased food costs, professional clothing or uniforms, dry cleaning, and tolls. Once I crunched the numbers, it was clear that even with my work income we barely came out ahead. It's crazy that for some women their own adult work can cost a family money. Unfortunately, in America this if often true. We also need to consider the less tangible benefits of employment. By working, I was keeping up my professional skills. Those skills and that involvement in paid work life, bring huge personal benefits and retirement income. That has real value. However, we weren't having fun, and we were exhausted!

In retrospect, I encourage couples where both parents work to seriously consider hiring a nanny. A good nanny in your life can be a wonderful thing, especially if you have more than one child. As well as providing a loving presence for your kids, they can greatly ease many burdens of the first few years of parenting. You don't have the frantic rush to get out of the house with two little kids in tow or race to leave work early to pick them up. The nanny can have the kids bathed and fed before you get home. They can get some laundry done and sweep the floor. If you're working, these things can help you find the room to breathe a bit...maybe actually enjoy your kid's early years. If you can arrange for the nanny to cover a regular date night, you'll find it an excellent investment in the integrity of your family's foundation. In many cases, hiring a nanny can be cheaper than paying for two children in daycare or preschool. In addition, a nanny whose Covid vaccination status and risks match your family's could also help everyone weather the next viral surge.

If you can also afford a house cleaner 1 to 2 times a month, do that as well. These expenses don't have to be forever. The challenges won't go away, but as the kids get older the help you'll need will become more manageable.

And if you are a lower income single parent with twins? Sigh. Find a social worker and get all the help you can. Call in favors from friends. Move close to family. Contact a local multiples mother's club for help. Do whatever you can to create a network of parents, moms, family, and friends who will help you through these first difficult years.

To be clear, I have nothing against daycare. My kids thrived in a daycare environment. If you have flexibility at work or family who can help with pick-up/drop off and caring for sick kids, then many children can find enrichment in a multi-age group setting. There are also other ways to make your days run smoother. You can hire a "mother's helper" for the after-work hours. Less costly than a nanny, a mother's helper can give you a hand with dinner, baths, clean up, and laundry. Or you could hire a teenager to play with your preschoolers while you make dinner. There are many ways to get yourself some help. Don't feel bad about looking for support. It really does take a village to raise a child.

4

THE NEW FATHERHOOD: OPPORTUNITY IN A QUIET REVOLUTION

ON ANY GIVEN DAY, YOU can now find fathers walking the park or cruising the coffee shop with little babyo's strapped to their chest. That's really a new thing. Certainly, there have always been fathers who loved their children, and were involved in their lives in many ways. However, since women have become more involved in the work force, fathers have had the opportunity to begin quietly breaking into a new world. The realm of newborn, infant, and baby care with all its challenges and joys is finally an opportunity allowed to men. Many new dads are stepping into a role that was largely denied to their fathers and grandfathers. Think about it, moms. If you felt clueless when your babies were born, just imagine the terror of a man who never had the skills of early fatherhood modeled for him. Baby care was, in all probability, not exactly on his radar as he grew into adulthood. It might be easier for him to stand back pleading incompetency... and then run away. Yet, many men find they want the opportunity to care for their newborn. They want the experience and connection that comes from changing the diapers, feeding bottles of milk, rocking a baby to sleep, and meeting the many needs of their children. Fathers of twins don't really have any option. They *have* to step up or no one survives! Fathers with multiple little ones who *don't* step up are taking a *big* risk with their spousal relationship. Still, there are many men who maintain peripheral involvement when their kids are very young. It's unfortunate. They miss out on so much.

My husband has said that he wouldn't trade the early years for anything. Despite the sleepless nights, despite the poop explosions, the inconsolable infants, the feverish babes, the vomiting, and spitting up, despite all the exhausting physical and emotional challenges of those first years, he wouldn't trade them for a more distant relationship. He treasures the intimacy of that time loving and caring for and raising his kids. And he's rightfully proud that when the kids were 2-years-old, he could send me off to Cambodia with a friend while he held down the fort...twin toddlers and all. He had taken several overseas business trips after the twins were born. Each time I stayed home and solo juggled the kids. It was his ten day trip to India, complete with an invite to a week-long Indian wedding, that pushed my jealousy over the edge. "You're going to India? INDIA! For 10 days? Including a lavish traditional wedding? How nice. (grit teeth, grit teeth) I've always wanted to go to India. You'll have fun. (Aaargh!)" That's what I said to his back as we rode our bicycles on a rare post-twins ride.

Then a week later he said, "You know, if you can take care of the kids while I'm in India, then I can take care of them while you take a trip. Maybe you could go somewhere with your friend Caroline?" As it turned out, Caroline's partner had a penchant for month long medical volunteer trips to Africa. And Caroline had also held down the fort while yearning for the kind of travel that was a bit difficult to swing with young kids.

So, that's what we did. Caroline and I took a week off from being stay-at-home moms and went to Cambodia. We explored the floating villages of Tonle Sap, and hired an awesome local guide for Angkor Wat. It was amazing! Truly eye opening. In Phnom Penh, Caroline visited, "the killing fields." She is a woman of great integrity who felt it was a moral obligation to bear witness to the horrors and crimes that had been committed there. I couldn't do it. I could only handle part of the tour of a Khmer Rouge prison. Halfway through I had to sit down on a bench under a tree. I couldn't look at photos of the prisoners or into the eyes of the street kids without seeing my children's faces. This trip was suffused with the most intense contradictions of life. Here was an ancient, exotic, and beautiful culture wrapped in a lush and green landscape. Here was a population that had lived through widespread genocide and torture. Here was a world of people busy and industrious, clamoring into the future. Here was deep corruption, child prostitution, and old deep pain. Here was an intelligent man, our guide, whose depth of knowledge about Angkor Wat bespoke years of study. A man, kind and open, who shared with us his story, and thus gave us a glimpse into the heart of his family and home.

All of this was about as far from American-suburban-stay-at-home-mom life as one could possibly get! Which was a very good thing for this mom. It felt like my brain was alive again. As for Dad? He did just fine. He accepted help from grandma, hired our old nanny to cover for a night of hockey, got the kids off to day-care each morning, made and fed them dinner each night, gave them baths, tended them in the night, got them dressed, did the laundry, proudly taking care of his 2-year-old twins.

Some father's involvement goes even deeper these days. Our neighbors decided to take turns as stay-at-home parents. The first two years he stayed home, and then they swapped. When the father went back to outside work, he did have difficulty at first. He was in the sports and recreation industry. Unfortunately, some found it strange that he had been focused on childcare for two years. With a bit of effort, however, he eventually found an excellent professional position that he really enjoyed. Despite the hurdles in returning to the work force, this father said he was immensely glad he'd had those two years of caregiving for his son. He spoke of a closeness with his child that he would not likely have managed without that time. This did not mean he found those years easy. He struggled with the same issues many stay-at-home-moms face. The difficulty of learning new skills, the subjugation of your own needs, the simultaneously challenging and mindless nature of caring for little kids, and the feelings of lost identity. In addition, his isolation at home was even worse than it is for many moms. He never quite felt accepted on the playground by moms with kids. He literally felt like the "odd man out" at play dates. So, he formed a stay-at-home-father's club. They took trips to the zoo and the beach, had picnics, and helped each other with the challenges of fatherhood.

In Sweden, which has one of the most generous parental leave policies in the world, fathers are required to take some of the leave that is allocated to each child. Dads often take 3 to 9 months of paid leave to be their child's primary caregiver. Apparently, "latte dads" as they are called, are a regular sight pushing strollers and hanging out with other dads. Swedish parents of both sexes are entitled to a combined 16 months of paid parental leave at about 80% of their salary. You get extra days for twins. Parents *must* share the leave. Swedish dads are required to take some of those 16 months. The days don't expire until your child is eight years old.

Despite all this parental leave, Sweden's per capita GDP (gross domestic product) continues to show robust growth. In addition, their life expectancy in 2017 was 82 years versus our 78 years. Hmmm, maybe we have something to learn from looking at other cultures.

Personally, I think this quiet revolution in fatherhood is a tremendous opportunity for men. While women in our culture have been denied access to careers over the years, men have been denied the challenges, joys, and intimacies of early childcare. It's not like that's some "natural" state for men. There are many cultures around the world in which fathers pick up and tend to crying babies just as much as mothers do. So, you newbie Daddyo's, step into your infants life in a deep way. Your life will be richer for it. And moms? You have to let go, and let them in. You just might get a trip to Cambodia out of it!

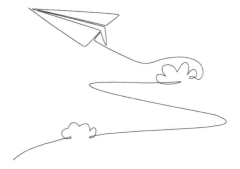

5

IF YOU'RE GOING THROUGH FERTILITY TREATMENT

THERE ARE MANY BOOKS THAT help couples through fertility treatment issues and logistics. I recommend getting an up-to-date fertility book to learn the terminology, techniques, and possibilities. Most clinics offer or require an orientation lecture so do that too. However, if you find yourself deep in a struggle with repeated trials and failures, then you are going to need some additional help. Infertility can be an emotional minefield. The heartbreak bombs will be going off left and right. Chances are good that friends and family will be unable to offer any useful support or guidance.

So, here's your map in the form of a book, *The Infertility Survival Guide: Everything You Need to Know to Cope with the Challenges While Maintaining Your Sanity, Dignity, and Relationships*, by Judith Daniluk, Ph.D. This book is an excellent guide through the many issues unique to fertility treatment, and the trauma it inflicts on those who endure. It addresses everything from how to deal with the anguish and emotional conflict generated by a good friend's baby shower to how to handle well-meaning, but clueless family members. I highly recommend it to anyone facing this often soul-crushing process.

Another useful tool is the CDC (Center for Disease Control) website for Assisted Reproductive Technology success rates. (see appendix C) This website displays the required reporting of procedures and success rates from all fertility clinics in the U.S. It provides a wealth of useful information to anyone trying to pick a clinic. You may find that one clinic you're considering has a better success rate with endometriosis patients, and another with decreased ovarian reserve or sperm motility issues. So, look them up, and be an informed shopper. If you find the information on the site confusing, then seek help from someone who's already been through the process.

A great place to find other couples going through fertility treatment is a RESOLVE support group. I didn't learn about RESOLVE until we were three years into fertility treatment. Initially, I was reluctant to consider a support group, and my husband considered it only because he felt I might find some comfort. Neither of us had any idea how valuable the group support would prove to be.

The RESLOVE support groups are led by people who have them-selves been through fertility treatment. Our leader was also a trained psychiatrist. Each week she would begin the meeting with a new and highly relevant topic. Our group consisted of one couple with a new infertility diagnosis who were trying to decide whether to proceed with treatment or not, another couple who'd just started treatment, three couples who were several years into treatments, and one woman who came alone as her husband was too uncomfortable to attend. All of them would become very dear friends. Long after the official support group ended we continued to meet. Most of us managed to have kids.

When you are in a RESOLVE group, everyone gets the chance to talk about the topic of the day. This means when you speak to the group, your spouse hears what you are thinking and feeling. Usually, someone else in the group feels the same way as you which validates your experience. Next, your spouse gets to speak on the same topic while *you* listen, and other people help your partner talk it through. On the way home from the meeting, you can say, "I never realized you were worried about xyz." Thus, opening a deeper conversation and understanding with your partner. The structure of the support group and the limited, but committed, time to talk each week can open lines of communication about very difficult topics. My husband will now urge anyone willing to listen to join a support group if going through fertility treatment. It will help you get through it. It will help you with hard decisions. It may save your marriage. It will certainly help you and your partner understand each other with far greater insight.

My last fertility treatment recommendation is one I've not found in any book. Fight hard for a "singleton" pregnancy. A twin pregnancy is not easy. We humans are made for one at a time babies. Whether you are youngish or oldish, the strain on a mother's body when carrying two babies is huge. HUGE. We tend to think of triplets as crazy and twins as, well, kinda normal. But the truth is that most twins are born prematurely. Many wind up in the neonatal intensive care unit after birth. Complications both during a twin pregnancy and after delivery are very, very common.

All of this adds up to a very stressful and emotionally exhausting pregnancy. If you've been through all the strain and agony of fertility treatment, it would be nice to hope for a simple singleton pregnancy. And once the baby is born, you want to be able to just snuggle down and cuddle. But if you have twins, you don't get to do that. Really. With twins, you'll find yourself holding one, and constantly looking to see if the other one is about to wake up and fuss. You are so busy juggling babies that you rarely relax. Moms who've had singletons prior to twins will frequently comment on how they miss the cuddly bonding they had with their singleton. After all the stress and anxiety of years from fertility treatment, it would be nice to be able to just snuggle and bond with one baby.

This is not just my personal experience speaking. I belong to a very active club for mothers of multiples. This subject comes up again and again and again. Seriously, and I mean *seriously,* consider transferring only one good viable embryo at a time. It is, of course, a different consideration if you're dealing with old eggs or embryos with a low chance of viability.

Remember that if your chance of getting pregnant on a single embryo transfer is, say, 33% then your chance is 66% after two transfers and 99%

after three transfers. So, think hard and talk with your doctor before you decide you want to transfer two embryos at the same time. Certainly not all embryos carry a 33% fertility rate. If you're dealing with "old" eggs, then you may have embryos that offer only a 5% chance of successful pregnancy. In that case, you're likely to throw in as many as you've got. But, keep the goal in mind of a nice, safe, pleasant singleton birth.

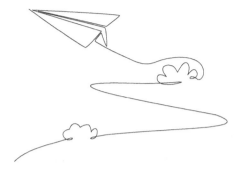

6

IF YOU'RE EXPECTING TWINS OR MULTIPLES

KAY, SO I SCARED YOU with my admonition to avoid having multiples. Oops, too late! You're having your own gaggle of goslings. No namby pamby one at a time stuff for you! You're gonna "get 'er done" all in one! Woohoo!

Truthfully, there may be some things that are harder to enjoy while juggling twins. Still, there are also many joys unique to twin parenting. Stepping into parenthood brings you into a previously hidden world. Twin parenthood is a special sliver of that world, and the people who walk that path can be astoundingly kind and supportive. You will get to know these people. You will also have a chance to see infancy and childhood from the unusual perspective of watching two different babies as they go through the same stages. They may go through those stages a year apart, and still be totally on track. And while the early years can be harder with twins, the later years can be easier. Sometimes. I make no promises. Kids are all different.

If you're pregnant with multiples, you may have greeted the news with excitement or anxiety. Often people feel some combination of the two. In general, I find the more informed I am on something the less worrisome it becomes. During times of uncertainty in life, my wise mother's advice has always been to "get more data." The idea is the more you know about an issue, the less conflicted, ambivalent, and anxious you feel. When you make decisions from a place of knowledge you feel more confident in your choices. So, you're having twins? A bit anxious? Get more data.

The one caveat to this recommendation is that for some people the hormones of pregnancy can trigger a great deal of anxiety. I've spent my life reaching for books in search of "more data." However, when I was pregnant each book bumped my anxiety up even higher. I had to turn over all the reading, research, planning, and baby gear buying to my family. If this sounds like you, then hand this book over to your partner and wait until after the babies are born to read it. There will still be stresses, but the hormones will settle down and you'll get your brain back.

So, what's useful to know if you're pregnant with twins? One of the best resources for support and information is a local mother's club for multiples. Ask friends with twins, your obstetrician, or do a web search to find a group in your area. Many offer meetings for expectant parents and provide fantastic in-person and on-line support. The group I belong to has meetings for expectant and new parents, offers a bed rest support team, arranges home cooked meal delivery to new parents, runs a volunteer buddy system, hosts multiple annual events for parents and kids, arranges semi-annual sales for member's used equipment, supports needy families of multiples through donations and gifts, and maintains an active on-line support forum where parents can get ideas, advice, and concrete help from other parents of multiples. It was my lifeline during my first year of parenting twins. I highly recommend that anyone expecting multiples find a group, and become a member. You'll gain access to volumes of wisdom and support. Start your search at Multiples of America.com.

You may be surprised to realize that twins are automatically considered a high-risk pregnancy. Since there are particular issues along the way, you'll likely wind up with more medical monitoring than for a singleton pregnancy. In addition, many women are surprised by how exhausted they become while gestating twins especially in the later months. If you have been pregnant before, be aware that this pregnancy may be different. Some women find they are able to work well into the third trimester, while others find they need to either reduce their work hours or stop entirely.

A good friend of mine who was having twins wound up with hyper-emesis and a dilating cervix. As a result, she was on bedrest and in-home uterine monitoring for many months. Her job was flexible and she was able to work from home, but many jobs don't have that option. The point is that you need to be responsive to your body's unexpected demands during this time. All your family leave benefits, if you have *any*, may be used up *before* the babies even arrive. After delivery, many twins come home with you. But others spend weeks or months in a neonatal intensive care unit. This can become another enormously stressful time as you struggle with both work conflicts and the emotional turmoil, logistical challenges, and financial strain of preemie care.

I know all this sounds really scary. But remember that *none* of these things may come to pass. I was a 45-year-old fertility treatment patient going through a known high risk first pregnancy. It wasn't easy for me, but some people cruise through with smoother sailing.

During your pregnancy, I encourage you to listen carefully to your body. If you feel good, then keep going. If you don't, then slow down. Consider some pool walking, especially later in your pregnancy. You will feel a tremendous relief when that water supports those big babies you're growing. Your back will also thank you! Eat as well as you can, but don't beat yourself up if eating becomes difficult. The babies will take what they need from you. Really, they will! I also encourage you to ask your doctor for help if you're having a lot of trouble eating. They can help with nausea. They can also help with constipation, which can be a major cause of nausea and lack of appetite.

Do take your multivitamin and folic acid. Those are important. Do drink lots of water. Really. Drink lots of water. Sip it all day long. If you're tired, rest. Your body is working amazingly hard to grow two new little people, and you may find you need to cut back on many activities. If you feel great then have fun! If you don't feel good, then focus on one hour at a time. Ask yourself, "what will I do for the next hour." Then do the next hour, and the next hour. If you aren't feeling well, don't focus on the months extending ahead. You'll feel overwhelmed. Instead, focus on one hour at a time.

Every twin advice book will tell you to line up help in advance. This is very good advice. Personally, I didn't know how to ask for and organize help. My husband was home for two weeks. My mom lives nearby and came over daily. This wasn't nearly enough. After ten days of severe sleep deprivation we realized that three adults to two newborns was not a workable ratio. The nighttime needs are especially exhausting. Get extra help.

One friend with twins lined up the grandparents. Her parents came right away and stayed for the first three months. Then her in-laws came and stayed for another three months. My friend took six months off work and juggled the nights with her husband. Thus, every day two fresh grandparents arrived, and stayed all day to help. Between the two sets of grandparents, there was *one* day when the family would have no helpers. My friend was very nervous about how to manage that *one day* alone. At the time, I was pre-twins and didn't really understand her anxiety. Now I do. The ratio of two newborns to two parents is scary!

There are other ways to get outside help. It could be family, a mother's helper, or a nanny. Where I lived *night* nannies for twins charged a premium. We thought we could manage without one. We were wrong. By day ten we were frantically searching contacts and websites for someone to help at night. It's possible you will need help at night for several months. We could only afford to hire a night nanny three nights a week. We'd wait in desperate anticipation for her arrival. Then we'd pass off the babies as fast as possible so we could dive into bed. Your body needs consolidated sleep. When you get only an hour or two at a time for night after night you'll find yourself more than a bit frayed. I urge you to figure out some nighttime help before the babies arrive.

You're probably going to need daytime help too. The early days are an intense, nervous juggling act between two newborns. There will be a million and one diaper changes, feedings, burpings, spit-ups, clean ups, soothings, and clothing changes for baby number one. Immediately followed by the same for baby number two. And repeat. Generally speaking, baby number two will *not* be waiting patiently for their turn! This type of work is hugely challenging if you are fresh, showered, and rested. If you are none of those things, you'll find the world starting to blur as it slips out of control. You'll be frantically trying to swim while barely keeping a nostril above the water. Having a fresh, rested adult show up every day will be really, *really* helpful.

There are a ton of jobs your helpers can tackle. The constant spit ups and diaper leaks will generate *tons* of laundry for babies and adults. Nor is there time for cleaning the house. Dirty dishes? Getting groceries? If you can line up family and friends to clean your house once a week, do it. If you can hire a house cleaner to come every two weeks, do it. Once a month? Do it. Remember that all of these expenses are not forever. The craziest time with twins is the first year. But the really, really craziest time with twins is the first six months. Get as much help as you can for those first six months. This is not the time for "I usually like to do things on my own" kind of mindset. The more help you have in place the more everyone can enjoy those babies.

If there's no help available, then let the housework go. It's good practice anyway. The mess goes on for a long, long, loooong time, and you might as well get accustomed to a higher level of dirt. You will not be able to keep your home in anything like the state you managed with only adults in the house. It's one thing to clean up after yourself. It's another to negotiate with a partner to clean up after themselves. But once you add a couple of kids to the deal, well, the whole house of cards kinda caves in.

The first few months with twins are probably going to feel pretty intense. Just keep breathing through it. The crazy days pass. You'll earn your stripes. And you'll move on to new crazy parenting stuff, and more stripes to earn. You've got this. At least as well as *any* of us have ever "got" the first months of parenting. Which is to say, crawling through the mud, under the barbed wire, hoping the rain will stop and the finish line will show up!

(Psst, you'll also find a ton of first year nitty gritty advice in chapter 22.)

7

ISSUES FOR THE OLDER, NEW PARENT

STARTED FERTILITY TREATMENT AT THE age of 39 and was 45 years old when our twins were born. Part way through treatment, one of my doctors began urging us to not waste time with treatments that had low probability of success. As an older parent, he was warning us that it was physically challenging for middle-aged parents with young kids. At the time, my husband and I were avid bicyclists who would train for long challenging rides. We weight-lifted at the gym after work. We loved long hilly hikes. I was plump and slow, as I've always been, yet fit and long on endurance. And my husband was all long lean muscle with endless aerobic capacity. So, we scoffed at the doctor's warning that we'd find it hard to keep up with young kids. Nevertheless, pregnancy and its aftermath were *hard* on our bodies.

People have different experiences of the world. Some of us come with genetics of longevity and health while others struggle with genetics that bring the risk of illness or infirmity. For most of my life, I'd kept the "obesity demon" marginally at bay with high levels of exercise six days a week. Hiking, running, biking, swimming, weight lifting, roller blading, kayaking, dance, and aerobics have been part of my daily life. But my body has changed. Since the kids were born, via C-section, I've had carpal tunnel surgery on both wrists. Reconstructive ankle surgery on both ankles, and surgical repair of my left rotator cuff. That's six surgeries in three years! Both right and left thumb joints are bone-on-bone and need surgery. My right knee flared up requiring several steroid injections. I've a torn meniscus in my left knee. I have a new bunionette on my little toe that developed while hiking, and trying to get fit. I've had countless injections in my heel to combat plantar fasciitis. So, five years out from a twin pregnancy, I found myself managing chair aerobics and one arm swimming! In addition, I'm perimenopausal with horrendous night sweats. If all of that is not enough of a challenge, well, the gestational diabetes that reared its head during my pregnancy is lingering as pre-diabetes. Whew!

So how much of this developed because of pregnancy and how much is my genetic destiny? Who knows? I come from a family were many of us struggle with weight. We need to maintain a very high level of physical activity just to maintain pudgy, and anything less will let us rapidly trend towards bodies that are good and fat. I look a lot like my mom who is short and round and has bad joints. However, there is no doubt in my mind that pregnancy at the age of 45, and the demands of young twins has delivered a hard, hard hit to my body. If you come from a family where you're all slim runners who rack up the miles into your 80s then you might not struggle as much. But, don't be fooled by the magazine covers of 50-year-old new moms who look flawless and 30. Whether airbrushed or whitewashed, magazines are about fantasy and often have a tenuous to nonexistent grasp on reality. When my very tall son was five years old, he weighed 50 pounds! I'd sit him on my lap rocking him gently while my rotator cuff protested. Still, he needed that snuggling time. Your kids won't stop needing you just because your joints and tendons are going bad.

Moms aren't the only ones who struggle with the physical challenges of being an older parent. My husband won the genetic lottery when it comes to body type and metabolism. He's now back to going out for

70 mile bike rides up and down the steep coastal hills. Yet, even he lost some fitness during "our" pregnancy. He herniated a disc in his back, has chronic pain in his foot, a bum shoulder, and needed hernia surgery when the kids were four. More and more we find it difficult to wrestle on the floor with the kids. He'll be guarding his back, and I'll be guarding a myriad of stiff, tender joints. We both routinely pass out on the couch, jaws slack and snoring, within an hour or so of putting the kids to bed at 7:30. We both now admit that the doctor who warned us about the physical strain of caring for young kids was right. It's hard on older bodies. Even fit older bodies, and 50 is an older body when it comes to parenting young kids.

So, what to do if you find yourself struggling to keep up with your kids? First, I suggest you forgive yourself for not being perfect! No parent is perfect. No parent can give all things to their children. If you were in a wheelchair, would you berate yourself for not being their karate teacher? No. You'd find them a karate teacher, and teach your kids something else that you are good at. If you can no longer backpack, then go car camping or hire a mule train! If hiking is hard on your joints, go kayaking instead. I had imagined long treks with my kids on my favorite steep granite trails in Kings Canyon. Instead, I have ankles and knees that can only do short walks on flat dirt trails. So, this summer we got kayaks for everyone and ventured into the wilderness by floating on our butts instead of using my ankles!

In addition to the physical difficulties, older parents often face emotional challenges. A midlife crisis a is often accompanied by a fair amount of emotional intensity. Much of our focus during this life transition is directed inward at one's own wants, desires, and needs from life as we glimpse our mortality. Now, throw a couple of needy helpless infants or toddlers into the equation, and you're pretty well set up for conflict that's riddled with angst. You can't sacrifice your kids' needs so you sacrifice your own. That hurts too much, so you try to find a balance that you never successfully find. Meanwhile, other people your age will have kids that are grown. They will be traveling, starting new careers, eating out with spouses at nice restaurants without juggling toddlers. They will be noodling away whole afternoons with a book, making sudden changes in plans, taking sailing lessons, rekindling loves and friendships, reviewing their bucket list. You, on the other hand, are left wondering if you'll still be physically able to enjoy those empty nest years. I try to focus on staying fit, but my joints are failing and my kids have needs. There is never any balance. So, I fear the possibility that by the time we've gotten the kids through college, I'll be too incapacitated to enjoy those last years of freedom. Life is "now," of course, but you really do give up much of your own life interests when your kids are young.

This pressure to abdicate your own needs in favor of meeting you kid's needs is a challenge for any adult. But I think, it can be particularly hard for first time, older parents. You're just so used to a different lifestyle and view of the world. As much as you want the new challenges of parenthood, the degree to which you need to sublimate your life for theirs is surprising. This continues until the kids get a bit older. At that point they are marginally easier to be out and about with or send off to school for a few hours a day.

Despite all of this, part of the maturation process of becoming a parent is the gut level knowledge that it's *not* all about *you*. It is, in fact, all about the babies' needs first and foremost. On the one hand, I encourage you to try to hold onto some little interest that feeds your soul. Consider thirty minutes twice a week with a book or music or painting or gardening or yoga. Whatever touches your deepest soul. On the other, other hand, try embracing the fact that it *is* all about the kids at this point in time. You will be more able to fight for time for yourself when they are older. Oh, and daddios, this crazy conflict applies to you as well.

Saving for retirement and putting kids through college at the same time is not a trivial challenge. In addition, you may discover that you are also caring for your aging parents. How do you swing the needs of a frail parent who is on a long slow glide into dementia, while also caring for two infants or hyper toddlers? If there is an older adult who is delicate or impaired in your home, consider making a fenced area that is safe for them. Then they can have some peace and still be present in the household. Do think about how to protect them. Human bites from little Neanderthals are loaded with bacteria. If your elder is frail, they will require protection until the "cavemen" gain some of the skills of civilization. If that grandparent is not financially stable, then how do you add the cost of their care to your own retirement and the kids college savings?

There are, of course, advantages to being an older parent. There is no doubt that my husband has come to fatherhood with the full focused attention of a man grateful for the opportunity to have children. So, if like my husband, you spent your youth in wild endeavors, you may be content to settle in and focus on family. If, like me, you were too timid to be wild in your youth, then you may find yourself plotting how to have wild adventures with young kids in tow. Either way, you will have been around the block a time or two. You will be familiar with the ebb and flow of easy times and harder times. You may bring more patience and tolerance to your marriage and kids than you might have in your youth. And that sense of mortality on the, hopefully, distant horizon has its benefits for your kids too. You will greatly value the time you have with these wonderful young beings. You will know that young and old alike get hit by cars, felled by aneurysms, and killed by melanomas every day. We can't predict the future. Much of it is truly uncontrollable. Knowing this, on the deep gut level that comes from life experience, will help you really embrace the little people evolving before you.

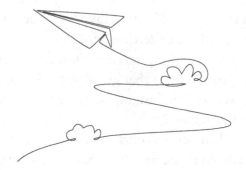

8

LIVING OUR CHILDREN'S LIVES vs FOLDING THEM INTO OURS

As PARENTS OF TWINS, MY husband and I were routinely amazed by the sight of infants snuggled in car seats, while their parents sat in a restaurant at 9 p.m. Long after baby bedtime! "How do they do it?" we'd wonder. Generally, the baby in question would be sleeping happily while mom and dad enjoyed a nice meal and time out of the house. Wow, talk about bliss! This seemed like an utterly impossible option for us to try with infant twins.

Perhaps it had to do with our kid's temperaments. Ours were neither calm stroller babies nor contented car-seat-kids. Ours did not continue in blissful slumber when moved from a car seat to a crib. Perhaps there was also the factor of two babies, not one, with a resulting adult to infant ratio of 1:1 as opposed to a more reasonable two adults to one infant. If you have two parents and your infant wakes up, then one parent can tend the baby while the other parent eats. However, if you have two fussy babies, then you need two parents to tend them...and no one gets to eat!

This is why so many parents find the arrival of baby number two is far more difficult than they expected. You might have been getting along okay by tossing the football-baby back and forth as you meandered through your family of three weekend. Once the adult to child ratio changes, all bets are off! Now, you find yourself with vocal beasties on different schedules with different needs. Divide and conquer no longer means that one adult is getting a rest. Instead, it means that *no* adults are getting a rest. At this point, parents only get a reprieve from duty when one or both kids nap. Thus, you may find yourself in a slavish dedication to your children's sleep schedule. This, among other things, can result in rotating your adult lives around your children's needs.

To some degree this is a normal lifestyle when you have infants. And yet, there are those babies sleeping in car seats or strollers as families and parents continue with their own activities. Do you subvert your life to conform to the needs of your child's life? Do you stay home for dinner so you can put your kids to bed on time and in crib? Or do you cart them along for a dinner out while folding your child's schedule around your own?

Ultimately, I think it is healthier for kids and adults if the child is folded into the adult life. The other way around puts too much pressure on the child to be all things in the family. They become too much the center of all adult attention. They become too much the adult's primary life project. That's just not good for an emotionally balanced family life. Furthermore, parents who lose connection to their life interests, industry, and *spouse,* suffer greatly for the loss. That's not beneficial for anyone.

So, *how* do you fold your child into your adult life? Frankly, this can be difficult in America. It is especially hard to do when you have twins or more than one young child. You see, not all babies respond with rational understanding when you attempt to mess with their schedule. In fact, some babies get downright *pissed off* if you change their schedule. Yet, to maintain some adult life, you need to have some time dedicated to adult activities. That often means you need to have helpers for the babies. However, in our culture, grandparents, aunties, and uncles are frequently scattered over great distances and are busy with their own lives.

It *does* take a village to raise a child. The village of extended family. The village of childcare providers. The village of adult friends. The village that watches out for your kids when they play in the cornfield, school yard, or skate park. The village that drops off meals and mows the lawns for families with newborns. The village that assumes, universally assumes, that everyone goes home on time to be with family, to have a life outside of work. Unfortunately, this village has disappeared. It evaporated into the mist like Brigadoon.

The next question becomes: How do we live within our *current* society and keep a healthy balance that allows our kids to live as kids and parents to live as parents? As a parent, how do you maintain some adult life while raising babies in an environment that makes so little allowance for their existence? I suspect there are subcultures within our country that are better at offering this child-life vs. adult-life balance. Some communities have successfully maintained stronger bonds within extended families and friends. They have much to teach us about maintaining a healthier balance between adult, child, and family needs. I suspect they make choices about where they live, and how they spend time that keeps them physically closer and more involved with relatives. If you place a higher priority on a weekly extended family dinner than you do on soccer practice, then you are more likely to maintain family and community connections that become a web of support. Similarly, you can decide to avoid "kid activities." Avoid spending time at the kiddie fairyland, birthday parties where you don't like the parents, and bouncy house activity centers. Instead, do a family friendly activity that *you* enjoy. A bike ride, the beach, music in the park, a barbeque with friends are all places where you can enjoy adult interactions while your children engage in their own way.

Another problem that tends to force parents to turn their life around the needs of their kids is the physical environment in which we now live. In the past, four-year-old children could roam the backyard and nearby neighborhood or fields with older kids. But there are no longer neighbor kids nor many corn fields to run through. Even in the suburbs, houses are built so close together that everyone has fences for privacy.

This means that wandering children are pushed to the street. Where I grew up there were no fences. Suburban homes defined their spaces with plants, and kids cut through the back and side yards of friendly neighbors to reach friends or streams or playgrounds. Today the fencing of yards and fear of crime has eaten away at the spaces of childhood.

Despite the fact that the crime rate today is lower than it has been in a very long time, parental fears for their children are high. Many people worry that a child who is out of their sight for even brief periods is in grave danger of abduction. This is simply out of proportion to reality.

The truth is that abduction by a *non-custodial parent* is fairly common. Stranger abduction, however, is rare. Which is why it hits the news so hard when it does occur. It's scary and unusual so the media goes over it again and again. This big news coverage distorts the reality of its rareness, leaving parents anxious and fearful for their children.

Perhaps, you're old enough to remember those milk cartons with pictures of missing children on them. Again, the vast majority of those were kids taken by a *parent* in a custody dispute or were kids who had run away from home. Compared to today, the violent crime rate was much, much higher when I was a child. Yet, I casually walked to and from school by myself from the age of seven. By ten years old, I wandered neighborhood paths through winding woods for miles. Many parents today will not even let their kids wander an established neighborhood or bike path.

Our suburbs with their fenced off backyards are empty of children after school and on summer days. Rather than letting kids explore their free time, their neighborhood, and nearby friendships, they will instead be signed up for one round of adult supervised activities after another. Often parents discover that if they want their children to have the chance to play with other kids, it has to be arranged by an adult.

So, we sign them up for soccer and karate and dance because that's where you find the other kids. Playdates may involve kids who live far apart. If a child is going to hang out with a friend, it often requires complex parental navigation, orchestration, and transportation. A child who can go next door to see if a neighbor can come out to play is fortunate indeed. The fact is many of our kids can no longer find other kids to play with in their neighborhood.

One of the consequences of this is that the early parenting phase of intense involvement and sacrifice of parental life continues much, much longer than it did in the past. The real solution to this problem is to change society so that it better meets our children's needs and our own parental needs. But, to build that world we have to first believe *we* lowly workers are worthy of societal investment. That *our children's lives* are worthy of a kinder world.

Many western cultures allow parents more time and flexibility outside work. This can make the work-family balancing act more successful for families. If other countries can do this, then why don't we? There is an unspoken fear in the U.S. that focusing on quality of life for our families will result in lower productivity for our economy. Ironically, when governments create support systems for families, it frees the parents to remain in the work force.

So, I have no quick answer for you about how to *not* rotate your adult life around the needs of your kids. If you can, live close to family. If you can, put your foot down and insist on leaving work on time. If you can, block work email and calls in the evening and on weekends. If you can, look for a home where there are no fences and kids are safe to run around. If you can, get to know your neighbors up and down your street. If you can, keep your kids out of too many after school activities and encourage other families to create free time in their kid's days. If you can, build a community of supportive friends. All of these choices can build time and space in your life that allows you to hold onto a bit more of your adult life.

If you can't do those things, do the best you can to attend to your personal adult life. And, vote for people who will make this lifestyle possible for your children when they are parents.

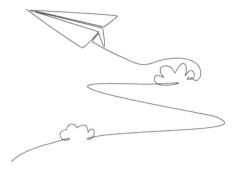

9

BUILDING A COMMUNITY OF PARENTS, A PEER GROUP, A SAFETY NET

O WE'VE LOST OUR NEIGHBORHOOD-BASED communities. Friends and family are often scattered over a large geographic area. Our kid's friends are also scattered, and many families move every few years. We've lost our village.

In addition, our children have lost the opportunity for free, unstructured, inventive play. Yet, we know this free time is the core of childhood. It is the time in which each child's own individual self evolves and grows. It is critical space in which we move along the slow path from immature wild beast into mature adult human. This process takes years and years in humans, and the protected space and time of childhood is critical to its success.

It's not just kids who have suffered with this loss of community. Parents have lost their adult support system. In the past, a parent would not only know the kids next door, but their parents, and the neighbors up and down the street, and the farmer in whose corn field the kids were playing. If your son rode his skateboard home from school in the street without his helmet, *someone* would call you. This kind of community that exists from simple geographic proximity and longevity in one location is disappearing. But we need it to parent well. We need it for sharing the burdens of child rearing. And we need it for companionship, support, and friendship through good and bad times. Our kids need it so they can have a window of time preserved for childhood immaturity and exploration. So, you're going to have to build some version of your own village.

My neighbor is a stay-at-home-mom with young kids. She has managed to create a whole network of friends with whom she swaps kids, hangs out at the park (aka her office), shares cars, and takes day trips. On any given day, her house and yard are full of kids. Some are hers. Some are mine. And some belong to her friends. She has found her own kids are happier and fight less when other kids are visiting. Sometimes the moms come and hang out as well. Other times they are working, taking classes, getting a break, focusing on another child's needs. Creating this kind of community of friends can take some effort in our scattered culture, but it is truly precious once you've built it.

When my kids were very young, I organized a multi-age playgroup. We gathered in the back yard on Friday afternoons. The kids ran loose while the moms sat around a table talking. It can be so refreshing to just shoot the shit with other parents. And simply having older kids and other adults present, makes "watching the kids" easier. If you time your afternoon right, then working parents can join the group as the evening wears on.

Another way to build a village is to make a standing playground date with other parents. Let the kids play, while the grown-ups talk. Be sure to welcome other parents on the playground, and invite them over for an afternoon. Go on outings together. All trips with kids are easier and more fun with another adult along. Remember, you're not the only parent in town feeling cut off and unsure. If your kids are in a half-day preschool, then arrange to stay late at a playground with the other families. Introduce yourself to the other parents.

Once you have these connections, start helping each other. Offer to watch someone's kid while they run an errand. Swap clothes your kids have outgrown. Share your snacks with a mom who has run out and has fussy kids. Drop a meal off at the home of parents with a newborn. That's how you grow a village. But, it won't happen by magic. You'll need to step up, and put some effort into meeting other parents.

The first five years of parenting are hugely challenging. Find a way to build this network of friends with kids. You will find enrichment and grounding through some crazy years.

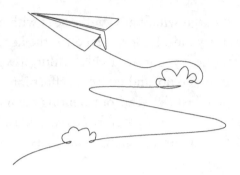

10

MOM IS PART OF THE FAMILY AND HER NEEDS COUNT

When you become an American mom, you cease to be a person in your own right. It's all about what you will *do for* your baby. What you will *be for* your baby. Drug-free natural childbirth, breastfeed for a year, making organic homemade baby food, attachment parenting, co-sleeping, and on and on. You, as a human being, cease to be. Except, as defined by how you are related to and attached to and have sacrificed yourself and body for, your child. I gather that Europeans think our parenting style is nuts. *Why* do we believe a woman needs to sacrifice her entire consciousness to thoughts of how to ensure psychological perfection in her children? *Why* would we believe it is *desirable* for an adult woman to not have time to engage in adult thought? To read and discuss and pursue activities of adult interest? Wouldn't we become dull if we only ran around sacrificing ourselves for our children?

Yet, American motherhood seems absorbed in this cult of doing *all* for our children even when we know it's not good for them. I mean really, why do we have a million parenting articles telling working mothers that they should be spending hours cooking and freezing food on the weekend so they can serve "homemade" food during the week!? The poor mom probably has little free time, and you want her to use it to cook and freeze giant batches of family food? And to buy all the organic ingredients and clean up all of the mess and supervise and feed the kids while she's cooking too? What's dad doing? Watching football!? How come he gets to chill out when mom is supposed to sacrifice her time? Well, because in this culture, you don't count when you're a mother. Your kid's needs count, your husband just assumes his needs count, and yet everyone knows that yours do not. That's just bullsh**.

It's important to recognize that you will see endless magazine articles about how to feed your family healthy meals, decorate cupcakes, create holiday traditions, make bento box lunches with smiley faces, raise entrepreneurs, raise philanthropists, raise strong girls, raise gentle but not too gentle boys, and even how to revive your sex life. There will be a million articles about what you should do for your children and your husband. But for you? You get to dream of a spa day. That's it. Where, I ask you, are the articles in women's magazines that recommend a mother take a college course, join a professional group, attend a conference, commit daily time to reading about an area of interest, or simply spend time vegging out watching TV?

How many articles have you read about how much TV time is good for kids? Probably 55 gazillion. Have you ever seen *one* about the minimum daily TV time required by the average mother to remain sane? While parenting a 2-year-old? While parenting 5-year-old twins? No. No one even does that study! Because your needs don't count!

In this country, mothers feel guilty if they take the least amount of time for their own indulgence. Fathers don't. But women have been saturated with the idea that if you aren't committing every ounce of your being, every second of your time, every moment of your presence to mothering your children and your family, then you're somehow not "mothering," not "nurturing." It's ridiculous. Even stay at home moms from the last generation spent less time with their kids than working moms do today!

You, my dear mother, are also a part of the family. You are a woman separate from being a mother. You should not live your life as if you have to sacrifice it all for others. You get to have your own life. Your own interests, and pursuits, and the time to engage in them. You will have less time when the kids are little (a lot less) and more time as they get older, but resist the guilt trip and spend some time on things that interest you. Remember you are not your child's play thing or entertainer. If you like playing with your preschooler on the floor, helicoptering on the playground, or watching swim practice, then go ahead and have fun. If you don't, then pull out that book or that screen or that article your friend mentioned and enjoy your time! You have years, and years, and years of engagement day after day! You do not need to be engaged with your kids 24-7-365. You *do* need your brain alive, active, and occasionally refreshed.

But how? How, you ask, do I get to have a life too? Yeah, I must admit, easier said than done. Here are some of the key points. First, your partner needs to understand that this is non-negotiable. If you can, talk this over before your kids are born. Our society is in flux right now. Some dads have heard the quiet male revolution and embraced the chance to grow into a new kind of fatherhood. They change diapers, rock fussy babies, hook up breast pumps, mix formula, and lose sleep. They dive in and "get" the whole messy, endless, exhausting role of parenthood. These partners will understand later, when they've gone back to work, that a stay-at-home-parent will need regular time for a mental health activity. A stay-at-home parent will need to maintain adult interests. So, work it out together.

If you have twins and zero help, well, it's gonna be a while before you get much time for yourself. But the day will come if you both work for it. As your children grow teach them to care for themselves. Step back little by little from the micromanaging that we all do when they are very young. When they start to fly a bit on their own, *you* will also get to fly a bit on your own. Finally, step away from the guilt laden, time soaking, "happy homemaker" and "perfect mama" imperatives you could waste your time obsessing over. (Yes, if you really, really like doing these things then, of course, have fun!) Instead, look up that subject you wanted to learn about in college, or that hobby you've never had time for, or reach for that professional journal you've been wanting to catch up on. Watch a documentary. Learn a language, an instrument, a skill.

Try to find some way to connect with who you were pre-mommyhood or you may go wacko. Try to carve out a block of time once or twice a week when you can do something that acknowledges your inner "you." Or that challenges you to learn something that is not related to motherhood.

I found an open studio art class and started painting for two hours a week. I never managed to paint at any other time, but I loved getting lost in the colors and paints and the challenges of a new skill. Look for something that floats your boat and try to weave a bit of it into your life. It will help you maintain your sanity when your kids are little. Remember, a mom is part of the family and her needs count too. Whenever I get a break, I come back refreshed and open to enjoying "the here and now," which makes everything nicer for everyone. I'm a much better wife, friend, daughter, and mom whenever I take time to take care of me. The problem is no one is going to "give" this time to you. You're going to have to "take" it for yourself. I think many fathers know how to do this better than mothers do. We women start to second guess ourselves and then feel guilty about everything! Despite all the ridiculous, unrealistic expectations and judgements that are dumped upon American mothers, you're going to have to take this time for yourself.

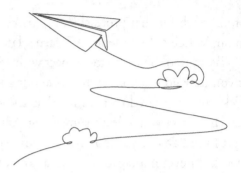

11

OUTSIDE CRITICISM AND FEELINGS OF INCOMPETENCY

IF YOU HAVE AN IN-LAW or a grandma or so called "friends" who boast of their "superior" parenting skills, I suggest you develop a mantra you can repeat to them over and over. Like, "I'm so glad you had such easy kids." Or, "Wow, you must have been the most perfect mom!" Maybe, "It's great that your kids have such easy personalities." If they don't get the message to back off, then limit contact with them. Spend your time with more supportive people.

Parenthood takes such great courage. We learn the skills of adult living as we grow, and yet, none of them have anything to do with parenting. Suddenly we find ourselves struggling to raise treacherously adorable, wild cave creatures who keep changing. It can completely gut your sense of competency and self-worth. Nevertheless, day after day, we come back to this often soul shaking challenge. Because we're moms and dads and we're needed. That is true courage. And it will get better. You will accumulate skills and experience and suddenly you'll find you have advice to offer a newbie parent.

Whether that critical parenting voice is coming from a family member or your own head, tell it to back off! Then give yourself a bit of time for on-the-job learning. I promise you, you're not alone out there. We're all dancing as fast as we can and trying not to miss the beat.

12

PARENTING IN A WORLD OF UNREALISTIC EXPECTATIONS

I**T IS TRULY AMAZING HOW** much righteousness and judgement complete strangers will feel free to fling at mothers. Fathers usually get a pass for all but the most obviously egregious behavior. Fathers are expected to be barely involved, which means anything more is golden. Mothers, however, are expected to be perfect according to someone *else's* values. No wonder moms become overloaded with stress and guilt when the kids arrive.

This is where it can help to be a non-conformist. If you've lived your life wearing your own wild style, walking to your own wacko beat, insisting on your own skewed perspective, then you're accustomed to not really giving a crap about what other, less brilliant people, think about you! I suggest that as you move into parenthood you cultivate a bit of this attitude. We have tons we can learn from each other, but you're also going to get hit with some really irritating and ridiculous stuff.

One of my favorite judgements shows up over and over in parenting articles. Parents who spend time actually playing with their kids on the playground get accused of "helicopter parenting." This, we are told, is a no, no! Instead, we should let kids explore on their own without robbing them of the ownership of their own growth and discovery. Oh. Okay, you say. So, you take the kids to the park, and let them go a bit. You sit on the bench and after a minute you pull out your phone and...gasp! You read your email! Now you are judged as a horrible parent because you're looking at your phone when you could be "engaged" with your kids.

Sure, we can talk about cell phone overuse. However, we need to recognize that we don't know what's happening in other people's lives, and let go of the urge to judge.

Let's see, what other crazy expectations will come your way.

1. Look sexy and not "momish."
2. Don't look tired. You can *be* tired, but you can't *look* it.
3. Make all baby foods from scratch, with only organic food, and store it only in glass containers.
4. Bond with you child and keep them attached to you.
5. Let you child roam free and don't become overly enmeshed.
6. Breast feed exclusively for a year or more even when you work outside your home.
7. "Lean in" at work.
8. Maintain a robust professional life, family life, married life, parental life.
9. Meet the needs of your children, your spouse, your elderly parents, your friends, your dog, your cats. If the goldfish dies, it's probably your fault. (Forget your own needs...no time for that!)
10. Spend your few free weekend moments making large batches of food from scratch and then organize and pack them for the family's next week of meals.
11. Get up an hour early to go running every day.
12. Give up on your little bit of free time at night, and go to bed early, so you can get up early, and go running in the dark.
13. Organize everything in your house into bright colorful containers. (Ha! Like it's going to last more than 30 seconds!)

14. Go through everything in your house and throw out anything that "doesn't make you happy."

15. Stay on top of all vaccines, doctor visits, dental care, preschools, nannies, babysitters, spouse's schedule, your schedule, your kid's school schedules, kid's activity schedules, work schedules. Cross reference all of this into one master schedule that no one but you will look at.

16. Volunteer at your kid's schools.

17. Volunteer at a soup kitchen with your kids.

18. Bake cupcakes for school birthday parties and bake sales. Use cute decorations. Slip in a bit of wheat germ, chia seed, flax or other "healthy" ingredients.

19. Keep a clean and stylish home. (Ha, ha, ha, hee, hee!)

20. Purchase only environmentally friendly toys. When the wooden toys get left outside and grow mold, be sure to dispose of them properly.

21. Use a diaper service rather than disposables.

22. Potty train your twins or triplets at 1-year-old. They do it in China, right?

23. Use only organic laundry detergent and hand scrub every stain before it's washed.

24. Convert your car to vegetable diesel to save the planet for your kids. Okay, you'll only get this one if you live in Berkeley or Madison.

25. Make sure your kids get fluoride.

26. Make sure your kids *don't* get fluoride.

27. Never feed your kids fast food even if you're a single working mom with three jobs and your kids are bonking.

28. Make ends meet after years of no pay increases, and multiple kids in daycare, while you "Lean In" at work, and take care of your aging parents, and...

It just goes on and on. At some point, you've just got to throw out the crazy stuff, love your kids, do the best you can, and trust that it will be good enough. Because that's all any of us really manage anyway!

13

LESSONS IN HUMILITY, FORGIVENESS, AND RECONNECTING

ONE OF THE MORE DIFFICULT areas of personal growth and development in the first years of parenthood are the ever recurring lessons in humility. When you are exhausted and drained by the continual challenges of our modern family life you may find yourself, well, yelling at your kids. I'm sure you never, *never* thought you'd be one of *those* parents. And yet, there you'll be, yelling at a small child.

On one hand, you'll feel angry and defiant and justified in your right to be angry. And then, you'll step back and feel like a bullying shit for yelling at a child who really has no power in the hierarchy of his life. Here is where you step away, swallow your pride and righteous frustration, and come back to your kid with love and apologies. "I'm sorry I yelled, sweetie. I love you very much. I love you even when I'm mad and frustrated. I wasn't very patient, and I'm sorry I yelled." It's a good phrase to practice. It's highly likely you'll need it again. You're allowed to not be perfect. Forgive yourself your imperfection. Forgive your children their imperfection. Believe me, the better you are at apologizing for your flaws, the better your children will become at apologizing for theirs. Swallow the pride, embrace the feeling of being humbled and allow yourself to grow from the whole messy process. You're going to have many opportunities to experience these feelings as your parenting becomes a mirror that reveals your oh-so-human imperfections.

And it's not just your kids who will aid you in your unsought quest for life lessons. Your partner is going to help you with this as well. Oh, goodie! As you journey through all this growth, and loss, and change, you may at times find things become uncomfortable. And you will want things to be easier, and better. It would, of course, all be better if "he" would just blah, blah, blah. Why can't "she" just do blah! Then it would all be manageable! Your life will be out of sorts and you may find yourself feeling that if your partner would just do "something" it would all be okay.

Unfortunately, your partner is dealing with their own joyous journey of growth and development. They may not have a whole lot to give right now. Besides, it's not something they can rescue you from anyway. Here's where you forgive them for not being able to rescue you from challenging times. Here's where you forgive them for feeling overwhelmed themselves, and not at their best. Here is where you dig deep, and look for the inner strength to reach with compassion and support for your partner. Even when you don't feel like you have anything left to give. Because you're a grown-up, and relationships are long journeys. And if you really think about those humbling moments, then you might realize you need to ask forgiveness for a few failings too.

Sometime during the first few years of parenthood, you may find yourself in a relationship that feels a bit drained. You love and appreciate your partner. You respect and care for them, but maybe the connection feels lost. Perhaps you will find yourself feeling lonely in the context of your marriage. Or angry. Or frustrated. Bored? Lost maybe? Infants and toddlers really do demand so much of parents that many find their adult relationships feel diluted, scattered, and disconnected. Well, when the going gets tough, the tough get reading! So, look for a book called *The 5 Love Languages* by Gary Chapman. It's a short, easy read and offers great insight into how to re-establish feelings of love, connection, and intimacy in a relationship that feels empty. If your marriage challenges seem too, too great, then imagine how much more complicated and challenging it will be if you divorce.

Many parents go through a time of discontent with their love relationship. Don't be afraid to turn some conscious attention to rebuilding and reconnecting. Some time and money spent on marriage counseling can prove to be an excellent investment. Paying a sitter for a whole weekend so you can get away with your spouse? Way cheaper than divorce, and more fun too! I'm not saying that divorce is never the best choice. My parents were divorced, and I don't believe they should have stayed together even though they remained supportive friends. The point I want to make is that it's not uncommon after kids are born to go through some years in which your love relationship seems to falter. When you can, try to come back around and fight for it.

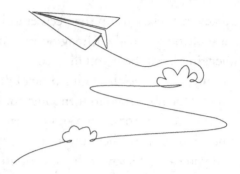

14

PATIENCE, PATIENCE, AND MORE FREAKIN' PATIENCE!

It TAKES AN AMAZING, MIND boggling amount of patience to raise kids. There's the repetition of rules, over and over again. "No hit. Gentle!" "No hit. Gentle!" Then there's the constant testing of boundaries and counting to ten waiting for a response. (Secret tip: counting to ten may work for a long time *if* you consistently enforce follow through in the early years.) The endless kid questions that go on and on, "What? What? What? Why? Why? Why? What would happen if?" It's exhausting and can become extremely irritating. I think my kids were 18-months old when I started saying to my them, "Mommy is losing patience!" I think it's good for them to hear that. Over time they gain a greater understanding of what it means. I also give myself a "calm down time" during which I step away into another room when I'm about to blow. I also rely on my husband being "kid fresh" when he comes home from work. I let him shoulder more of the load in the evening.

The other thing that I found helped me with frustration and recovering my patience was to carve out some regular time for me. (Pay attention, this idea may come up again!) No one will hand this to you.

You'll have to work to arrange time for yourself, and then you'll have to fight to keep that time for yourself and not just fill it with errands. If you manage it, you'll find you have more patience with the kids. Challenging phases come and go, and come again, and go again. Kids cycle through periods of being off balance and difficult and then relax into months of smoother sailing. Each period of challenging behavior usually precedes a big developmental jump. This means that arranging "mommy time" to maintain your sanity is a great investment in meeting long term childcare challenges. You're in this for the long haul, so carve out time for you.

It can also help if you can get some assistance during the evening hours when the kids are tired, and you're worn thin. Help can be a teenage neighbor who comes to play with the kids while you make dinner. Or it can be an experienced mom who can shoulder a bigger work load. Really, any fresh adult or young adult can help the crazy evening hours go smoother for everyone. You can even try easing off on the pressure you may be putting on yourself. Dinner doesn't have to be a four course meal. Soup and bread or cereal and fruit may be all you need some nights. Buy some extra underwear so you can go longer without doing laundry. Decide that dust bunnies are cute. No need to sweep them away quite so often. Cut yourself some slack. A little wiggle room in life can create space for patience.

15

FEELINGS OF ANGER

I HAD A YEAR OR TWO (yeah, a long time!) during which I was often angry and irritable. I dumped my frustration on my husband and mom. (Neither of whom remotely deserved it.) At some point, I picked up a book I'd read years ago, *The Dance of Anger* by Harriet Lerner. While it's a bit dated, the gist of the book holds true and hit the mark for me. Lerner points out that when we are feeling regular anger or annoyance, it can be a sign we've compromised too much of our self and identity. Often this happens when mothers only focus on the needs of family and kids. When we lose too much of ourselves, our distress comes out in the form of anger. When we meet our own needs, we are able to let go of the anger. (Hmm, does this sound similar to the advice on fostering patience?) Once I realized what was going on, I embarked on a process of reflection on my life. Over the next year I completely reworked my life into something that allowed me to begin recapturing some of what I needed. This has resulted in a happier me, and thus, a much nicer wife, daughter, mom.

No one will do this for you. Let me repeat that. *No one will do this for you*! Your kids will not be "making time for you" to do your grown-up things. They have no concept that you have any needs at all! You have to make it your own priority to take care of your emotional and intellectual needs. Okay, let's repeat that too. *You have to make it your own priority to take care of your emotional and intellectual needs!*[3]

In addition, I've learned a few everyday things to do when I'm at wit's end with the kids, and my anger begins to simmer. I know they pick up on that under current. So, I make sure that when things are calm I talk to the kids about how "I love them all day long." And that even when I get frustrated, I still love them. Then we list things that have happened that made me get upset with them, and I'll say "yes, when you don't -xyz- it makes me mad but even then, I love you. I love you all day long." We also have a book that has a similar theme that my kids enjoy, *I Love You All Day Long* by Frances Rusakas. I used this story to help establish that even though people get angry they can still love you.

You should also be aware that post-partum hormone changes can cause a lot of irritability. If you've experienced PMS symptoms of irritability, the same feelings can be longer lasting after delivery. If you think that's part of what's going on for you, then seek help from your medical provider.

But, I must say that the best thing I did in order to feel less angry was to ask myself what *my* needs were and then to make the changes to get those needs met. If you're reading this book from front to back, you may have noticed that I've already hit this point several times. That's because it's really, really key to modern motherhood. You do not need to be a martyr to be a good mother. In fact, resisting martyrdom will make you a better mom and a saner woman. You are a parent. You have responsibilities. Take care of yourself so that you can attend to those responsibilities.

---

[3]   Hmmm, does all this sound familiar? Over the last several chapters, I've suggested that taking time to meet your own needs can help you 1) not go wacko, 2) have more patience, and 3) feel less angry. Interesting!

16

PERINATAL MOOD DISORDERS

SOMETIMES PREGNANCY AND ITS AFTERMATH can leave us feeling pretty shitty. You're *supposed* to be feeling so happy, and joyous and contented, but instead you feel anxious and overwhelmed and depressed. Well, you are not alone. Disorders of mood and mixed feelings are very common during pregnancy and after delivery. "Baby blues" refers to a milder form of depressed mood that lasts less than 1 to 2 weeks after childbirth and is experienced by up to 80% (!) of new moms. Post-partum depression is more severe, longer lasting, and a much more life disrupting episode of depression that occurs in up to 15% (!!) of moms after delivery.

Less commonly discussed and often dismissed as "normal stress" is post-partum anxiety. Unfortunately, many women suffer from anxiety that is beyond normal stress. Like a major depression, severe anxiety can make it very difficult to function in the processes of everyday life. Like depression, it's painful to exist in a state of constant anxiety. In a 2020 Parents Magazine article, Dr. Jonathan Abramowitz says, "We call postpartum anxiety 'the hidden disorder' because so few moms recognize it and it goes undiagnosed." "You constantly feel worried and on edge," says Sarah Gottfried, M.D., author of *The Hormone Cure.* "I think of postpartum anxiety as the loss of the normal sense of balance and calm, and postpartum depression as a loss of heart."

Often, health professionals, who are in a position to help women with postpartum mood disorders, do not recognize the symptoms. The mental health screening questions a woman may be asked to answer at her first post-partum check-up are focused on post-partum depression, and are not designed to pick up symptoms of clinical anxiety. This, combined with a general lack of recognition of post-partum anxiety, can lead to dismissive health providers when a woman most needs help. For women who are experiencing post-partum anxiety, it is not uncommon to experience upsetting and intrusive thoughts, obsessive concerns, a constant state of worried hypervigilance and fear, nausea, rapid heart rate, or racing thoughts. Many are exhausted, yet unable to sleep. Treatment with anti-anxiety medications, hormones, stepped up maternal support, talk therapy, and sleep aids can offer enormous relief from suffering to a woman experiencing this anxiety.

Newer guidelines for post-natal medical follow up encourage moms to get checked by a provider no later than three weeks after delivery. This can be a good time to talk with your doctor about how you are doing emotionally. Seek help sooner if you need it. I would also encourage you to bring someone with you who will advocate for your needs. There are numerous stories of medical providers who either overreact and try to have a woman committed or underreact and dismiss a woman's emotional pain. If you're not sure about the person you're seeking help from, then bring your partner or a friend or family to advocate for an appropriate response to your needs.

Perinatal mood disorders are common. They cause a great deal of suffering. And, they are also very treatable. There is no more important way to take care of your baby and family than to take of your own emotional needs.

For the National Suicide Prevention Hotline, dial 988 anywhere in the U.S.

A LETTER TO MOMS WITH POST-PARTUM MOOD DISRUPTION:

People who go through a major depression or severe anxiety, often feel like they are at the dark end of a tunnel with no light or clear path to the other side. They feel they will never find joy in the simple things of life again or that they will never again see the world through a normal lens.

The process of getting to the other end of the tunnel when you don't see the light or the path is one of faith. It's about having faith in the process of therapy and medication applied over time. It's about having faith that you will find your way back into the light of a lovely and reasonable world. You may not see how that can happen right now, but you *can* return to a more balanced life. You can get back to a place where you find joy in life. In the process, you will grow as a person and in the end you will be stronger for it.

A period of personal growth is often uncomfortable. Okay. Sometimes it's downright painful. Yet, when we face the things in life that we fear, we find the doors to the world open for us. You don't need to go through this alone. Do it with the support of a good therapist who will help you understand what is going on in your thoughts, and with medications that can help rebalance the chemistry in your brain and the hormones in your body.

So, what comes first? The chicken or the egg? Is it the biochemical imbalance in the brain or the life events that cause depression and overwhelming anxiety? Frankly, it doesn't really matter which goes out of whack first. When they are both really out of whack, you treat both. You try to understand the thoughts and feelings you're having through cognitive therapy. And you start nudging those neurotransmitters and hormones back into balance.

Be aware that finding the right anti-depressant or anti-anxiety medicine, for *you*, is a process of trial and error. What works for a friend may not help you and vice versa. However, there are many very well tolerated medications available. Most people can find something that helps them feel a bit more normal, a bit more stable, and a bit more able to function.

So, keep in communication with whomever is prescribing your medication as you work through what helps you. A doctor or therapist will help you find the right one if you need it.

The process of therapy is an investment in your health and wellbeing. Make sure you're comfortable with your therapist. The choice will become the best investment of your life. You will be building the foundation of self-understanding that can become a solid bedrock for your life ahead. You will also be developing the mental and emotional skills for handling life's slings and arrows with more resilience. Be gentle with yourself during this process. At the same time, with the support of your therapist, look hard at the things that scare you. Understanding what is behind the fear can set you free. Therapy doesn't have to be something you do for years on end. Often a modest period of crisis intervention can help people get back on an even keel.

Another tool you can employ as you fight the battle to regain the life you want is "guided imagery." One of the main goals of these recordings is to stimulate a relaxation response. This can be especially helpful for coping with anxiety. During my pregnancy, I struggled with anxiety that was way, way, way beyond anything I'd personally experienced before. My obstetrician directed me towards a series of audio recordings by Bellaruth Naparstek.[4] You can easily find these online. The one I found most helpful was for was labeled for insomnia, but I also use it for general stress relief and anxiety. Download the recording onto whatever mobile device you have so you can spend 30 minutes a day listening. She guides you through a series of images. The process helps trigger a hormonal relaxation response. It's a form of meditation that doesn't require years of training. It can be done even by someone who is anxious and has trouble getting their mind to quiet down. I highly recommend trying this technique.

We all go through some really, really hard times in life. You can find your way through to a good place again. It will be a process. It will

---

[4]   *Meditations for Healthful Sleep* audio CD by Bellaruth Naparstek. Health Journeys, 2000.

be hard at times. As you work your way through it, you will become a stronger person. As you get older the accumulated strengths from meeting life's hardest challenges will make each successive challenge easier to manage. The best thing you'll ever give your kids is your own emotional health. Focus a bit on you, and they will be fine.

Good luck and hang in there! Have faith in the process and the work of healing. Don't go it alone. Seek out some professional help.

About Postpartum Depression:

Postpartum Depression Fact Sheet NIH
https://www.nimh.nih.gov/health/publications/perinatal-depression

About Postpartum Anxiety:

Postpartum Anxiety: The Other Baby Blues We Need To Talk About, Parents Magazine, Stacy Collino and Nichole-Gabian Weber, 2/10/2020.

Strong As A Mother, an excellent book by Kate Rope.
For the National Suicide Prevention Hotline, dial 988 anywhere in the U.S.

17

PARENTING THROUGH QUARANTINES

THINGS ARE CRAZY RIGHT NOW. Even more crazy than typical for American parenthood. Some of you may have found yourself in a prolonged cloister with young kids. I hope we are done with this phase of the pandemic, but it's hard to know what the future will so generously lay on our doorstep. So how do we muddle through when the times are tough, the kids are young, and the days are long and lonely? Try some of these practical approaches to rough patches.

Baking

It doesn't matter if it is cliché. It doesn't matter if it comes from a box or is produced "from scratch." Just bake it. Eat it. Give it to your kids. Think of it as Covid vitamins or an old fashioned anti-depressant. If your baking involves chocolate or cinnamon or frosting, all the better. It's important that it appeals to both little kiddies and to household grown-ups. If that seems contradictory in your home, then remember that you can bake for adults and just add a huge layer of frosting to make it "kid friendly." It can certainly come from a pre-made tub of buttercream. The kids will be quite happy as will many of you "frosting eaters" out there. I'm a cake person myself. I scrape off the frosting and offer it around while I go back for a second slice of the cakiness.

If you fear that all this baking is excessive, then remember that our ancestors used to bake every day! It's true. I'm sure. Apple pies, cakes, biscuits, pancakes, and steamy butter rolls used to be the daily mark of a well cared for family. In addition, if you're really feeling guilty you could use this as a "learning activity" with the kids. In the future they will need to have the skills to provide and care for themselves. What better skill to teach them than how to cook comfort food! Bake. Eat. Share.

TV

Turn on the cartoons or give the kiddos a device, and walk out of the room. Unfortunately, this only works if your kids are old enough to have a shred of attention span. But, if that includes two out of three kids, then it's still a win! If you're purely in the infant stage, then TV may not offer much for engaging your babes. However, television and other electronics are not only therapeutic for children. Adults can also benefit from their many charms. If you find yourself descending into Stuck at Home Syndrome, then go to YouTube and watch "funny animal videos" or "acts of kindness" or "epic wins." Watch old musicals. New musicals. (I love me a good musical!) Or Mongolian throat singing. Look it up it's amazing! YouTube is kinda like crack, but with slightly fewer unhealthy side effects. At the very least, you can get yourself a little dose of happiness hormones and laughter endorphins. Or for a more serious topic you can watch permaculture documentaries, and save us all from global warming. Under the cover of Covid, daytime screen-time becomes resourceful survival instead of lackadaisical laziness. Might as well take advantage of the times.

Not Drinking?

Maybe not too much alcohol. Maybe. Just a little. As a medical professional, I have cared for people who have drunk themselves to death with alcohol. So, I'm genuinely cautious on this one. It seems all fun and "good spirted" for parents to break out the beer or wine when hanging out and debriefing over their parenting travails. But for some, too much can easily become a habit and lead to more and more. If you find yourself reaching for more than one average size drink a day, then it's time to stop for a six month alcohol break. You can revisit the issue after that. And no, you cannot wait for Covid to be over, your job to get better, or your kids to start school. I suggest parents under a lot of stress keep a lid on too much alcohol. Sorry to be such a party pooper on that one, but we're already losing people to this coronavirus we don't need to up the ante with newly minted stress induced alcoholics.

Human Contact

It's a good thing. Get a texting group of friends going and text every day about your successes and struggles. It's hard to call everyone every day, but it's amazing how much that contact with friends can help. Pick one person a day to actually call and have a conversation with. You may think the texting is enough, but once you actually shoot the shit and laugh with your friends, you'll realize how much better it is to just talk with them.

Get Out Of The House

Even those of you with the best of hibernation skills are going to need to get a bit of sunshine at some point. And children have this need to run. Preferably in the sun, wind, or rain. Snow play sounds good, but it involves all this bundling up in snowsuits and mittens and boots, and they can't move so they come right back in all fussy. Or if your kids are older they will insist on wearing knit gloves in wet snow and freeze their hands into painful popsicles, then come back in crying that their hands hurt. So, you'll need to be in a strong place emotionally before you embark on snow play. But otherwise, find an empty field and let the kids run for a bit. Scream for a bit. Jump in a stream, and get wet for a bit. Obviously this is harder to do if you live in a city. In that case, consider sending the children to spend the summer with someone in the country. People have been doing that for wars and epidemics as long as we've had wars and epidemics.

Count A Blessing

Be glad you're not raising babies in a war zone. Our stresses are very real. Many people are losing loved ones to Covid, but at least we don't have bombs falling on our children's heads.

Let It Go

Let go, and go with the flow. There's a lot of parenting stuff that you just can't control right now. And truthfully, "parental control" is really all just a grand illusion. Now that I think about it, that's one of the main parenting themes of my book. Ease up on attempts to keep everything in control because you don't really have control anyway. Parenting 101, ta da!

Velvet Paintings

Yeah, I know, most of you don't remember the days of curbside stands selling large velvet paintings of Elvis or fully framed velvet nature scenes. They seemed to be on every corner in my youth. Who would ever imagine that these atrocious, neon bright roadside attractions would become a quarantine savior. Life is full of strangeness.

I discovered the more modern version of velvet paintings while cruising the aisles of a craft store. There they were. Black and white color-in-posters where the black part was velvet, which quite frankly makes it *much* easier to stay in the lines! I have since discovered that you can go on-line and order "velvet posters" or "fuzzy art" in an endless variety of subjects and difficulties. There are kittens and monster trucks for kids and swirly koi or graphic patterns for adults. I know, I know you're wondering if I went off the deep end. But really, they are fun and mindless. You just play with colors and work on it here and there, now and then. You can do it. The kids can do it. And in the end you get this wonderfully bright thing laced with cheap velvet that goes with nothing in your house. So, you order another one and more makers. Remember, not everything in life needs to be a great accomplishment. If you are suffering from boredom and confinement, consider a velvet poster and a bright pack of magic markers. I'm sure art therapists everywhere will condone the practice, so we can call it legit.

Alrighty, now that I have covered *everything* a parent needs to know to survive during confinement with young kids, we can move on to some of the everyday issues that may have concerned you pre-pandemic.

If you have lost someone to Covid, please know that you have my deepest sympathies and condolences. I am so sorry for your loss. I wish you all peace and comfort.

PART II:

HISTORICAL FORCES INFLUENCING AMERICAN FAMILIES

18

BIG CHANGES IN THE LAST 100 YEARS

I SUSPECT MOST OF US TAKE the job of parenting pretty seriously. We want to do the best we can for our children. How much time we have to invest in figuring out *what* we feel is best for our kids is pretty variable. Most of us grab what information we can when we can. If we are lucky, we have time to pick up a book or two as we muddle through our crazy lives. We're always speeding ahead. Looking ahead. It's human nature to look at life and simply accept how things are. We feel as though life has always been this way. This is probably why I was taken by surprise when I started looking back just the littlest bit in time.

In the last 100 years, the nature of the relationship between parents and children has undergone a profound change from what it was like for most of human evolution. These very recent changes to the parent-child relationship affect everything about how we raise, relate to, and educate our children. If you know what existed before, if you recognize what has changed and why, then you can understand parenting through fresher more accurate eyes. This is not some esoteric academic discussion. You may soon be picking a preschool or daycare for your child. The type you pick may be different when you understand how we got to be where we are in parenting beliefs and education agendas. So, don't skip the next few chapters. They are not a philosophical exercise nor just for parents with older kids.

19

FEAR BASED EDUCATION AND PARENTING

PARENTS TODAY OFTEN FEEL THEY need to provide their kids with numerous opportunities and activities to "develop" their children's skills. This mindset can start at a remarkably young age, and puts enormous stress on both parent and child. I think it's worth looking at how some of this pressure to "develop" our child's skills came about. Stick with me for a few pages. I think you'll find some interesting new perspectives on educating your kids.

Many of us take for granted that raising our children has *always* been about "schooling" their potential. But let's go back in time. Let's go way back to when we lived in hunter-gatherer groups. This is where we have spent most of our evolutionary history. That's about 200,000 evolutionary years as homo sapiens and 2 million years if you look at earlier hominins. For almost all of that time we proto humans, and then homo sapiens lived as *hunter-gatherers*. We still have a few pure hunter-gatherer societies in this world, and through them we get a glimpse into how childhood has been experienced for most of our human timeline. It's important to understand that hunter-gatherer societies are typically more egalitarian than ours is today. Everyone is considered valuable, whether male or female, young or old. Children are considered fully formed individuals whose wants and needs have legitimate worth. They are not forced to "learn" nor be "educated" by the adults. It is expected that children will learn what they need to learn on their own. As they mature, they will contribute to the wellbeing and activities of the group. The children learn almost everything through self-initiated play. One of the main structures of child growth and development in these types of societies is the multi-aged play group. Young children, ages 2 or 3, will be carried around by older children, ages 8 or 9, who are following around the 10 to 15-year-olds who are play-practicing what they have learned hunting with the men, gathering with the women, or just watching the older members of their group. As they grow, the children begin to contribute work and take on more of the tasks of life. It is certainly vital that each child not only masters but also excels at many of these life skills. Hunting, fishing, identifying and gathering plants and herbs, animal behavior, seasonal variations, making tools, making medicines...the volume of information along with the detail and complexity of skills that kids master is truly monumental. They learn this by "doing and playing," not by sitting for a lecture, taking notes, or doing worksheets. Activities are initiated by the children generally without adult involvement. These children will be deciding what to learn on any given day. They will also have a whole village of experts to learn from not just their parents.

Now, let's jump forward in time to the era of farming societies. This transformation got underway about 12,000 years ago, but it took a while before most humans lived in permanent settlements. In early Western cultures, the growth and proliferation of settled villages generates the concept of land ownership. This resulted in the development of cultures with land "owners" and landless "laborers." Society became hierarchical and the few "haves" began to rule the many "have nots." For a looong time the vast, vast majority of the world population were basically land-less peasants or slaves. Only a very, very few lived in a wealthy house or a castle on the hill. This transformation meant we now had social "classes" rather than the egalitarian society of the hunter-gatherers. Most peasant children grew and learned alongside siblings, parents, and neighbors. They still learned by doing, but likely with less time for play. Because now parents needed the labor of their children in the fields and animal pens. Their parents nurtured in them and taught them the skills that went with the family work. Farming, animal care, blacksmithing, baking, weaving, knitting, food storage, and more farming. Generally, children were making significant contributions to the family's success from a young age. The exception, of course, were those rich aristocrats living on the hill. Their children would be sheltered from the drudgery of work and settled down at a desk for a one-on-one tutored, academic education.

Slowly, during the late Middle Ages and early Renaissance, a small middle class developed amongst wealthy European traders and craftsmen. These families could then seek tutors and schooling for their children much as the wealthy aristocracy had long done. Then, just a few hundred years back, the French and American Revolutions would come along and embrace ideals of "the self-made man" and the emerging concept that a person might, through hard work and brains, actually "move upward" in class![5] This was truly revolutionary. Then just 150 years ago, came the Industrial Revolution. Farming was becoming mechanized, and many parents were leaving the country side to work in factories. They were reaching and striving for "a better life." And the children of the poor masses followed, learning the skills of their parents while working in the same factories.

By the early 1900s, the labor movement hit the United States. Laborers began demanding a fair, living wage. The concept that workers had rights, that women had rights, and that children had rights spread throughout the cities. Social progressives started campaigning to ban child labor in factories and provide expanded education to the masses. Learning became a way to move *up*. And the middle class in America exploded. For the first time, educating your children became something achievable for a large number of families. It was no longer for the rich

---

[5]   I know, I'm compressing a lot of world history into a few Eurocentric lines here, but this is a book about American parenting not history. Stick with me. I have a point to make.

aristocracy alone. The self-made-man (provided he was white) now had the right and the opportunity to raise children who could continue to move his family *up* the social and economic ladder.

Think about it. These are massive social and cultural shifts that are relatively new in our world. They are still not fully evolved or understood.

1. Lower classes can aspire to move up in wealth and class.
2. A primary route for upward mobility is education.
3. A child's *job* is schooling, which allows them to reach higher than their parents.

How we attempt to implement these ideas in daily life is a new and on-going experiment. We've only been living with these ideas for about 200 years. Not very long in the grand scheme of humanity. The concept of upward mobility can be very freeing. However, it can put a lot of pressure on a child.

Individual, tutored, didactic education of children has been practiced by the wealthy for a long time. But, generalized education that reaches all children is a rather new creation. How then has childhood education evolved? Prior to the early 1900s, school, for those who had access to it, often started at age seven. Some kids started later if the family needed the child's help at home or could not afford to pay for school. Sometimes called "The Age of Reason," seven years of age is when children begin to become capable of more complex thought. This is the earliest age at which it was felt children were developmentally ready for school. Kindergarten, for younger children, is a relatively new idea that began in Germany during the mid 1800s. Friedrich Froebel first coined the term "kinder-garten" and felt that young children could learn a great deal through the *play*ful exploration of the world. He started "*pre*-schooling" for children 3 to 7 years of age. The original goals of this "children's garden" were to use supervised *play* to prepare a *child socially, emotionally, and morally* for the academic school environment that would come later. German immigrants would bring the idea of kindergarten to America. In the U.S., the idea was adopted into an English format by the philanthropist Elizabeth Peabody. By the late 1800s many women were working in the factories of the Industrial Revolution. Young children would often be placed in "day nurseries" were they had little supervision or stimulation. Kindergarten became a better, more enriched environment for the children of the working poor. And as child labor laws pushed kids out of the factories, the burgeoning public school system pulled them off the troublesome streets. Over the ensuing years there was, of course, debate about what kind of learning should be incorporated in kindergarten.

All education includes a certain amount of indoctrination. Religious schools teach their view on the world, and even public schools present history and the world through a choice of lenses. Many early public school advocates in America were wealthy, and wanted a working class that supported the underlying capitalistic beliefs of our economy. Thus, early public education tended to focus on basic literacy and math that would create a work force that functioned in the new factories of the Industrial Revolution. However, literacy is an insidious beast that leads to the "evil" spread of information, knowledge, ideas, and opinions. Pamphlets, fliers, newspapers, and all the radical ideas they contained became accessible to the newly literate poor. Now the lower classes could *really* see there was an emerging economic power inherent in being knowledgeable and educated. So, they too became invested in the idea of educating their children whenever they could. In the early 1900s these forces would come into play in the formation of unions and the push for worker's rights. World War I and the Spanish Flu pandemic were followed by a devastating economic depression that would reinforce the underclass appreciation of education's protective potential. Thus, by the middle of the 1900s, an American child's early life no longer revolved around supporting the family. Instead, children were expected to spend their energies on learning. Over time this would evolve into a much more intense and potentially troublesome academic race.

By the 1950s, cold war anxiety would lead to a push for starting academic studies at younger ages. While Sputnik circled overhead, Americans panicked that we were "falling behind" the Russians. This led to a kind of "fear based" and politically driven academic policy that continues to this day. This political fear of "falling behind" intensified with the rise of a successful Japanese car industry in the 1970's, and today with a fear of "falling behind" China. Part of this panic led to the idea that for America to "keep up" in the world's economic and political race, *our* children, *your* children, need to start academics at younger and younger ages. And so, we see the age range for kindergarten shifted from under seven to five years old. Most school systems now require that a child attend school by age six, and parents often fear their child might "fall behind" if they are not in *pre*-school by age three or four. Many teachers will tell you that the play based *learning* of the "children's garden" has given way to the rigors of first grade academics and worksheets pressed upon flighty brained 5-year-olds.

We're going to come back to this situation, but first we need to understand another element of recent history that has had a huge impact on the nature of *our* children's educational experiences.

Let's have a look at the history of the Head Start Program. (Stay with me!) In 1965, President Johnson launched his "Great Society" campaign with the goal of improving social justice. The civil rights movement was in full force, and the hope was to raise disadvantaged children out of poverty. The Head Start Program began as a summer program, and evolved into a comprehensive plan to address emotional, cognitive, social, and nutritional issues. This early childhood education program was based on the idea that kids from "disadvantaged backgrounds" could get a boost in academics if *their parents* were given resources and skill development while the children accessed time in an enriched environment. Head Start was aimed at reaching families with low income and low levels of parental education. Think Appalachia, "company owned" mining towns, and sweatshop workers. Think people of color who had been subjected to racism, repression, and systemic terrorism across generations. It has been noted that children from these backgrounds are, on average, exposed to far fewer new words per day compared to children from homes with educated parents and better income. This is often called "the word gap," and it can correlate with worse academic outcomes. By providing disadvantaged kids and *their parents* with a more enriched environment in Head Start, the hope was these children would get a boost to bring them up to speed in school. They would have a greater chance at academic and economic success than they otherwise could expect. And, basically, though it is a hard thing to measure, it seemed to help. Disadvantaged kids given early Head Start pre-school *and parental education,* did seem to do better in school *than their disadvantaged peers* who did not get these Head Start interventions. The most important aspect of this intervention was felt to be the parental education component. Modeling new ways of parenting allowed parents to internalize new skills which they could continue to use with their kids as they were growing up. Unfortunately, this vital parental component was not truly recognized. Instead, people became focused on the pre-school component. What happened next is even more interesting. There appears to have been a general extrapolation of the early intervention idea to other groups of children. If early pre-school was good for disadvantaged kids, then it must be good for all kids, right? And the world is now competitive, so we don't want any other kids getting ahead of our kids, right?

This idea fails to recognize several facts. First, young kids are not mini-adults. Their brains do not work in the same way. I mean that literally. Their brain structure and function are not like an adult's. It takes years and years for a brain to mature. In fact, recent studies using technologies that look at brain function show that the brains of 20-year-olds are still evolving. Children are programed to develop various skills as they grow, and as their brain matures. No matter how early you start math, you can't teach calculus to a 5-year-old. At five children are just starting to wrap their heads around vague concepts of time. Really. Try explaining time to a three-year-old. They are only going to grasp the bare periphery of the concept. Some things are learned only when the child's brain development allows for it. If your child is growing up in a family where parents read to young children and a pile of chocolate chips becomes an opportunity to teach addition and subtraction, then your child is already growing up in that enriched environment.

Many researchers, parents, and teachers feel that early academics are a problem. It pushes children to learn in ways for which they are not yet developmentally ready. They may try, but their brains are too young. This leads to failure and frustration for the child, who may be demonized as a "behavior problem." Worse yet, they may be pathologized and given a diagnosis that may haunt them for far too long. The result is that kids can turn off to the joy of learning and tune out for the duration of their grade school years. Studies have shown that kids who are pushed to read early are reading at the same level as those who are not pushed when measured at age ten. If we then reassess these two groups at age 15, we find that kids who learned to read *later* are, in fact, reading significantly more. Huh! Why is that? Seems counter intuitive, doesn't it? Perhaps there are other developmental tasks that the late start readers get more time to master. Such as a capacity for internal motivation. Or perhaps the gift of time lets them simply enjoy reading. We in fact have no evidence...no evidence... that early reading or early academics leads to long-term improved academic outcome. We certainly have no evidence that it leads to personal or professional success. In fact, we have considerable evidence to the contrary. Too much pressure early on can backfire. Young children have other developmental tasks to master and maturation to complete before they are ready for didactic education.

This is not to say that good child-initiated *play*-based *pre*-school can't be a good thing. An open, free, play filled environment with a teacher who facilitates a child's individual development and exploration of the world can be a very good thing. Many early childhood development experts recommend a *pre*-school that allows *child*-initiated activities guided by a teacher who focuses on verbal language, social and emotional skills, and the development of thought processes. On my son's first day of pre-school, at age four, the teacher noticed his keen interest in the hole puncher she'd used. She set him up with the puncher and stack of paper with which he proceeded to occupy himself for an hour. Mechanical engineering, fine motor skills, hand eye coordination, cause and effect, and one boy punching holes with complete freedom. I know he loved every second with that hole puncher. That's a great teacher, and a great environment in which to grow and learn with joy.

So, we have this child with a brain that is unlike our own. The wiring is different, and the connections between the wires are different. It's certainly not an empty receptacle into which information simply needs to be dumped. It is in fact, a complex, rapidly growing, evolving, and changing network of brain connections and revisions. Further, each child's brain is evolving in its own pattern and time frame. It's reasonable to believe the educational needs of such a beastie might be worth some real research. In fact, a great deal of research has been done, and our knowledge is rapidly evolving. Unfortunately, many of the decisions about *how* to teach our children continue to be fear based, often political, reactionary and uninformed. I was surprised to learn that large policy decisions about what and how a child should learn are often made by people without expertise in childhood development or neuro-educational science. Furthermore, most school systems in the U.S. do not require teachers to have training in child development! Our teachers may have little to no instruction in how a child's brain works and grows!? As of 2021, twenty-seven states did not require early education teachers to have instruction in the science of literacy teaching. This includes phonological awareness, phonemic awareness, learning the alphabet, and concepts of print. There is a science to teaching reading. We really do know what works. Yet, many states still practice outdated, and soundly disproven methods, such as "whole language." Unbelievably, Only 11 states require a *special education teacher* to pass a test of early literacy teaching skills! On-going teacher education requirements and assessment also vary enormously from state to state. In addition, many states have rolled back GPA and basic testing requirements for students entering a teaching credentialing program. Isn't that a bit crazy?

Okay, what's the point of all this discussion? Well, we haven't been attempting universal education for very long. Much of the form that our American public schools currently take is a reflection of historical, political, cultural, and emotional forces from the last 150 years. It's not some tried and true format that has been developed by experts in child development. Actually, it's quite haphazard and in no way reflects the types of environments that human children evolved to live in. In fact, we are just barely beginning to understand human brain development, and the wide range of learning differences our children bring to the educational table. Furthermore, it's almost impossible to predict the future world our children will inherit. Technology is moving so fast that we can't even really predict how we will be living ten years from now. I recommend we keep an open mind about how this public education experiment needs to evolve. It's entirely possible that emotional, inter-personal, and mental flexibility skills may offer *your* child the greatest buffer against an uncertain future. These are some of the things we *used* to focus on in kindergarten and the early grades. Fifty years from now, whether your child started reading by age 4 or age 8 will have no bearing on their economic or emotional well-being. If your child is not doing well within the educational system as it currently exists, don't assume it's your child that has a problem. Your child may be perfectly normal. The problem may be a dysfunctional school system. Furthermore, what your child may need in life may not be what they are getting from that school system. Other countries, like Finland, do education completely differently. Once you understand these concepts you become more empowered to help *your* child in a substantial way.

A few great resources on this topic:
1. *The New Preschool is Crushing Kids. Today's Young Children are Working More but They Are Learning Less.* Erika Christakis, The Atlantic, Jan/Feb 2016.
2. *The Importance of Being Little: What Young Children Really Need from Grown Ups*, great book by Erika Christakis
3. *What if Everybody Understood Child Development*, great book by Rae Pica.
4. *Early Childhood Education in Finland: In Finland's Early Primary Years, Space, Time and Free Play Come First!*, Becky Searls. Map Mates.org, 5/5/2017.
5. *Early Academic Training Produces Long-Term Harm Research Reveals Potential Risks Of Academic Preschools And Kindergartens.* Peter Gray, Psychology Today, May 5, 2015.

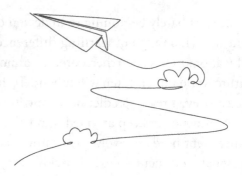

20

CONCERTED CULTIVATION vs ACCOMPLISHMENT OF NATURAL GROWTH

L ET'S TAKE A LOOK AT *how* our child-centric approach to education plays out in everyday life. Many parents have internalized the concept of "concerted cultivation." Annette Lareau, author of *Unequal Childhoods: Class, Race, and Family Life,* coined this term when she was studying the impact of race and class on the long-term success of children. Her study was aimed at identifying ways that success was either hindered or facilitated in families of different backgrounds. She found two different approaches to raising children. In middle class families with educated parents, there was an attempt by parents to carefully "develop" their children's skills through school, sports, classes, languages, and activities. This "concerted cultivation" model involved extensive scheduling of children's time in primarily adult supervised activities. These kids developed good skills in navigating the adult world outside the family. They were accustomed to interacting with adult authority in the form of coaches, teachers, and club leaders. They also became familiar with forms and applications, photo IDs, deadlines, commitments, and the logistics of dealing with the bureaucratic structures that oversaw their activities. These skills had value when as young adults they entered the working world. On the other hand, their parents were often strained by constant conflicts between work, transporting, and supervising their kid's highly scheduled time. The kids were often exhausted, stressed, and rarely had any "down time." These families were not as bonded since little time was spent in family focused activities. The exception to these findings was in middle class African-American families where children were still "cultivated," but time with extended family was also maintained. However, the middle-class kids of all races had little opportunity to engage in self-invented play with friends and carried high levels of stress. So, if a balanced work, play, and family life is important to your definition of "success" for your child, then this approach may need a bit of revision.

In Lareau's study, the flip side of "concerted cultivation" parenting was termed, "accomplishment of natural growth." Lareau found this attitude towards parenting was more common in lower income homes. These parents typically had little time or money to facilitate sports, dance, or music lessons. In these homes, kids were allowed to schedule their own free time, and create their own forms of play. Much of their time was spent playing with neighborhood kids in spontaneously invented games with extensively negotiated rules. These families often had deep binding ties to extended family and community. Children in these homes typically had a large network of aunties, grandmas, and cousins to rely upon through much of their lives. And yet, these kids often internalized their parent's mistrust and suspicion of organized authorities. This lack of trust in and exposure to adult organizations could result in young adults who lacked the confidence and bureaucratic fluency that can be so important in negotiating the professional world.

It's important to note that Lareau published her study in 2003. If you were to interview Baby Boomers and their parents, none of them would have experienced "concerted cultivation." I suspect (in a non-scientific analysis) that even those with the most advanced degrees spent their childhoods in a manner more in line with the "accomplishment of natural growth" style that Lareau describes. My siblings and I certainly spent our free time unsupervised and roaming an ever expanding territory around our suburban home. My parents also share childhood memories of their neighborhood turf and gang of friends. I get it that we may want to offer our children an opportunity that was not available to us. A chance at some of those fun things the "rich aristocrat" kids always get to do. My mother got piano lessons and I got dance class, but there was no "pre-school" nor "cultivation" nor constant parental supervision. And there was a lot of time to work on developing those less tangible skills of empathy, curiosity, and exploration.

I am not a digital native. During my last year in high school, the "computer club" was born when four bulky terminals with green type became available to the geeky few who wanted to learn Fortran. Yet, as the world has changed, I have learned the technical skills I needed for my professional and personal life. Do we really need concerted cultivation of our kids for them to live happy successful lives? We truly don't know what the world will be like in 20 years. 50 years? We have no clue what skills our children will rely upon.

Almost two decades after Lareau's study, middle class concerted cultivation has reached a fever pitch in America. A desperate competition has evolved. The youngest children are now scheduled with foreign language class, dance, gymnastics, karate, art, engineering, music, early coding and on and on. Within this frantic race in an apparently constricting world, we have both students and teachers caught up in cheating scandals. Teen suicide rates are rising across ethnic groups. High schools and colleges alike are struggling to help students who are stressed and lost as they try to jump through every hoop we put before them. Yet, many lack any grounding that ties them to family, community, friends, cause, or reason for being.

So, where did this parental idea that we need to "cultivate" our children's skills come from? And why has it reached such a fever pitch? We have to look back at those monumental economic and cultural revolutions of the last century. In this country, men, and for the first time women, have internalized the idea that we can achieve whatever success we want through hard work. Yet, we are also aware of the unspoken truth that the playing field is most certainly *not* level. That it is easier for the rich to get richer than it is for the poor to get less poor. Our parents did better than their parents. And so, we are supposed to do "better" than our parents. Unfortunately, twenty-five-year-olds are moving back in with mom and dad, debt is way up, wages are down, suicide is up, healthcare is out of reach, elders struggle in poverty, and college tuition seems stratospheric. So, we look at our kids and think, "they need to be the best, the *very* best to make it in the coming world." And we've been told that education is the way *up*. Therefore, we get behind and puuuuush.

There lies a tangled web of disordered thinking. The first problem is the social-political idea that everything is fine in the world. That if people aren't doing well they just need to start pre-school earlier, or work harder, longer hours…without a raise…or benefits…or regular hours? We have this idea that if we aren't successful that it is intrinsically our own fault. That the poor are poor because of their own flaws and failings. These beliefs ignore the very real truth that laws, rules, prejudices, history, societal structures, and even bad luck can deal us massive and even insurmountable obstacles. In fact, many of the laws that set up the growth, development, and protection of middle class Americans have been slowly dismantled over the last 80 years. We act as if state supported childcare is a luxury rather than a necessity for working parents. We fear that "healthcare for all" is the same as Communism, and that funding education is bad for our country. When we think that pushing our kids to be their academic best will let them succeed in the world, then we are ignoring the very real forces that are arrayed against them. And if we ignore the problems, then we can't fix them. If we want our kids to have a good life, then we need to repair the social, political, economic, and environmental damage that's been done over the last 80 years. It's not early pre-school that will help your kids live a good life. It's building a better society.

How can *every* generation "do better" than the last one? If by "better" you mean have a bigger house, more cars, and more possessions, then at some point we'll eat up the world and all its resources. Instead, how about we hope our children have a "good" life. Perhaps we could aim for balance. A place where everyone's needs and comforts and creative endeavors are nourished, and the earth can regenerate and be in balance. At the very least, we as parents can work to make the playing field more even for our adult children. So that once again, the self-made common man or woman can have a fair chance at a good life. If we can build that world for our kids, then we don't need to stress about whether the right pre-school will launch our child into the old boys network of Ivy League alumni. Or fear that breaching the halls of the rich aristocracy is the only path to a life without homelessness and despair. We could let our kids be kids again.

If this sounds revolutionary, well, maybe it kinda is. But the voices are out there. Economists, business leaders, environmentalists, and parents are looking to change the very goals and structures by which we run our lives. The Agricultural Revolution and the Industrial Revolution both dramatically changed the structure of society. How will the Technology Revolution change our future society? What shape do we want our society to take as our kids become adults? The dystopian world of Blade Runner? Or the utopian vision of Finland? Whatever it will be, it's *our* job to build it for our children.

Here are a few books to inspire you:

1. *The Nordic Theory of Everything: In Search of A Better Life,* Anu Partanen.
2. *Range: Why Generalists Triumph in a Specialized World,* David Epstein.
3. *Doughnut Economics,* Kate Rayworth.
4. *The Year of Living Danishly: Uncovering the Secrets of the Worlds Happiest Country,* Helen Russell.
5. *The Danish Way of Parenting: What the Happiest People in the World Know About Raising Confident Capable Kids,* Jessica Joelle Alexander and Iben Sandhal

The other thread to consider in this tangled web of frenzied concerted cultivation is basic child development. I'll say it again. A child's brain is not wired like an adult brain. They are not mini me's. They need and deserve the time to be young and immature. We are the most intelligent creature on the planet because we take foreeeever to grow our young to adulthood. There's a lot going on in that foreeeeever that needs to happen.

It may seem strange to be discussing issues of concerted cultivation, free play, overscheduling, and restructuring of society in a book aimed at parenting the youngest of children. Yet, these issues have so permeated the conscious anxiety of parents that some grounding in their origins is useful. The pressure to engage in concerted cultivation is starting at crazy young ages. It's easy to get sucked into it even as you try to resist. Moms who keep their 4-year-olds out of soccer will be told by other moms that their kids won't be able to keep up when they are 10-years-old. It's not true. The 10-year-old may start out behind, but their motor cortex and cerebellum are much more developed than a four-year-old's. If it's in their nature, and they are interested, then they will pick up the skills much faster. But it's hard to argue this when all the other moms fearfully argue that you have to start them at age four. If you do keep your kids out of activities and try to set up playdates, you may find most of the other kids are booked into scheduled activities.

But, don't give up. You will find other kids that can run free with yours. Children need a chance to be young. They need time for free play. They need a lot of time for free play. They don't need parents displacing the world's anxiety about global outsourcing and competitiveness onto their earliest years. Consciously limit how many activities you allow your children. It will facilitate family time, and allow for the deepening of important bonds. Place value on teaching the life skills of making regular meals, cleaning a bathroom, doing the family laundry, and caring for pets. This gives kids truly vital skills they can take to any college or job. Coach your kids not to perfect scores, but instead to find a balance of school work and fun time, industry and friendships, giving and community involvement. This can be key to helping them find a more rewarding life balance with meaning and connections. Before you pick a preschool, before you set your little one's feet upon life's path, think about where that path might lead her. Ask yourself if it looks like it goes where you want her to wind up.

To get you thinking before you pick a daycare or preschool for your little one:

1. *What if Everybody Understood Child Development?* Rae Pica.
2. *Importance of Being Little: What Young Children Really Need From Grown-ups,* Erika Christakis.
3. *Reading Instruction In Kindergarten: Little Gain And Much To Lose.* Nancy Carlsson-Paige, Geralyn Bywater McLaughlin, & Joan Wolfsheimer Almon, Alliance for Childhood
4. *Early Academic Training Produces Long-Term Harm Research Reveals Potential Risks Of Academic Preschools And Kindergartens.* Peter Gray, Psychology Today, May 5, 2015.

21

THE PATHLESS JOURNEY

> Two roads diverged in a wood, and I?
> …I had no idea which one to take..[6]

ONE OF THE CHALLENGES OF modern parenthood is that there are often no "right" answers. The days in which children were raised on the same schedule and clear rules of child rearing are long gone. Which means, what works for your family and your kids is the "right" way. If your kids are eating and happy with your schedule, then it's good for them and you. If it isn't working, try something new. Certainly, there are generalities that apply to most families and children. For example, you can expect that over the first year your baby will gradually eat more solid food and less formula or breastmilk. But even this varies a lot. Some infants are eating lots of formula at 1-year-old while others take very little. Your kids may have a strong opinion about this. One baby may like the solids, and lose interest in the formula. Another baby may not care for the new and strange foods you're offering and cling to liquid meals. It's okay.

---

[6] A mutilation of *The Road Not Taken* by Robert Frost.

If you look at what is considered normal or "best" for children in different cultures around the world you'll see it varies tremendously. A !Kung infant sips breast milk every 4 to 5 minutes all day and night, and often continues long after eating solids. Those foods are first chewed by mom then transferred to the child's mouth. The French see breastfeeding beyond three months as an unnecessary burden on mothers. Yeah, really! Therefore, it's not considered advisable for family bonding and unity. Many of the U.S. theories regarding early introduction of solids and allergies have now been found to be incorrect, and some recommendations were recently reversed. Beliefs about what is good and appropriate for children can vary enormously in different cultures and over time. Nevertheless, children grow and thrive within a huge range of situations.

In 2014, Malia Wollan and Hannah Whitaker produced an article and photo journal for the New York Times. They photographed young children around the world sitting with their breakfasts. Japanese children sat before spreads of fermented soybeans, miso soup, rice, salmon, beans with dried fish, and squash. In Malawi, well off children ate fritters, cornmeal porridge, sweet potato, pumpkin, and sweet tea. Many South American children start their day with coffee and milk along with bread, cheese, and ham. In Amsterdam, they had buttered bread with heavy doses of sweet chocolate shavings. The French child ate chocolate cereal, bread with butter and jam, orange juice, and fruit. I know many an American parent who would shudder at the sugar content of those last two meals! Just think of the different standards around the world for a "good" kid's breakfast.

We all need ideas and input from other parents and pediatricians with experience, but I encourage you to not worry about whether you are doing things "the right way." There are many "right ways," and a healthy kid is basically genetically programed to thrive. Take a deep breath and ask yourself what works for *you*, your kids, and your family. Experiment if you're not sure, and don't forget you can make decisions based on what is best for the adults in the family. If daycare is working for your kids, but both parents are overwhelmed with juggling jobs and transporting kids, then it's not working for *the family*! You may be able to tough it out for a bit, but it will strain the family relationships. So, don't be afraid to consider a nanny or different daycare with better location or a pick-up/drop-off nanny or a mother's helper or an au pair or inviting grandma to live with you for a year.

It can be tough not having a clear set of predetermined steps and sure answers. However, as your kids get older, you'll realize that families have a variety of structures and routines. In the very early days of parenting, many of us (myself for sure!) have felt less than confident. Seek out advice and ideas. Pick and choose from those offerings, and then trust yourself.

22

THE TRUTH ABOUT AMERICAN MOTHERHOOD: SO HOLY, SO LOWLY

REGARDLESS OF THE REALITY OF working mothers in the U.S., we tend to imagine "motherhood" with visions of a stay-at-home mom whose life moves to the rhythm of her kid's needs. Always present. Always solicitous. Steady and unwavering in her focus on the slightest needs of her children and family. We have a twisted ideal of "good" mothers as unfailingly devoted to the all-consuming task of caring for others. This ideal completely lacks any allowance for a woman's selfhood. It ignores the value of the numerous other contributions she can make to this world. It obliterates the needs of the female adult, while elevating her work so stratospherically high that it becomes beyond worth. To pay for such purity would be disrespectful. No, a mother's work is beyond and above such dirty things as pay or Social Security or - gasp - healthcare! At the same time that it is too holy to be paid for, ironically, it is denigrated as unskilled and unworthy of pay. This is especially true if the mother is a woman of color.

An American *mother's* involvement in the adult world is not *really* expected, nor *wanted*. That would pull her attention from its focus on the ideal of endless self-sacrifice. In 1963 Betty Friedan wrote *The Feminine Mystique*. This groundbreaking and culture shifting book argued that an idealized definition of femininity was constraining and entrapping women in certain roles and behaviors. In the ensuing years, much of that mystique has been dismantled as women stretched for liberation. But the idealized "American Motherhood" lingers as a left over residue of that repressive "feminine mystique." It's now okay for a *woman* to wear pants. It's now okay for a *woman* to work. It's even okay for a *woman* to pursue a career. Right up until it clashes with the idealization of American *Motherhood*. Once a *woman* becomes a *mother*, she is expected to sacrifice her inner self for her child. She is no longer allowed to have her own needs. Furthermore, her own life industry becomes of no value to society. Only silent unpaid laboring for the needs of her child and family is an acceptable path for a mother. As her career and industry are sacrificed so too is her financial independence and security. If she fights to maintain her career, interests, and income, then she will often do so while *still* attempting to meet the silent expectations of the self-sacrificing, perfect American Mother.

If she is a mother-of-color, the rules and expectations change. Then she is considered lazy if she stays at home raising kids, and negligent if she keeps working outside the home. No win there!

If my criticism of the idealized American Mother upsets you, then consider Daddyo. Fathers are not expected to give up their life's industry to be a good father. They need to be present, yes. They need to be loving, yes. Today's fathers need to be involved, yes. But they are also expected to take business trips, go to the gym without kids in tow, meet friends for basketball or biking or a beer every now and then. There is no unspoken expectation that they obliterate their own adult needs and contributions to the world. Sure, they need to compromise and give up a thing or two. However, they are not only allowed, but *unconsciously expected* to continue personal adult pursuits.

We have this concept of motherhood that is emotionally unhealthy, and also a ridiculously unrealistic reflection of modern life. Yet, many new mothers find themselves blindsided by these crazy expectations just as they are hitting professional stride. Young women today have been exposed to other women in positions of power, of accomplishment, and as heads of household. They have often worked hard to gain the skills of independence and financial solvency. But as soon as they grow a baby, they are expected to fill a role of endless under-valued emotional giving and caretaking…*without pay.* Women in our culture are expected to be the primary influencers on the growth and worthiness of our next generation of American adults. They are expected to do it for free. Out of their pure and selfless heart. Out of our motherly love for our children. Fathers love their children. Yet, they do not risk financial destitution in order to have children. In fact, so many men fail in their obligation to nurture, care for, and provide for their children that we require entire legal systems to go after deadbeat dads. So far our feminism has made it possible for mothers to engage in outside work provided they continue to work fulltime within the home. Yippee! We can have it all…except we get paid less than a man…and get nothing for the second shift. Yippee?

I know you're all uncomfortable now because I have implied that a mother should be paid for raising our country's next generation. Here's the thing. We no longer live in hunter-gather societies where food and property are shared. Where social structure is egalitarian as opposed to hierarchical. Where babies are genuinely raised by the whole village. No, we live in a capitalistic, hierarchical, competitive world where privilege and comfort must be worked, fought, and struggled for across a very uneven playing field. Systemic sexism and racism are still embedded in the fabric and laws of our society. Nevertheless, you want women to sacrifice their whole life and attention to raising the next generation? And you are going to take care of them how? That paternalistic marriage thing never worked and is now fully broken. We can't count on that. So, what do we Americans do? We expect women to seek employment for their own personal needs *and* dedicate themselves to a second job that requires far more hours of labor, endless on-call demands, endless innovation, endless drudgery, endless giving, and zero pay. Then, of course, just to make the ideal even more crazy, we expect centerfold bodies, Pinterest lunches, perfect children, etc.

Wowie! We need to work on this a bit! A good first step is to recognize the economic value of traditional "women's work." The unpaid labor that is contributed by women to the economy or "home production," as it is termed. The economic value of unpaid women's work was much discussed in the 1940s. Over protests, women's financial contribution to the U.S. economy was *not* included in the calculations of GDP. However, many economists now recognize that as women have entered the work force, this unpaid labor of house work and caregiving is, in fact, a vital contribution to the economy of America...and the whole blinkin' world! As women move to jobs that provide income, power, and retirement without poverty, we as a nation, will need to ask how we will fill the very large labor gap they leave behind. Frankly, we are going to have to pay for it. Whether childcare workers or elder memory care specialists, these caregivers will want a working wage and benefits. As family members, we will want those workers to be educated, highly trained, and well paid. They are caring for our loved ones. So, why not recognize the same value in a stay-at-home parent? That is what extended paid parental leave really is. It's paying American mothers or fathers to raise the next generation of American citizens because...we *don't* live in hunter-gather societies, and women have the right to a decent life. Other Western countries seem to understand that we, as a society, are going to have to *pay* someone to raise our next generation.

In today's America, we tend to see children as an expensive privilege that parents must work to afford. They are a luxury of those with money. But the truth is that without children to grow into our culture, to work and invent, and create, without *children* America will cease to exist. Our entire culture and economy would collapse. The birth rate continues to decline across the Westernized world. Other countries have come to realize that if they want to continue as a culture and a country they *need* children. Plain and simple, they need children. They see that there is great economic value in *raising* children. That it is a legitimate need of a country to financially support the birthing and raising of kids. It cannot remain a luxury meant for the rich. Children must be recognized as a valued contribution to our society.

We need to understand that in America the unpaid, undervalued woman is now free to get a job and work for herself and her future. If we want these women to consider a job that is 24 hours a day, 7 days a week, 365 days a year without bathroom breaks or status, well, we're gonna need to pay them and offer a few benefits. This is, of course, exactly what most countries do. We're the only westernized country to fail the next generation by devaluing children and parenthood.

Modern economists are actively working on how to include the economic value from the unpaid labor of women in economic assessments. So why *wouldn't* we include the unpaid work of women in economic measures? Psst, it's because the status of women and women's work is still rock bottom.

Finally, we have lessons from WWII. In America, women were desperately needed in the paid work force. We all think of Rosie the Riveter, but what about her kids? During WWII, the *federal government funded daycare centers* across the country *so that women could work outside the home*. Let's say that again. The federal *government* funded *daycare centers* across the country so that women could work! We want women to work now too. We need their insights and skills and education and life's industry. So, imagine if you will, daycare. Federally funded daycare. Good quality. Well paid staff. Safe and full of adults with master's degrees in early childhood development. Bright, light, joy filled spaces with lots fresh air and outdoor time. So, then mothers don't have to quit work when they can't find good care.

Here's what I want my kids to inherit when they have their own children to care for. Eighteen months of federally paid parental leave per child that can be used at any time until the child is 8-years-old. Require that at least 40% of that leave be taken by the father or second parent. This will avoid discrimination against women of childbearing age or those who use their parental leave. Businesses will *have* to adjust much as they have successfully managed to do in many Nordic countries. Fund Social Security and healthcare for all stay-at-home parents. Aim for equity and access to parental leave for *all* parents in America. Require daycare and childcare workers to have a bachelor's degree in education with extensive child development courses. (Can't outsource that job!) Pay them very well. Since our knowledge of brain and child development keeps growing, I'd require yearly continuing education credits in learning differences and brain development. Fully fund or highly subsidize infant and childcare for all. Allow parents to decide whether to use the childcare funding for daycare, or a nanny, or other kind of childcare helper.

Don't tell me *our* country can't do this. The Danes do it. The Swedes do it. The French do it. The Italians do it. The Finns do it with excellent results. Pretty much *every other* country does some variation of this concept. Don't tell me we are too weak, too diverse, too incompetent to build this country wide infrastructure. We are quite capable. Frankly, we really have no other choice. We are not egalitarian hunter-gatherers with a village raising our children, caring for our elderly, and feeding all.

There *is* one alternative. It is widely practiced in some parts of the world. Lebanon, Dubai, India and other countries have their own way of dealing with the labor gap as women work outside the home. It's even practiced here in the U.S. All you need is a source of poor or low status women. You import them to do the work of raising your kids. You bring in desperate women from the Philippians or Chad, Mexico or El Salvador. Pay them a pittance, and work them all day long. In some countries, you routinely take away their passport and confiscate their phone. Then you're all set. Just maintain this hidden economy of underpaid, undervalued foreign women. Be careful not to notice the pain they suffer when separated from their own children.

Remember that in the U.S. we *enslaved* people of color up until 1865. Jim Crow laws, segregation, racism, systemic terrorism, and lynching kept many American citizens of color in positions of low pay and menial jobs. For example, as "domestics" who did "women's work" for little pay. Or as crop pickers, road workers, dam builders whose labor built the infrastructure of America, but who never got credit or cash or status for this work. Personally, I don't want an economy built on the subjugation of one group of people whose unpaid or underpaid labor fuels the wealth of everyone else. That type of economy still very much exists in many parts of the U.S. and the world. In some places it is a caste system or clear discrimination against a group which creates the low pay labor pool that supports the rest of the economy. Often it is based on immigrant labor. But, by far the most common unpaid or underpaid labor that fuels the world's economy is the domestic work of women.

Remember that in the United States of America, "the land of the free," women did not have the right to vote for their own representatives until 1920! Remember that in the United States of America, women and their money, were legally considered the *property* of fathers and husbands in many states until 1900! Remember that the subjugation of a wife to her husband was coded into law. "The legal codes of the southern states classified *master and slave* and *husband and wife* as parallel parts of the law of domestic relations." Remember that women in the United States of America could be legally beaten by their fathers and husbands up until 1920! Remember that women in the United States of America, who were later *illegally* beaten by their husbands, still did not receive police protection until laws that required police to *act* in domestic violence situations went into effect in the 1970s! (That's about 40 years ago. *I* remember when the news began reporting this change.) Remember that in the United States of America women often had to be married *and* have their husband's permission to seek birth control until 1972. Remember that in the United States of America, many "public" libraries would restrict women's access to certain books well into the 1900s, and women of color would wait even longer for access to information. Remember that in the United States of America, women could not have their own credit card until 1974! Remember that in the United States of America, women could not run in marathons until 1970. Remember that in some parts of the United States of America women were not allowed to serve as jurors until 1975.

Okay, we as women and as a culture, have come a long way in a short time. But our journey is very recent and far from complete. We may have allowed women, especially white women, to embrace roles that were traditionally male, yet we still devalue traditional domestic woman's work. We so devalue this work that any stay-at-home mom who does this underappreciated work becomes one of two things. If she is a woman of color, then she will come up against systemic racism and will be seen as a "welfare queen" leaching off the largess of the more worthy. Whether she is poor or middle class, a mother of color will fight presumptions that she is lazy. The fact that she sacrifices her own life's industry to raise our next generation of citizens is of no import. And since no one wants to give money to a "lazy queen," it means that poor children of color become unworthy of the benefits that would pay a woman fairly for the work she does. Thus, we perpetuate child poverty.

On the other hand, if the stay-at-home-mom is white, then she becomes a "saint." And that holy, pure, white American mother is too beautiful to sully with dirty money. Whether poor or middle class, a white mother is above such things as pay for motherhood. And this too perpetuates child poverty.

So, whether you are a "lazy mother of color" or a "holy white mother" your work does not warrant monetary valuation. Because, a mother's work is seen as either menial and unskilled or sacred and too precious. It all sounds like a crock of shinola to me!

Both of these distortions of motherhood are standing in our way. By failing to recognize the monetary value and contributions of poor mothers, we leave them trapped. Middle class mothers face a double standard that is preventing women from engaging fully in the world. It creates the so called "second shift" of work after work that drains American women. This idea that saintly mothers can somehow magically manage to do the unpaid labor of the past *and* the modern work hours of today is absolutely magical thinking.

In addition, the all sacrificing mother ideal leaves no room for dad. Really, if mom is meeting all the family's emotional and physical needs, then what is he supposed to do? All that's left for him to do is to excel at work, car maintenance, and lawn mowing. If we want fathers to be actively involved in the emotional aspects of childcare, then we need to dump our current idealized myth of mother-who-is-all-things.

If you are new to parenthood, remember that there is a history to ideas, attitudes, and beliefs. If you are a new mother or father, be prepared for an onslaught of judgements and assumptions. Be prepared to question them.

PART III:

THE NITTY GRITTY OF PARENTING

23

COMMON ISSUES OF THE EARLIEST YEARS OF PARENTING

STAYING SANE IN THE FIRST FEW MONTHS

Okay, THAT WAS A TEASE. Basically, nobody stays sane during the first months with newborns! For many parents this is just a really hard time. Mostly all you can do is wade through it until the babies grow a little. At this age, they grow and change very, very fast. However, when you are getting no sleep and no break it seems like it's going on forever! Keep reminding yourself that your babies will change a lot in one month. Really, a lot. Regardless of what *you* do now, they will be doing things completely differently in a few months. Then a few months after that, they will be in a totally different phase of sleep, growth, and development. Take a deep breath. You can do this. One hour at a time. One day at a time. You will wade through the unknown. In the beginning, you will be too tired to see it, but you are slooowly becoming an expert! You're not going to feeeel like an expert for a veeery long time, but this is how you get there.

Let's review a few books that offer good advice for the early days. *The Happiest Baby on the Block by* Harvey Karp, MD, is definitely on the "must read" list. This book will help you understand how to effectively sooth the fussiest of babies. It will also give you a good sense of how your baby's brain is changing over the first year of life. This book is extremely well done and available on CD so you can watch swaddling techniques. Swaddling is very useful. I strongly recommend you practice swaddling your baby before you leave the hospital. If you ask, the nurses will walk you through it again and again. When done well swaddling can be very comforting to a young baby. We loved this technique so much that when the kids outgrew the smaller blankets, I went to the fabric store to buy large pieces of cloth to make jumbo swaddles.

During your baby's first year, you will become obsessed with sleep. Yours and theirs. The better they sleep, the more you sleep. It's a simple equation that is somehow difficult to actually balance. There are numerous books written on sleep. In the early months, I read everything I could get my hands on. We were exhausted and frantic to get our kids sleeping in some kind of remotely consolidated way.

Finally, my sister-in-law sent us a book that really helped. I highly recommend, *The Sleep Easy Solution,* by Waldburger and Spivack. The information in the book is well organized. Best of all, their approach is respectful of the emotional and sleep needs of both child and parent. If you need to sleep train, it will give you clear, step-by-step instructions. It will help you prepare your child for sleep training. It will also walk you through solutions to various obstacles, like how to wean off night-time feedings. If you can, read this book before your baby arrives to set yourself up for an easier process. Regardless of your kids ages, you'll find real practical help in *The Sleep Easy Solution*. You'll also find more help in my chapter titled, "Sleeping Babies."

Before your baby is born, do some pre-arrival prep work to lighten the everyday work of the first few months. If you have space, invest in a small extra freezer. We stocked ours with quiche, an assortment of organic frozen meals, and food prepped and brought by friends. You can pull out a meal for one or a quiche to last a week of lunches. You could also practice ordering groceries delivered from a local store. Set up a favorites list and get comfortable with the ins and outs of your local service. Stock up on your basics like toilet paper, tissue, and coffee. Order your first set of diapers delivered to your door so that re-orders are easy. Get familiar with the process now before you're struggling with breastfeeding, pumping, and bottles. I know some moms even set up calendars so friends can sign up for helper duties or meal deliveries.

Now is a good time to look for help from nannies, night nannies, family, or friends. Whether you hire them or they are volunteers you want people who will really *work*. You don't need "visitors" who need *you* to entertain them or for whom you need to clean before they arrive. Just say, "No, come later, when they are 6 months old" to those would-be guests.

STAYING SANE...WITH TWINS, WHAT ONE BABY DOES, THE OTHER BABY DOES

There is one key to help you stay sane with newborn twins. "The Schedule." With twins, you will get zero breaks during the day if they are each eating and sleeping on different schedules. I followed the rule of: "what one baby does, the other baby does."

This is going to sound crazy. Sometimes you have to wake a sleeping baby. "No, no, NO!" you say. Why would you *ever* wake a baby who is finally sleeping?! I, too, thought this was crazy. The idea was downright painful. But if you have twins, you will find yourself in desperate times. If baby #1 is sleeping while baby #2 is awake, then baby #1 will surely wake-up once baby #2 has fallen asleep. This means that you get absolutely NO break. And that is a problem. A big problem. With twins, it's vital to get them eating and sleeping at the same time. The way you do this is the rule "what one baby does, the other baby does." If one wakes up and eats, then you wake up the other one and feed them too. If you keep this going a bit, they will sync up. Then you will, of course, need to learn how to juggle two babies at the same time. Sigh. But, it's better than no break.

I'm keenly aware of just how hard it can be to do this. In the first month, we fed our twins on demand and let sleep run its course. But we got very few breaks, which left us exhausted. Finally, I told my husband and mom that we needed to follow a friend's advice and "wake the sleeping twin." No one wanted to do it. Even the idea is painful when you are that exhausted. Well, do it! Once they are in sync and eating and sleeping on a schedule, you will get just that little precious break when they both sleep at the same time. Most likely, once you've got them together you will adhere to the schedule with great rigidity. It is the backbone of infant and toddler twin care.

AVERTING DIAPER DISASTERS

This is for newbies. There are a few vital mistakes you don't want to make in the "baby diapering" department. First, projectile pooping. It's real. It does occur. I've seen it. Young baby poop is not formed like adult poop. It's basically soft, liquidy, yellowish, lumpy, mush. Fortunately, it doesn't smell nearly as bad as the poop you know. (wink, wink) I am highly sensitive to, shall we say, aromas. Yet, I did okay with odor of baby poop. The consistency, however, lends itself to some unexpected poop potential.

One day, when my babies were a few months old, I was changing a diaper. Babyo was on the changing table, and I was doing the "one hand holds the feet up while the other hand slides in a new diaper" move. Thankfully, I had just leaned back to reach for a wipe when there was a "toot" and…an arching stream of golden poop sailed across the table and splattered on the curtain. Whoa! Talk about a get your attention moment! As it happens the curtain was left over from my husband's bachelor days and was itself baby-poop-gold. Can you say, "uuuugly!!" I hated those curtains. Now I could throw them away! Heh, heh. An unexpected benefit of projectile pooping. But, you dear newbie parent, remember the possibilities and position yourself appropriately when engaged in diaper related activities!

It is also important to consider all surroundings when opening the Pandora's box that all "in use" diapers can be. An acquaintance related the tale of her husband's travails. It seems parable worthy. First time parents, they were out with their newborn. Desperate for some fresh air and sunshine, they headed for Shoreline Drive in Santa Cruz. They had somehow managed to get the infant car seat in the back of their sporty little roadster. Upon arrival, Daddyo urged mom to get out and soak up the day while he did the diaper change. She was leaning over a railing watching the waves and surfers when the screaming started. Racing back to the car she found a half-naked baby on the front passenger seat…with nothing under him…except a large puddle of smeared, yellow…poop. Daddyo was frantically wielding diaper wipes, but it was clearly too late. You must. MUST. Always. ALWAYS. Put a changing pad or new opened diaper under the baby BEFORE you remove the used diaper. Failure to do so can result in: having to sit on a towel on top of smeared baby poop in your expensive sports car for the hour long ride home. While your wife drives in the only clean seat in the car. Gotta be a parable in there somewhere.

Yes, your boy baby can also hose you in the face, the suit coat, or the party dress midway through a diaper change. So, open up a clean diaper and cover that end while you work the other end. We have been there. You do not need to go there. Learn from us and go forth forewarned.

SOOTHING FUSSY INFANTS

Baby soothing is best taught by Dr. Harvey Karp in his book, *Happiest Baby on the Block*. It details the five "S"s of soothing: swaddling, side/stomach position, shushing, swinging, sucking on a pacifier. Often people try one of these techniques without success and give up. If you have a really fussy or colicky baby, then you want to do all five and do them right. And Dr. Karp can help you do that. Even if your baby is not colicky, you'll find many infants respond well to Dr. Karp's techniques.

My babies mostly had ordinary levels of infant fussiness. They loved a good swaddle, and my daughter liked the swing. But my son found a swing too stimulating. He did better with a quiet crib or a calm snuggle. I tried very hard to get my kids to take pacifiers in hopes of having a nice soothing tool. But, kids have their own opinions and mine refused the paci's repeatedly. However, when my kids were really upset, I'd pull out all of Dr. Karp's maneuvers. Infants are all different from day one. Some are easy, and some are really tough. A friend of mine has a new baby. He is an easy going, easy to comfort, smiley little guy. Watching my friend with him I finally understand why some parents love this early infant stage. If you're getting all this snuggly feedback from an easy baby, well, it's pretty rewarding.

But not all babies are so easy. Another dear friend of mine had a baby with full on colic. She and her very involved husband were completely overwhelmed. She tried swaddling, but it didn't seem to work. So, I bought her a copy of *Happiest Baby on the Block*. Two weeks later she told me her boy was still colicky, but when she swaddled tightly and followed all the five soothing techniques, it actually did help. The other very smart thing she did was to welcome her father-in-law into their home. Grandpa came from overseas to live with them for a year and help with his new grandchild. If you have a difficult, fussy infant, one of the best things you can do is to get as much help as possible. These friends of mine are both professionals with demanding careers. I doubt they both would have made it back to work without grandpa's help. Ultimately, as their family grew, they relocated across the country to be near even more family as they raised kids.

Loving and caring for fussy, irritable, or colicky babies is very, very difficult. Fortunately, they do grow out of the worst of it. If this is what you're struggling with, you get five gold stars, major parenting points, the right to bitch and moan, and a big hug from me! You also need to read Dr. Karp's book. Get the swaddle right. You may find it a lifesaver during the first six months.

When the crying just won't stop, try putting on noise canceling headphones paired with aroma therapy in your favorite soothing scent. (Except avoid lavender and tea tree oil per a recent statement from the Endocrine Society. Sorry.) You can put your baby down in a safe place and walk away to recuperate. Call a supportive friend and vent. Breathe deep. Have a snack. And go back in. Maybe with a white noise machine for the baby, and those headphones for you!

Be aware that babies can have reflux without much spit up. If there is any correlation between eating and when your baby is fussiest, then keep your baby at a 45 degree angle after feeding and see her pediatrician about possible reflux medication. The medicines can offer tremendous pain relief to the baby if it is indeed reflux.

REFLUX

Reflux occurs when the muscle at the base of the esophagus is loose. This allows stomach contents to move backwards up the esophagus. The acid in the "refluxed" stomach contents is very irritating to the esophagus and causes pain. Babies who suffer from reflux will often cry after feeding and may be difficult to console. The trick is that all babies spit up some. However, babies with reflux may spit up more or very little or not at all. This can make it hard in some cases to recognize that reflux is causing an infant's distress.

Reflux is more common in premature infants and, thus, in twins. If you think your baby may be having reflux pain after eating, then make an appointment to discuss this with their pediatrician. If a trial of an acid blocking medicine helps, then it could relieve your child of a great deal of suffering. There are two types of medication used to treat reflux in infants. The H2 blockers have been used for many years and are well tested in babies. The proton pump inhibitors are a bit newer, but have a good track record with infants. This second class of drugs are stronger acid blockers. When babies get only partial relief with an H2 blocker, they often do better on a proton pump inhibitor. All of these medications are available in infant dosing. To minimize reflux, it is important to keep to small, frequent feedings, and to keep the baby upright or at a 45 degree angle after eating. For some infants, these simple techniques are enough to provide relief.

Babies gradually outgrow reflux. Often this occurs around 6 to 9 months when the child's abdominal muscles develop enough to allow them to sit unassisted. My daughter's reflux lasted a full 12 months, so we had to readjust her dosing as she got bigger. Many babies will continue to grow well even with untreated reflux. However, sometimes babies can get so turned off to feeding due to pain that they don't gain weight well. This was true for my daughter. Before she was treated, her spit-ups were not large, but her pain after eating was enough to make her push away from her bottle. Once we had her on medication she became a happy eater and caught up on growth. We tried tapering her acid blocker at 9 months, but she wasn't ready. Then at 12 months we tapered again and all was fine. Any child who has reflux symptoms beyond 15 to 18 months of age should be evaluated for other possible health issues.

BREASTFEEDING vs. BOTTLE FEEDING

One topic sure to generate anxiety in many a new mom is the question of breastfeeding vs bottle feeding. Again, there are options. Again, they are all okay. Yes, really! It's okay if you don't breastfeed for any reason! Your body, your life, your choice. Feel good about whatever you decide. If you do want to breastfeed, then seek some experienced help. This is especially important if you have twins. Tandem breastfeeding is possible for some people. One friend with twins who managed this almost gave up in the early months. Her advice is to get a lactation consultant who will come to your home. Having someone help you in the actual physical place you feed the babies can make all the difference. If you want to breastfeed, it is a small investment to have someone come to your house. Many, but not all, insurances will cover a home visit from a lactation consultant. If you're worried about the cost, then compare it to a year's worth of formula! Another benefit to breastfeeding is that it appears to reduce a woman's chance of developing diabetes. Gestational diabetes can occur in any pregnancy, but is especially common with twin pregnancies. If you do develop it while pregnant, your risk of developing diabetes later may be as much as four times higher. Some recent studies have shown that if a woman breastfeeds or pumps she significantly lowers her risk for diabetes at a later age. Breastfeeding for as little as a month has benefits and the longer you can produce that milk the more your long term health can benefit. The baby, of course, gets all those wonderful antibodies from breast milk. There are definitely some advantages to breastfeeding, and you will hear them over and over from many well-meaning sources who believe they know what is "best" for you.

On the other hand, according to Pamela Druckerman author of *Bringing Up Bebe*, in France breastfeeding beyond three months is considered an undue burden on the mother, and therefore "not beneficial to family bonding." So, don't get too bent out of shape if you find you don't want to breastfeed for any reason. Work and commuting are far from conducive to breastfeeding, and why should you have to sacrifice everything? Your breaks, your lunch, your privacy, even your boobs suddenly belong to someone else! And what's with the little parasite sucking off you all day long? Who wants that? And maybe you're a bit, well, FREAKIN' exhausted! Oh, and the pump thingy! There you are stuck in a corner like a cow in a stall while the pump sucks your nipples dry! If this, or anything remotely like it, is how *you* feel about breastfeeding, then consider some formula.

Some moms don't like breastfeeding. Gasp! Yes, I said it! Some moms don't like breastfeeding! You don't need to apologize if it doesn't work for you. Nor do you need to explain if you were abused in the past and find exposing your breasts traumatic. Really. Your body, your choice. You may encounter enormous pressure on this one. Don't buy into to it. Just move on. Snuggling a baby in your arms while she thup, thup, thups away at a bottle is just as nurturing and bonding. Furthermore, some of us *can't* breastfeed. Isn't it wonderful that we live in a world where our babies can still thrive!

Since I had two breast biopsies with a microductectomy prior to having kids, I found that only one breast really produced much milk. Nipple variations, small baby mouths, and large breasts meant my kids weren't latching on. Even the lactation consultant didn't think it was going to work for me. So, I pumped for four months, and we supplemented with formula. By the end I had one giant boob (da-prah-ducer) and the other one was half the size (da biopsy boob). After more than 120 days of feeling shackled to a pump when I only made half the milk we needed, I gave up on pumping from sheer exhaustion. Fortunately, once I stopped pumping the "giant boob" slowly shrank back to normal size. (Whew!) So, we fed the kids formula, and guess what, the babies continued to grow!

Don't sweat this one. Yes, there are benefits to mom and baby from breastfeeding. Yes, some moms love the experience. Yes, we need to continue to fight for a woman's right to breastfeed and pump wherever and whenever! I am an ardent, vocal, almost rabid defender of the rights and needs of breastfeeding moms. But, your baby is not going to die or become mentally impaired if you give them formula. Bottle feeding means your partner can *also* bond while feeding babyo. This can lead to a more equable sharing of childcare duties which is highly beneficial to family stability. So, breastfeed or don't, or do some partial pumping variation for a while. If your babies are healthy and growing, then do what works for you and yours. What makes life work for you is also good for your baby.

TANDEM BOTTLE FEEDING AND THE DOUBLE JUGGLE

If you're bottle feeding twins or two babies under two years old, you'll need to learn the juggle of feeding two infants at the same time with one adult. Here's how you do it. First, mix up a day's worth of formula or pumped breast milk in the morning or the night before. Then divide it into the number of bottles you think you'll need in a day. This will require a lot of bottles and refrigerator space but will make the day much smoother. When it's time to feed babies, you can use a bottle warmer for breast milk. If it's formula you can microwave the bottle. You CAN NOT microwave breast milk as it will destroy the good antibodies in the milk. But you CAN microwave formula. HOWEVER, if you are warming with the microwave, you must do some test bottles to see how long you need to nuke it to get to lukewarm and not hot. You will also want to gently invert the bottle a few times to mix the formula after warming. This will ensure there are no hot spots in the formula that could burn your baby's throat. You can start out testing temperature by microwaving for 5 seconds per ounce of formula. However, you may need more or less time depending on your microwave. You do not want your baby to suck down hot scalding formula, so be sure to practice and test!

Wherever you're feeding, you'll need a ready stash of diapers, wipes, hand sanitizer, burp clothes, and a changing pad. When babies eat, they poop and spit up on everything. You'll be juggling back and forth between feeding, burping, and changing each infant. Don't forget to clean your hands between diaper changes and feeding! Usually, one of your babies will be easier to soothe than the other. If they are both hungry and crying, then start with the *easy* baby first. Once you get that one settled, then you can focus on the fussier one. Here's where it's helpful to have multiple baby holding devices at hand. If you're alone you won't be able to hold both babies and both bottles at the same time. You'll need a way to get the babes into a good "hands free" position to eat. There are lots of ways to do this, and you'll likely use several systems depending on where and when you are feeding.

At home, you can use two Boppy pillows. These are horseshoe shaped pillows designed to prop up a baby or support them while nursing. (At my first expectant parents meeting, everyone kept talking about "Boppy pillows?!" I had *no* idea what they were talking about and felt completely lost. So, now *you* can be in the know!) I liked to sit on the floor with my back against the couch, and a Boppy pillow on either side of me. You place the babies so they are facing you then hold the bottles for them. You stop feeding part way through and do the burp and change bit on one kid and then the other. You can do the same thing with any good "containment system." So instead of Boppy pillows you can use bouncy seats, swings (good idea to turn them off), strollers, or infant car seats. Just be sure to have a spot at home or a stocked travel bag with everything you'll need, including a change of clothes for everyone involved. You'll need to be able to safely leave one baby and step away with the other to change clothes or deal with unexpected issues. Make sure that whatever you set up is secure and safe. After the final burp and diaper change, you can either enjoy a brief awake time with the babies or swaddle them up and hope for sleep.

This is obviously the bottle-feeding version of the double juggle, but tandem breast feeding can take a similar form. All of this is much, much easier with at least two adults, but the day or night will come for the first solo juggle of newborn twins. It's not easy or snuggly or remotely relaxing, but you can do it! Once you've got this kinda figured out then you and your partner can each cover half of the night. That gives mom and dad 5 to 6 hours of consolidated sleep! And that is a very good thing.

SLEEPING BABIES

Many people sleep train. Some do not. This is a highly personal issue without a "right" answer. So, too, is where babies sleep. Children around the world grow up in "the family bed." If this works for you then, well, it works! However, remember if you have a gaggle of gators, even a big bed with two co-sleepers can get crowded fast. Further, if you have four or more people all tossing about, it may make for less than restful sleep for all. I have one friend who was rather rudely awakened when her 5-month-old stuck his finger up her nose. He went in deep enough to draw blood. Yikes! Nevertheless, some members of my twins club found co-sleeping worked best for them. You could also wind up with one kid who wants to sleep separately, and another one who does better co-sleeping. Personally, I need the quiet peace of my own bed at night. The demands of constantly caring for the myriad needs of my kids wears on me through the day. By bedtime I need my own space. I am also someone whose sleep needs are on the high end of the scale. For us, sleep training worked amazingly well. Our only regret was that we waited longer than we needed to start.

So, here's the short and sweet on sleep training. First, a baby's ability to sleep through the night is dependent upon brain maturation. Thus, all things sleep related are calculated from the baby's due date not their actual birth-date. So, if your kid arrived early, then you need to adjust all sleep expectations based on the number of months from their *due date.* Next, your baby's sleep patterns in the first several months are *not* a reliable predictor of their later patterns. Babies change and grow at a phenomenal rate over the first months and sleep development is no exception. Your baby who only cat naps for 30 minutes at a time during the day and wakes up fussing frequently in the night, may evolve into a great napper and consolidated nighttime sleeper. Much of this is simply out of your control. Their brains develop. They change. This will be an early sampling of a long-term pattern. You'll finally get them on a schedule. You'll finally have adjusted yourself to the schedule. You will have mastered new skills and then they will change. You'll discover you need to toss out much of your old routine, and figure out a new one along with a new set of skills.

But, back to sleep issues. From birth to five months (post due date!) you will soothe your kids to sleep anyway possible. We used 2 gliders, 2 swings, 2 bouncy seats, a Moses basket, 2 cribs, 2 Boppy pillows, and 2 floor mats. Yes, this was probably a bit excessive, but we were nervous newbies with twins. Your baby will already have individual sleep pref-erences. My daughter loved the swing. For my son, it created a sensory overload that could send him into a crying fit. He liked a nice quiet crib. Yes, in the beginning you can put twins in the same crib. How long this will last depends upon how fast your kids grow, and whether they are rolling into each other. If you need to sleep train, start when your child weighs at least 15 pounds *and* is five months post *due date.* This is when you follow all the steps in *The Sleep Easy Solution* by Waldburger and Spivack. This is an excellent book and, by far, my favorite pick from all the sleep advice books out there.

Sleep issues often feel monumentally overwhelming to parents. You're just so sleep deprived that you'll try anything. Personally, I was frantic for help. So, I repeat. Here's what you do. Soothe your baby any way you can until they are five months old and weigh at least 15 pounds. Read *The Sleep Easy Solution* so you're aware of what's normal, and what you're working towards. Follow *all* the steps they recommend if you need to sleep train. I repeat, follow *all* the steps in the *Sleep Easy Solution*. They will guide you in preparing your baby for easy, successful sleep training. What I love about this book is that they don't leave out any steps. Unlike other books nothing is vague. You follow precise, clear steps and track your baby's progress. The recommendations and techniques are very respectful of the emotional well-being of your baby. Follow all the steps and sleep training will probably go much better than you anticipate. I was unable to be in the house the first night we sleep trained. The idea of not going to them when they cried was unbearable to me. But, the progress wound up moving so fast that my anxiety was quickly eased. We actually had far, far *less* crying with sleep training than we did when we tried to soothe them to sleep. Really, much less! And we had tried every weird crib rocker, white noise machine, heartbeat music, shushing, bouncing, colored LED lights, holding, rocking, swinging, breathing, touching, binkies, massage, warm baths, soothing scents…whew. You name it. We tried it, to no avail. Until, we followed the steps in the *Sleep Easy Solution,* and it worked. (I get no kick back on sales of this book, but frankly it saved my life. And it might just save yours too!)

If you're sleep training more than one baby at the same time, it can be helpful to have them in separate rooms during training. This could mean putting one crib in the closet of another room or a hallway for a week or two. After they have the hang of getting to sleep on their own, you can move them back into the same room. Do expect a slight adjustment period, but don't panic. You can also sleep train both babies in the same room at the same time. It may be a little harder to juggle, but it's been done and can be done again if you have no other option. Understand that sleep training for overnight sleep and naps are not the same. Consolidated night time sleep often develops before naps schedules settle in. A child may be 7-months-old before becoming a better napper. Again, this is purely based on brain development. And if you try everything and your child never naps? Well, you have my sympathy. Those kids do exist.

Finally, there's one more step to sleep training that I feel is vital. I highly recommend you have a video monitor in the baby's room. There are many different kinds, but the main issue is to have some way to see how they are doing without going into the room. This will be very helpful and anxiety easing during sleep training and for years to come.

MONITORING BABIES or PEEK-A-BOO! I SEE YOU!

Do you set up video monitoring in your baby's room or not? Some people feel that a monitor becomes a device that gets between them and their baby. I get this. There is a difference between looking at your infant on a monitor as opposed to going into their room and looking directly at them. My husband and I were so fearful of waking up our sleeping babies that for a long time we didn't go into their room unless we could see on the monitor that they were awake. As the kids got a little older, I realized we were missing something by not directly gazing at them as they slept. So, I started tiptoeing into their room for a look at the slumbering beasties. I highly recommend doing this. It's wonderful.

However, I still found a video monitor very helpful through to age 5. After the kids were sleep trained I liked to check them on the monitor as I lay down to sleep. I could see my babies breathing or wiggling in their sleep and knew all was well. As kids grow they also go through all kinds of nap time and sleep time shenanigans. The monitor becomes one more tool in handling some of these behaviors. At some point, they outgrow cribs and move into beds without bars. This leads to a great deal of sleep time chaos, and a video monitor really helps. You can speak over the monitor, and become the "voice from above" that tells them to lie down for night–night time. When my kids were a bit older, my husband liked to wake them up in the morning by playing music over the monitor.

On one occasion, my toddler daughter, who had been quiet, began to fuss a bit. When I looked on the monitor, I realized she had gotten the long tag from her lovey twisted and wrapped around a finger. It was painful and cutting off circulation. (Watch out for those long tags on stuffed animals. My daughter loved to finger the tag, but they can wear down to a long string. Cut those tags shorter.) Without a monitor,

I might have waited longer to see if her fussing settled. Instead, I was able to run in, and get her finger untangled. And there will be other times when you want to see what's happening without going into their room and reinforcing unwanted behavior.

When they are 4 years old, you may hear wild shrieking giggles coming from the bedroom. You can check the monitor, and relax upon seeing they are just whacking each other with their stuffies. Or you could see they are poking each other in the face with a sharp stick that has somehow materialized. This would be a good time to yell into the monitor, "NO POKING FACE WITH STICK!" It's also probably a good idea to remove the offending stick from the room. But, that's advanced parenting.

We don't have that village of extended family and helpers that parents need when kids are young. We need help wherever we can get it. For me the video monitor became an extra set of eyes in the room that eased my anxiety. Many people do fine without one, but I've found it very helpful. Parenthood is loaded with anxiety. If a simple tool like a monitor can ease that anxiety, then I'm all in.

But what about having a monitor in your living room so you can check on your child and their nanny while you're at work? This is a more difficult question. Certainly, a nanny is not a family member, and when she's in your home she's working. People at work are often observed and monitored throughout their work day. It can be very hard to know what is going on in your home when you're not there, and it's reasonable to want some way to check up on your child and the nanny's activities.

If you do decide to have a monitor in the living room, I think you should let the nanny know. It's just creepy to be watching someone when the person doesn't know. I feel they have the right to know. In our case, we never had a monitor outside of the kid's bedroom nor one that was accessible online. There were other ways to check on a nanny's performance. You can leave for work, and then unexpectedly return an hour later. You can come home a few hours early. You can have a friend or family drop by unexpectedly. You can work from home for a day. You can video conference with the nanny on a regular basis. All of these things will give you insight into how things are going when you're not home. Frankly, I always had suspicions when things were not going well. And I came to fully trust our really good nanny.

HIRING HELPERS: WHEN DAILY LIFE ISN'T WORKING

Your family's needs are going to change repeatedly over the first few years. If you have extensive and helpful family nearby, then you may be set regardless of these changing needs. However, many people no longer have a family community to rely on. That doesn't mean you won't need them. You just won't *have* them. In that case, you may find you need to hire helpers. Keep the following ideas in your back pocket so you can reach for them as your family life changes.

Many twin parents will hire a night nanny for some portion of the first few months. And frankly, if you're adding a new singleton baby to a gaggle of other young kids, a night nanny may be helpful in getting everyone back to work. They are very expensive, but if you have no other resources to help you at night you may become severely sleep deprived. We lasted 10 days and then began a desperate search for a night nanny. They are often found by word of mouth or by posting on a mother's club website. We could not afford someone every night so we hired her to come Sunday, Tuesday, and Thursday nights. This let my husband get better sleep on three out of five work nights.

I'll cover hiring day nannies more extensively in the next section, but a couple of thoughts here. Nannies can be part-time or full-time. If they are a student then they may be content with working fewer hours. However, if you hire a part-time nanny who really needs full-time work, then the chances are good you'll ultimately lose her to a job with more hours. You can also hire a "mother's helper." It could be a teenager who plays with your kids while you make dinner. Or an experienced mom who picks the kids up from daycare, meets you at home, then helps with dinner and feeding the kids. You can also hire "pick-up and drop-off nannies" who just take your kids to and from daycare or school. If you work from home, a pick-up nanny might get you two more hours of quiet work time. Or you can hire someone to do your grocery shopping and laundry. You can pay for a professional housecleaning service or get a teenager to do a lesser job for less money.

There are many different kinds of helpers, so ask yourself what you and your family need right now. You don't have to hire them forever. Think of it as an investment in your family's sanity and stability.

HUNTING NANNIES

Nanny hunting is definitely a challenge for which most of us receive no prior training. Previous experience hiring employees will be helpful. But, there's a big difference between interviewing someone to work in your business versus someone you'll trust with your infant. In addition, anyone can bill themselves as a nanny, and it's not always clear what is the most important criteria you want to consider. Your needs may be different if you have long or irregular work hours. For example, let's say you find a candidate who is a warm and loving woman. She's an experienced mom whose own kids are grown, but her English is borderline. If you're going to be in the house or at an office around the corner, then she may be wonderful to have snuggling your baby. However, what if you work an hour away, your child has a fever, and you don't trust her English enough to explain how much Tylenol to give your child? In this situation, the language barrier can be a problem. So many things affect who and what you're looking for in a nanny. Sometimes you may not find everything you need in one person. So, let's go through the nanny hunting process.

First, you have to find nannies to interview. You can start by looking on Craig's List, mother's club listings, neighborhood groups, nanny services, and websites like Care.com. You might also hit the local parks on a weekday, and scope out a nanny who seems to be doing a good job. Then ask them if they know anyone who's looking for work. They may be just finishing up a position or may know other nannies who are available. You'll want to search online nanny services, but these often come at higher rates. Nevertheless, they're a good place to line up nanny temp services who can fill in on-call. You pay a premium for these services, but when you're working sometimes you need last minute help.

Now that you've lined up a few people to interview, you'll need to figure out how to evaluate them. Start by asking them about themselves. "How long have you lived here? Where did you grow up? What schools did you go to? What interests or hobbies do you have?" These questions are just to get them talking so you can get a sense of who they are. Remember, it is illegal to ask them if they are pregnant, married, or have kids.

When you are past the introductions, ask about their childcare experiences, and any training they might have. Some may have taken courses in early childhood development or have infant-child CPR certification. It's also important they can show current immunizations with a Pertussis booster, Covid series, and Influenza shot. You can ask for a copy of a negative TB test or negative x-ray screen from the last year. For each childcare job they have had, ask them about the age of the kids they cared for. What they did with them? What did they like about the job? What didn't work well for them? Get them talking a bit about each position. Again, this will give you more insight into how they think, and what they expect from a job. For example, do they mention doing any housework or kid's laundry? Do they have experience with infants? Twins? Were they juggling an infant, a 2-year-old, and a 6-year-old after school? Or were they caring for 8 and 10-year-old siblings needing transport to after school sports?

Next, you'll want to share information about yourself and your family's needs. The more you can be clear on your needs, the better. Let them know you'll expect them to take a break during the baby's nap. Be aware that how much housework a nanny can get done depends a lot on your children's ages. Newborns and twins are very time consuming for one person. You can expect nannies to wash bottles and baby clothes and keep things organized, but not much more. Once the kids are a bit older then the nanny can likely also sweep the kitchen and baby's room, and wipe down counters. When the kids are much older she may also be able to prepare family meals. If this would be your expectation, then discuss it to be sure your prospective nanny is on the same page.

Talk about cell phone usage. If you are interviewing an older middle-aged nanny who has had her own kids, then cell phones *may* be less of an issue. She'll want to use it to check in with her own kids periodically, and that's okay. You're going to want to call and check on your kids from work too! If you are talking with a younger nanny, then cell phones can be a potential problem. You will want to make clear that the phone is for emergency calls only, and that like any job, you expect them to be focused on work when they are with your kids. We had to let one young nanny go because we learned she spent all her time on her smart phone and ignored the kids. We discovered this when I came home early one day, and she didn't hear me come in. I was in the house for 45 minutes, and she was playing on the phone the whole time. The kids got progressively more wild until she yelled at them. Honestly, we'd been a bit suspicious beforehand. She was young and seemed to think she was just babysitting. I find that nannies who had their own kids often "get it" when it comes to pitching in and helping make a house run. They are also more likely to understand the kind of love and attention that's involved in raising kids.

Ask for references, and call all of them. If they tell you the nanny was loving and hard-working, but always late, then you know what to expect. If you need to get to work on time, then schedule her to arrive 30 minutes before you need to leave. That way you won't have to stress, when she's 15 minutes late. If they say she often cancelled at the last minute, then she may be okay if you work from home, but not if you have to cancel a day's worth of scheduled patients because you had to stay home.

Arrange some paid trial workdays for candidates that you feel might to be a good fit. You will learn a lot by having them working with you for a day. If you narrow it down to one candidate, then do a trial week. If no one seems right, then start your search over. Yes, you may need to start over. It's hard to start over, but this is one area where you want to be as confident about your choice as possible. During one trial week, a nanny lavished attention on my cute daughter, and nearly ignored my son. It was obvious and extreme favoritism. She also sang constantly in an annoying kid-like voice that drove me crazy. On another trial day a nanny left my infant daughter on the changing table to walk across the room. She had mostly worked with older children, and was out of her element. You learn a lot with trial days.

If your nanny will be driving your kids anywhere, do a DMV search as an employer. Let her take you out for a test drive to see if she's easily distracted by you talking to her. For practice, take the car seats out to check if she can put them back in correctly. I was surprised when my very experienced nanny improperly installed *her* own baby's car seat in my car. You never know when something's going to happen that requires the removal of a car seat. You want to be sure she can get it back in correctly.

If you are looking for someone to care for twins or multiple young children, I encourage you to look for an experienced mother with children of her own or an experienced nanny who has cared for multiple children at the same time. You will likely pay more for them than for someone with less childcare experience. But juggling multiple infants or toddlers is hard work! You want someone who knows what that entails up front. Finding the right nanny can truly be a wonderful gift to your family. But, trust your instincts and keep looking until you feel you've made the right choice.

Once you've hired a nanny, it's important to keep communication going both ways. In the beginning, I recommend doing a weekly sit-down to discuss what is working for her, and what is not. Your first instinct may be to tell her what *you* want her to do. But, I encourage you to start by asking her what she needs to make things work better for her. The more you take a team approach to figuring out the shape of her role, the more she'll be able to step up as the kids get older. When you're responsive to her needs she's more likely to be responsive to yours. If possible, encourage her to get out of the house with the kids every day. If she can meet other nannies at a park or playground, she'll be happier and so will the kids. A happy nanny is likely to stay. A happy nanny is a good thing!

I also think it's important to do unannounced drop-ins, early returns from work, and occasional days at home so you'll have a better idea of how it's going. You should give your nanny paid vacation and sick days. Some families will ask a nanny to coordinate her vacation with their family vacation. This is very helpful to you, but you may not want to make it a deal breaker. If you've found a good nanny who needs to take her vacations at different times, then you can use a nanny service while she's gone or take extra time off work yourself. One of the best investments in your own professional future is a good nanny. She can greatly ease the burden of working parents when your kids are young. With her, you'll be much more likely to keep two parents working outside the home. Without that help, you may find a parent burning out at work and leaving their job to "lean in" at home. Remember too, that your nanny may be a working mom just like you. Traditional women's labor and the women who do it remain at the bottom of our socio-economic ladder. But don't confuse traditionally low status with low value. As a working parent you should recognize the true value of her work. You should recognize that she faces many of the same work-life-family conflicts that you do. Respect, flexibility, and appreciation can go a long way in creating a partnership that works. So, if you find yourself with a good nanny, take good care of her!

HOW TO ESCAPE THE HOUSE WITH MULTIPLE BEASTIES IN TOW

Getting out of the house with more than one wild critter presents certain challenges. It's especially hard when you're doing the solo juggle. The main component that makes it possible is what I call a "containment system." These can take the form of car seats, strollers, shopping carts, high chairs, fenced areas, harnesses with a leash, baby backpacks, or any other device that allows you to safely turn your back on your "runner" baby while you tend the other little 'un. If you are going to a playground with multiple youngsters, you'll want to scope out ones that are fully fenced and gated. You'll go from car seat to double stroller to playground, then reverse for the return trip. Or you may use a single stroller and a strap on baby carrier. But, remember that will mean you don't have a place to safely put both kiddos down at the same time. You will do this even when the playground is quite close to your car. When the kids are less than a year old, your grocery trips will often involve pushing the double stroller ahead of you while you pull a shopping cart behind. Once they are able to sit, you may carry one into the store while pushing the other in a single stroller. Then you can put one kid in the cart seat and leave the other in the stroller. Don't assume that once they are walking that you can all hold hands and walk into a store that has double seated carts. You may find yourself in the middle of the parking lot with one kid who just sat down, and another pulling in the direction of an oncoming car. Sometimes you can cruise the parking lot until you see an empty cart with two seats. Then park nearby, and take it to your car. Pretty soon you'll know which of your favorite stores have double seated carts in good supply and which playgrounds are safely enclosed.

A friend, who also had twins, liked the harness and leash approach. Once her boys could walk, they didn't leave the house without their harness on until they were 3-years-old. They kept the harnesses by the door with the coats, and the boys just got used to wearing them. Two tips if you want to go the harness route. First, you need to practice. In the beginning one or both children will charge off in various directions. There will be crashes and entanglements until they learn that they can't run off. Second, it helps if you can find a harness where the leash attaches lower on the back. If it attaches higher, and the child runs they will get pulled up short on the leash. With higher attachments, they are more likely to fall back and hit their head. If it attaches lower, they are slightly more likely to fall on their bottom and spare their head. My friend was so happy with her harnesses that I tried them too. However, my son's learning curve seemed a bit steep. I gave up and stuck with other containment systems.

Frankly, we spent so much time transferring kiddos from one containment system to another that eventually we realized the kids had never learned how to hold hands while crossing the street! Some of this training depends on your kid's temperaments. Nevertheless, if you have even one "runner" you're gonna need containment and planning to get out safely with young twins or your average rumpus of baby rhinos.

Some parents find it challenging just getting their gaggle of littles to the car. If you live in an apartment or have on-street parking, then the easiest thing is often to load the babies in a double stroller and use that to move them to the car. On the other hand, if you have a lot of stairs to negotiate, it's going to be more complicated. You're not going to want to leave one kid in the house, and take another down the stairs to the car. You'd wind up having to leave them in the car seat unattended while you go back to get their sibling. That's not going to work. So, you need to carry two infants in front/back baby carriers, or carry two fully loaded infant car seats. I don't recommend carrying both infants in your arms. First, if you trip and fall you will not be able to protect your infants or yourself. Second, once you get to the car you'll need free hands to get both babies into the car seats and you won't have a good place to put one infant down while you buckle the other into their seat. If you have multiple young kids, I highly recommend a ground level apartment or one with an elevator. Of course, once you have yourself, your kids, your diaper bags, purse, snacks, bottles, all the necessities, packed into the car…someone will spit-up or blow out a diaper! Whenever possible just do the clean-up and change in the car, and get yourself out of there. Out to a change of scenery!

STROLLERS

Ah, yes. I do remember the fleet of crumby, gummy vehicles which packed my garage. In which fine chassis would we stroll casually today? Would we take the front-back tandem? Or perhaps the side-by-side tandem? Maybe we should split up and take two single umbrella strollers? How about the giant knobby wheeled all terrain double? So many options for our sleek and sexy adventure. Which one will I watch my children spit-up on today?

My twins were my first kids and my previous stroller exposure was… zip. You probably think buying a car is a big deal, but if you're a first-time stroller buyer you'll discover you don't even know what to consider. And they vary in price from about $30 for a single umbrella stroller to $1,500 or more for fancy doubles. So, what do you need? What's going to grow with the kids? What are the features to consider?

First comes infancy, right? In the beginning, you'll want a stroller into which you can clip an infant car seat. You will unlatch the car seat from the car, set it onto a stroller attachment, and off you go, babies still sleeping. Ok, *your* babies may still be sleeping at this point but *mine* always woke up. For early infancy, you can get a snap-n-go (single or double), or "invest" in a stroller with a car seat adapter that converts to a toddler stroller for later. The double snap-n-go is a long frame with places for two car seats arranged front to back. I never had one, but they are usually relatively inexpensive, and can often be found used. I gather they are not especially maneuverable, but you're not going to be taking your newborn infants on jaunts across roads strewn with potholes and granite boulders. You may get by for 6 to 9 months with a snap-n-go. At some point, however, your kiddos will be getting a wee bit too heavy to heave around in their car seats. And, they may want to be more upright to see the world. At this point, you'll leave the car seat in the car and move the babes into a stroller that's designed for older infants or toddlers. Usually, these work best with kids who are old enough to sit independently. If you bought a stroller with car seat adapters, then you can take the adapter off and you're ready for this next phase. As time goes on, kids get bigger and the activities you want to do with them will change. This can affect what you want down the road in your suburban hot rod.

There are many different strollers and ever-changing models. I'll hit some of the popular ones and review features that I found useful at different stages of a child's growth. However, this list is in no way comprehensive, so shop around for current offerings. Here's what to consider when "test strolling" different types of badass baby buggies:

Snap-n-Go's:
PROS: Cheap, easy to pop car seats in and out. Can often be found used.

CONS: Double has a long chassis and is not easily maneuverable. Wheels are small, may not convert to toddler stroller.

Front-Back tandem: like City Select or UppaBaby:
PROS: Narrow profile, which is good for small stores or weaving between clothing racks. Can take car seats at first and when kids are bigger convert to toddler seats. Often have good snack trays. Can have nice large carry space located underneath. This means if it's loaded with stuff and the kids climb out, the stroller won't tip over. When folded, they are often smaller than jogging tandems.

CONS: Tend to be expensive. Often need to keep heaviest kid in front to handle well. May need two hands to maneuver if walking where there are many driveway cut outs. Harder to control with older/bigger kids. Harder for kids to climb into on their own.

Side-by-Side or Single Jogging style: like BOB, double BOB, Mt Buggy, etc.
PROS: Large wheels, tripod shape, and wide handlebar means you can often maneuver these one handed even over driveway cut outs and uneven pavement. Many have infant car seat adaptors which you can later switch to a toddler seat. Can accommodate 5 to 6-year-old kids which can be helpful on some outings. Can be taken on wide trails and gravel fire roads. Often have under seat storage area and good sun shades. Very sturdy and long lasting which means you can buy them used.

CONS: Expensive when new. Big and heavy when folded. Small toddlers may need a fleece insert to fit well in the large seats. Snack tray options vary but can be limited.

Side-by-Side street style: small wheels like City Mini, Combi.
PROS: Some have many features and still are cheaper than jogging stroller. They are smaller and lighter than joggers. Some fold-up pretty small, have good snack trays, and are easy for older kids to climb in and out of on their own. Many have storage underneath, good sun shades, and small wheels that make them lighter and are fine for pavement. They can often be found used.

CONS: Not good for gravel, dirt, or trails. Some brands are less sturdy. Can be harder to maneuver with one hand.

Umbrella Strollers
PROS: Important if parents want to split up with multiple kids in tow. Wide price range but you can find them cheap. Fold up very small and light. If the airline trashes it, you won't care so much.

CONS: Usually no snack tray. Storage maybe located on the back of the stroller so that it tips backward when the kids get out of the seat. Usually no sun shade and limited seat reclining.

Stroller Features to Consider by Age:

Infant: Car seat adaptor. If you're expecting twins, make sure your arrangement can work with a car seat rated down to 4 to 5 lbs. since many twins are preemie. Not all seats are rated for the lower weights.

Young toddler: Snack trays are very helpful. If you're in line at a store and a kid starts to fuss you can throw a few cheerios or a toy on the tray to keep them happy until you can finish. You want a good snack tray! Good sun shades are also important.

Older toddler/ young child: Snack trays are still important. Look for a size that is easy for kids to climb in and out of when unbuckled. This makes trips to the zoo or fair easier on parents who won't have to lift the kids in and out of the stroller.

Young kids 4-6 y/o: These kids can do longer outings, but will tire by the end. Having a stroller that can still handle two heavy kids will allow you to take longer hikes. The kids can walk out and ride back. It makes the end of your day at the fair more pleasant since you don't have to try to cajole tired kids into walking back to the car. It can also be a gear holder for the first half of the day, and a containment system in large crowds.

Feature Notes:

Under seat gear storage: This can balance the stroller so it's less likely to tip over backwards when the kids get out.

Size: Important if you live in an apartment or have a small car. Check both set-up and folded size. On the other hand, if you have a garage and minivan this is less of an issue. I had both and rarely folded my strollers. Even a double BOB or a City Select would fit in the back of my minivan without folding. I never encountered a door that a side-by-side couldn't get through, but there may be areas with historic buildings and narrow doors that could be problematic for a side-by-side.

Weight: Lighter is better if you're going to have to fold and lift it a lot. Heavier and solid is better for longevity and durability. These things will take a beating!

Sunshades: Important, look for them.

Accessories: Many have attachments you can add like cup holders, phone holders, bag hooks.

Strollers can be big budget purchases, but you can often find good deals on used ones. I was gifted a City Select which we used with car seat adaptors for our newborns and with toddler seats when they were small. As my kids got heavier, I found this front/back tandem to be harder to maneuver. Later, I bought a used double BOB from Craig's list. At first is seemed a bit big for my kids, so we used a fleece insert. Ultimately, it became a long-lasting work horse, and was the last stroller we let go. Over the years, I also bought two used side-by-side Combi's, which we used quite a lot. The first one was very cheap and more beat up as it had been through three kids. It lasted about a year and a half of heavy use. The second used Combi was in better shape when we got it, and still good when we passed it on several years later. It is lighter and less sturdy than the big joggers. But it had great snack trays, sun shades, storage, and was easy for the kids to climb in and out of. That made it a regular go to stroller for a lot of pavement based outings until my kids were just too big for it. Even when new it's much cheaper than the double joggers. Hopefully, all this will give you an idea of what to start looking for and considering when shopping for a stroller. One of the hardest parts is to try to think ahead, and find a stroller that will grow with the changing needs and activities of your kids.

TEACHING BABIES TO ENJOY STROLLER TIME

So, you've got your stroller all picked out, now it's time to get strolling! Right? After all the months of immobility during my pregnancy, I was determined to get out and get walking with my babies. You've seen those parents. It's naptime so they put their babies in the stroller, and head out for a walk. The babies fall asleep. The parent gets some much needed fresh air and exercise. Perhaps they walk to a cafe and sit in the sun with a nice cup of coffee while the babies snooze away. Ah, bliss. Absolute bliss! I wish this for you. I really do. Unfortunately, this was not my reality.

I first tried to do the stroller walk when my kids were a few months old. My son, however, was highly sensitive to loud noises. We'd be walking along and a big truck would rumble by, the air brakes on a bus would squeal, or some playing kid would shriek. Whatever the noise, it would send my son into a startled screaming frenzy. It would take a long time to soothe him. Pretty soon my daughter would pick up on his distress, and start crying too! I could be a block from my house or a mile away with two wailing babies. Not fun! I remember being unsure of what to do about this challenge. I was a newbie parent, and I wondered if I should expose my son to more sounds so he could get used to them or avoid these situations? I called my sister and a good friend who were both experienced moms. They offered great advice saying, "You know, he's just so so little. Right now, you just need to protect him from this." I remember being so relieved by this wisdom. It felt right. So, I stopped trying to do stroller walks for a while. As he got older, my son outgrew his terrified reaction to sudden noises.

All right, now I've got toddlers and my son is over his "stage," so let's get stroller walking! I'd gather all my gear. Diaper stuff, bottles, snacks, clothing changes, my purse, bundle the kids into the stroller and set out from home into a moderately bustling neighborhood. After about 5 to 10 minutes my kids were done. "Ok, enough of this sitting around stuff. We want OUT!" I tried walking faster or slower. I tried different strollers with more upright positioning or more laid back seats. Bigger wheels with a softer ride. Sun covers. Wind covers. Walking at nap time in the hope they would sleep. Then walking after naps and eating in the hope they'd be less fussy. I tried driving to more interesting places to walk in areas with better scenery. None of it worked. I couldn't believe it. I did not have "stroller babies." They simply were not going to put up with being confined to a stroller for the duration of a walk. Brief jaunts to a location where they could get out and play were fine. But I was not going to get any exercise by taking my kids for a walk. Obviously *other* people managed this, so why couldn't I?!

As it turned out this was one of those early parental lessons. The fact is, "kids are like a box of chocolates. You never know what you're gonna get." You may really, really want "stroller babies," but you may not actually *get* them. And they are *not* little lumps of clay that you can mold into what *you* currently want or need them to be. They are already opinionated little beings. At some point, you have to let go and go with the flow. Really, parenting is a great lesson in what you can *not* control in life...which it turns out is quite a lot. We do like to be in control in our society. At some point, however, you may find you need to let go and learn to enjoy watching your kids grow into themselves.

So, how do you "teach" your babies to enjoy stroller time? Well, you can try all the things I mentioned above. Maybe it will work for you or maybe you'll just have to let it go.

DIAPER BOXES, PLASTIC CUPS, AND SCOTCH TAPE

What do these three things have in common? Well, they are by far some of the best kids toys ever marketed. I know! I know! The cost of them is prohibitive. But. They are toys with great longevity, and well worth the investment. First, came the big plastic yellow cup. Before my twins could even sit, they loved that cup. If one had it, the other tried to get it. No other object would garner such concerted effort to wrest it from a neighboring baby. They would turn it, and shake it, and pass it from feet to hands. Eventually, it became a vessel to pour from or stuff things into. You could pound on it. Chew on it. Scratch fingernails on its roughish surface. Oooh, and roll it!

Once you're a walking baby, you can put a cup inside a diaper box, and then climb in with it! Woo, hoo! You can get *under* a box or *in* a box. You can fill it up or dump it out. You can fill it up, and slide it down the stairs. Poke a hole in it for a string, and drag it behind you. You can put your sister in it, and push her around the kitchen until it's your turn. The options are truly endless for the cardboard box. At 12-years-old, my kids still love a good box. They will play with it for hours and days. When the kids were little, the diaper box was optimal size. Later, slightly larger was good, and now fort size is awesome. Laundry baskets can fill a similar role, but be warned they will end up cracked.

Then there's tape. Any kind will do, but often it's the clear wrapping tape that reigns supreme. The love of tape hits around 3-years-old, and appears to be nearly universal. Well, at least in my limited mom survey. It is an enduring love with, as of yet, no clear end in sight. This toy *can* get a bit expensive. They won't use it in little strips and bits…no, no, no. Great long pieces 3, 4, and 5 feet long will stretch across doorways and between furniture, from windows to floors, around and around stuffed animals, in the carpet, in the dog's fur. You'll turn from making lunch and find your living room has been taped from end to end, as though some giant psychotic spider had built its nest while your back was turned. "Mom, we need more tape," they will say. So, after banishing the spider, you will get more tape. A three pack for good measure. Then the next day, they will say, "Mom, we need more tape!" Whaaa? "I bought three rolls yesterday?!" "It's all gone. We used it," they say. "For what?" you ask. And they will bring you 25 tape mosaics. All of which, they expect you to prominently display. So, you will get more tape for putting the tape mosaics up on the wall. The next day, they will say, "Mom, we need more tape." Whaaa? "I bought six rolls. Six!" you'll say. "It's all gone," they will say. "For what?!" you ask. "I dunno? We need more," they say. "I'm not buying more tape if you're just going to waste it!" you say. Then, because *you* need some tape around, you buy three rolls and *hide* them. Heh, heh. You're so smart. Of course, when you go to wrap a gift, the tape will be gone. Grrr! "Look, Mom, we found some tape way down deep in that drawer, and look what we made!" They will take you to some obscure window in the house which they have covered in a million little bits of tape. "Isn't it pretty mom? It's just like a stained-glass window." The tape will have become baked onto the glass. After a screaming fit, you'll spend hours carefully trying to peel off miles of thin plastic and adhesive.

No. More. Tape. You'll be quite firm. But, you might as well give it up. Tape is a toy of endless invention, and kids love it. You'll never be able to keep it hidden nor live without it. Just buy stock in a tape factory, and then get it by the pallet load. I do encourage you to try to put some limits on taping locations. Teach them to avoid windows, carpets, hardwood floors…really any floor, antiques, pets, kitchen cabinets, sofas…sigh. Just get good at peeling it off. And when people ask what to get the kids for their birthday? Tape.

SAFETY, CHILDPROOFING, EMERGENCY KITS

Childproofing your home can vary from moving furniture in front of wall outlets to maximum lock down. If you have more than one kiddo, you will need at least one safe place to corral your mischievous critters while your back is turned. This can be a pack-n-play, a fenced off area, or even a stationary entertainment center. What you might need beyond that often depends not just on your home's layout, but on your kids' temperaments. Now, if we'd had two kids with my daughter's temperament, we might have gotten away with a gate or two and some basic childproofing steps. My son, however, was a different deal. If the possibility for injury existed, he discovered it. And while my daughter sat and watched the action, my son was moving fast. We wound up baby proofing to the max. We had gates everywhere, cabinet locks, latches to hold some doors open (to prevent him from crushing his sister's fingers in the door), latches to hold outside doors closed, special wall outlets, breakables hidden away, TV mounted high on the wall, stove shields. We also consulted a professional child-proofer since we were too exhausted to figure this all out ourselves. Best tip from the child-proofer? Don't bring plastic dry-cleaning bags into the house. All plastic bags are one of the deadliest things in the home. Our nanny taught us to pull plastic grocery bags into a string, then tie them in two knots before putting them away up high. If you buy paper goods in bulk, they often come in a large plastic covering. Take the toilet paper out of the plastic covering, tie up the plastic, and get it out of the house.

Remember there can be dangers just outside your door. Busy streets, ponds, pools, and drop offs can pose a risk within a few steps. At some point your child may want to wander outside without you. Yeah, really, they get out! Let's say you're sleep deprived or distracted by another child? A leaking washer? Something. One child gets the door open and wanders outside. What dangers will they encounter there? You can guard against this with door knob covers or by putting inside latches up high on your doors that lead outside. You can use the type often found in apartments. It has a chain that hooks across the door opening. Or use a simple hook and eye latch to prevent them from opening the door. Just be aware that determined kids will bring a chair to stand on, and learn to undo the latch. You can also use door alarms that buzz or announce which door has been opened.

Beware of door jams. This is a common spot for one kid to put their fingers in while another kid closes the door and crushes them. You can use the same hook and eye or apartment chain latches to hold doors *open*. Just change the placement of each part of the latch.

You may also want to block toddlers from whole rooms. Again, the hook and eye or apartment chain latch can be used to keep rooms off limits, yet allow adults easy access. Great for bathrooms or any place you want to keep kids out of.

When our kids were born we lived in earthquake country. Maybe blizzards, hurricanes, or tornados are visitors to your neck of the woods. You'll want to update your emergency kit to accommodate your newest little 'uns. The first year you're going to want to add things like diapers, formula, water filtration pumps, rash ointments and sunscreen. But by the next year they will be eating baby food and you're going to need to completely redo your kit. Check the dates on everything. You'll find one of the longest lasting products are backpacker's dehydrated food pouches. You can find various lists online of things to include in your kit. Make your kit. Update it as your kids grow. Don't forget. Check out these sites to get you started on creating emergency kits and how to baby-proof your home.

Baby proofing information site: Childproofing Experts.com
https://www.childproofingexperts.com/childproofing-checklist-by-age/

Emergency Kits: Ready.gov
https://www.ready.gov/build-a-kit

GROWTH CHARTS

The thing to remember about growth charts is that they were created as an assessment tool. Like any tool one needs to know how to use it, and what it can and can't do for you. Pediatricians use growth charts to alert them to a child who may need extra attention. After all, babies can't tell us if something's wrong nor answer our questions. We want things that can alert us to take a closer look. One of the main jobs of an infant is to grow. They put enormous energy into it so when growth isn't occurring normally, it can be a warning sign. However, like any tool, growth charts have their limitations.

The charts typically used in the U.S. are based on data for formula fed, Caucasian kids, from the U.S. Weight and height charts using data from other groups can be *very* different. Many countries produce their own charts based on the local ethnicities and growth patterns. The World Health Organization also makes charts based on breastfed infants. So, if your ancestors are from the Philippines, or Tanzania, or the high Andes, then the "normal" weight and height ranges on a U.S. chart may not be "normal" for your baby at all. If the child's parents are both well under 5 feet tall, then it can be completely normal for their infant to be well below the 5% on U.S. charts. If the parents are 6'6" tall gigantic Scandinavians, then the baby may well be literally "off the charts."

So, what's the point? Again, it's a tool and you need to know how to use it. A pediatrician should consider if your child's weight and height are in a normal range for their ethnic background, parental size, and gestational age at birth. Then, we can watch their growth over time. Does the child grow at a normal *rate*? This is also called "tracking on a normal curve" on the chart. Next, we can look at whether the child's weight is in proportion to their height. You're looking to see if they are roughly, *roughly* at the same percentile for weight and height. Are they well-proportioned? Unusually tall? Too skinny? All of these factors are most useful if you are charting the child over time to assess good growth. On the other hand, if a child is steadily "dropping off" her growth curve, then there may be some concern even if they are smack in the middle of the chart.

Growth information is, of course, non-specific. It doesn't tell you *what*, if anything, is wrong. It could be as simple as hidden reflux or as concerning as low growth hormone. Then again, a child could hit a growth spurt and suddenly catch up. But, unexpected findings on growth informs us to pay attention, look around, consider further assessment. The most useful question to ask your pediatrician is whether your child is "tracking on a normal curve."

There are many, many issues that can cause a child to have growth problems. Pediatricians investigate this issue all the time, and will watch changes closely. If they see a concerning trend, they may feel more assessment is needed. You can always ask them to explain their reasoning for why they are concerned or why they are not concerned. Remember, we still often wind up comparing children even when we shouldn't. It can be perfectly normal for kids to grow at wildly different rates. My son went from 5 lbs., 12 oz. at birth (below the 5%) to the 99% for weight and height by 3 months. My daughter was born at 5 lbs., 10 oz. She barely hit the 5% by 3 months and remained around the 10% for many years. Both were "tracking on a normal curve."

If you want more information on growth charts, here's a good article: *Growth Charts for Kids*, Elissa Strouse, CNN Health, April 4, 2018. https://www.cnn.com/2018/04/04/health/growth-chart-parenting-strauss/index.html

TALKING TO DOCTORS, DEALING WITH HEALTH ISSUES

I believe that clear communication is one of the most important aspects of good medical care. As a physician assistant, I strive to not only understand a patient's medical issues, but also their questions, concerns, and level of understanding of their care. As a woman who went through five years of fertility treatment and a stroke, I've also experienced medical communication from a patient's perspective. As a mother with a child who has some health issues, I've dealt with this challenge from yet another angle. Here's my take and advice: It doesn't matter whether a medical provider is an MD, DO, NP, or PA. Some people are good communicators who listen to their patients, and some are not and do not. If you feel that your child's pediatrician isn't listening to you, doesn't communicate well, or doesn't take the time to address your concerns, then find someone else. There are medical providers out there who listen, are careful, knowledgeable, thorough, respectful, and good communicators. Don't settle for less.

Having a child with a health problem can be really tough. Whether it's a serious condition or just chronically frustrating, it is often emotionally exhausting and very time consuming. Even modest issues can require huge investments of time and energy to manage. It can absorb your whole life. You will just want to make everything better for them. And you may not be able to do that. You may find you need to become a pushy advocate for your child's needs. Don't be afraid to be pushy. Children have no voice. You will need to speak for them and their needs.

If you are going through this kind of challenge, I encourage you to seek out other parents for advice and support. Facebook mother's clubs can be a great source of help, and you may find illness specific support groups. At the same time that you cultivate support from other parents, you'll want to develop a group of professionals that you trust with your child's wellbeing. Recognize that managing a serious or chronic condition in a young child can be so time consuming that you are not able to keep up with other parts of your life. Cut yourself as much slack as you can and seek out trustworthy caregivers who can give you a break. Perhaps you're wondering why your child's severe peanut allergy is causing so much disruption in your life? Well, constant hypervigilance over another person's life is exhausting! You're not imagining how hard it can be. Having to always be prepared. Having to always pre-research every environment you child goes into and every person they encounter. Having to constantly work with medical staff to decide how to manage the issue. Having to make risky decisions for your child…and then live with the choices. Having to double check every minor symptom your child has. The endless sense of failure when you can't "fix" it.

It's just hard, hard, hard. Get help. Accept hugs. Sending hugs your way!

PARENTING ISSUES OF THE LATER EARLY YEARS

GENERAL APPROACHES TO PARENTING

PARENTING BOOKS TEND TO HAVE their own lens through which they view children and parents. The problem is they view everything and everyone and every family and every environment through the same lens. When you're sleep deprived and desperate for help, it may sound like a wonderful all-encompassing guiding principle. When you're a little more rested, and a little more experienced, you realize that's just silly. People are complicated. Life is complicated. One shoe will not fit all feet for all occasions. While reading parenting books, I have found it useful to simply look for useful insights and ideas. I often wind up pulling helpful ideas from very contradictory perspectives. Do you need to make emotional connection? Manage behaviors? Develop relationships? Facilitate a developmental stage? Well, yes, all of that. You also might be curious about how the Danish do it today, and what our hunter-gatherer ancestors passed on to non-western communities.

Let's go through a few of my favorite parenting books, and see what they have to offer.

Happiest Toddler on the Block by Harvey Karp, MD is a great book that can help parents connect with their emotional little ones. We all want our feelings understood. And regardless of whether we are 40 or 4, we tend to have a hard time processing anything when we are upset. Instead, we lose our capacity for rational conversation. Our toddlers have not been on this earth very long, and have absolutely no experience managing their intense feelings. Nor do they have the best of communication skills. That combination can become rather explosive when a toddler's intense desire to run into the street is thwarted for reasons they can't understand.

So, yacking at a distraught toddler is unlikely to get you a calm response. In those times we need to connect with them on an emotional level that acknowledges their feelings. Later, when everyone is calm, we can help the little critters understand their feelings. This is where Dr. Karp steps in to help parents find ways to connect with kids who are emotionally distraught.

In addition, *Happiest Toddler on the Block* offers a perspective on the parent-child relationship that I quite like. Karp suggests that parents think of themselves as "ambassadors," and their child as a "Neanderthal" newly introduced to civilization. As an ambassador, we adults must remain diplomatic and respectful while guiding our charges. We may be teaching our children the expected courtesies and customs of our world, but we do best if we remain appreciative and respectful of the individual before us. And, well, we know what to expect of a Neanderthal. It may take them a while to learn because, well, they are a Neanderthal. Diplomacy, however, requires us to recognize their value and behave diplomatically and respectfully. In essence this means we think before we act. We avoid being reactive. (Psst. That can be hard!)

Looking at parenting from a completely different angle we find *The Kazdin Method for Parenting the Defiant Child* by Alan Kazdin Ph.D. This Yale child psychologist, focuses on how to change some of the often extremely bothersome behaviors of toddlers and children. Some times with young kids you just need a behavior to change! In fact, a lot of toddler parenting can seem like behavior management. Kazdin teaches us how to *successfully* use well applied positive reinforcement to get effective behavioral change. There have been times when using his techniques have helped our family go from screaming "NO, NO, NO!!!!" all day long to having a home filled with "Yippee! I'm proud of you for doing that!" The energy in our home flipped from very negative and frustrated to happier and more positive. And, we were getting the behavior changes we needed. There are a variety of techniques that Kazdin teaches, and he carefully reviews *how* to do them *effectively*. His ideas helped us to drop the "stern" voice and refocus on positive reinforcement of good or almost good behavior. As adults, we have the power to step back from the chaos in which we are embroiled and find a new approach. As parents, learning to take that step back, and take that second look is a vital skill. Avoid reacting. Instead, stop, think, plan, then act. (Yeah, easier said than done. But worth the work to get there!)

Kazdin teaches you *how to see* what you want the kids to be doing and how to then *set them up to succeed*. When they are set up to succeed with better behavior, you are also set up to offer praise for success. It can turn the whole emotional and behavioral dynamic between adult and toddler on its head in a very good way. You will find it makes for a much nicer home environment. The kids will be calming down and behaving better as you are able to praise them more and more.

I'll review one of Kazdin's techniques that you can use again and again. Let's say your young kids have hit a "wild and crazy" stage. Going to bed now involves little beasties screaming and running around, throwing things on the ground, jumping on the furniture, general mayhem, and parents screaming "No, NO! NO! STOP IT!" Previously, it had been going well, but now? Nothing you used to do is working. You start each evening with the plan to make it a good night. Before you know it, the kids are jumping on the bed and screaming. You just want them to stop screaming, and put their PJ's on! So, you try "consequences." And the next day that doesn't work so you try more severe "consequences" You wind up with crying kiddos, but no enduring compliance. Kazdin explains that negative consequences do NOT work when trying to change behavior. The escalating discipline is a common trap that parents fall into because *at first* it seems to work. But then, it doesn't, so we escalate the punishment. Then we look at ourselves and say, "Who is this harsh disciplinarian that I'm morphing into!" "What's going on with my kids!" "How am I supposed to fix this!"

Okay. First thing to do is step back and ask yourself, not what you want them to STOP doing, but rather what you want them TO DO. Then write down the behavior you want: "I want the kids to walk nicely to their room, put their pajamas on, and climb into bed for story time." You have now defined what you want which means you can start praising and rewarding all steps in the right direction. You can also set them up to succeed by practicing. First, you practice in the middle of the day when everyone is fresh and happy. "Okay kids, we're going to play a game! If you walk nicely to bed, I'll give you a chocolate chip. If you then put your pajamas on nicely, I'll give you another one!" Then you practice with immediate reward and praises. Suddenly, you're saying "Good job!" and getting compliance. It really works. Read up on all the fine points of making it work, what mistakes to avoid, how long to do everything. Kazdin's book has very useful information and can be a life saver in the early years when the beasties are sometimes wild just because…they are wild!

But parenting isn't just about behaviors. *Duct Tape Parenting* by Vicki Hoefle stresses the importance of teaching our children the skills of life and then letting them have the freedom to grow into their own competencies. For a child to develop competency, you have to first show them how to do something, then back away, put your hands behind your back, and the duct tape over your mouth. Let them learn by living. We have gotten way, way, *way* too focused on doing *for* our kids in these days of over parenting. It isn't a gift to rob them of their opportunities at learning and mastery. And it is a *huge* burden on parents to keep children in a state of constantly needing micromanagement. You don't turn a toddler into an independent creature by wishful thinking. But, this *is* when you start. They can set their cup on the table at dinner. They can "help" sweep the floor afterwards. By age 3, they can set and clear their cup and plate. At age 4, they can help set the family table. Little by little you add skills and expectations. Hoefle has compiled a great list of life skills, self-care skills, social and emotional skills covering four different age groups in her book. Use these as a guide for the kinds of mastery and skills your kids can be working on. Your 7 to 8-year-old can be waking for school with the help of an alarm clock, getting themselves dressed, brushing teeth, making some breakfast, feeding the cats, and packing jackets and sports gear for school. In the evening they can set tables, load or unload dishwashers, clean up after dinner, and take out garbage. On weekends they can do laundry, clean bathrooms, or vacuum. My 8-year-olds did these chores regularly. Execution of their jobs was far from perfect, but they had the capacity to master all of these skills and more. It's very good for them and it's necessary for parents. There are some parts of *Duct Tape Parenting* that I don't fully agree with, but this part is spot on and very important. Teach kids the skills of life and weave in the expectation that they take part in family work. At the same time, you must, *must* step back, close your mouth and avoid micromanaging. This can be very, very hard. But it is also truly liberating. You will find you get a bit of room to breathe, while getting to enjoy your children from a wonderful new perspective.

I have one caveat here. At the same time that you are giving your child the space to struggle and make mistakes in a new task, you also want to teach them about teamwork by helping them sometimes. Hmmm, sounds rather contradictory, doesn't it? Well, yes. That's one of the points I want to make. I've taught my kids how to get ready for school by themselves. They have check lists and generally muddle through most days. Yet, sometimes one or both are having a hard morning. I may ask them if they want some help or just get something together for them. Then I give them a high five and say "Team work!" Because I also want to show them they can rely on me. That, we as a family, are a team. That we can help each other. That we look out for those we love.

This brings me to another important parenting perspective to keep in mind. Your babies are growing into themselves. You want to get to know them. You want to think about developing a relationship with the person your child is growing into. Maybe you have a toddler who doesn't want to stop what he's doing and tends to dawdle. That's frustrating behavior when you're trying to get kids out of the house on time. But, it's not always just behavior. That child may grow into someone who lingers over a task until the project is fully done. Your child is already an individual. Learning to see them for who they are and value them for their strengths is worth doing even at a young age. It can be helpful to pull back from your child's crazy Neanderthal behaviors and wild emotions. Remember to love and embrace the individuals within.

Another particularly important book for stressed out Americans to read is *The Danish Way of Parenting: What the Happiest People in the World Know About Raising Confident, Capable Kids*. This eye opening book was written by Jessica Joelle Alexander, an American journalist while living abroad with her Danish husband and kids. It's co-authored by Iben Dissing Sandahl, a therapist and family counselor in Denmark. Together they have distilled some of the key features of how Danes manage to raise some of the happiest and most capable of kids. What Danish parents focus on is quite different from a typical American parenting approach. The differences are insightful and worth serious thought.

To start with the Danes don't focus on ensuring their kids get the "best" education. Nor do they push them to excel in sports or other endeavors. Instead they focus on nurturing play, empathy, social skills, autonomy, integrity, democracy, and self-esteem. Per Alexander and Sandahl, "if children are always performing in order to obtain something...good grades, awards, or praise...then they don't get to develop their inner drive. They (Danes) believe that fundamentally children need space and trust in order to master skills by *themselves*, to make and solve their *own* problems. This creates genuine self-esteem and self-reliance because it comes from the child's own internal cheerleader, not from someone else." The authors go on to explain that this internal cheerleader or drive is our "locus of control." When we have a predominantly internal locus of control, we tend to see life from a perspective in which we feel we have some degree of power. Certainly, there are many things in life which we cannot control that do affect us greatly. But having a sense of internal efficacy will leave one feeling much less powerless in the face of the slings and arrows of life. People who have a more external locus of control will feel that fate, other people, or outside forces are the determinants of their lives. These folks also tend to have higher levels of stress and depression. Unfortunately, over the last 50 years, studies of American children have shown a pronounced shift towards an external locus of control.

I believe an external locus of control is also a key factor behind racism, prejudice, nationalism, and even genocide. If we have an external locus of control, then other people, different people, strangers can easily be seen as one of many external threats in life. In that framework, joining and identifying with a group seems the only safe choice. If instead, we have an internal locus of control, then people are more likely to be seen as a potential source of community and strength, not a threat. With an internal locus of control, we can view "our group" as all of humanity.

The Danish Way of Parenting focuses on the importance of play, authenticity, reframing of perspective, empathy, and social networks. Notice how this is so, so, sooooo far from American parenting anxieties centered on discipline, success, building smartness, grades, sports, concerted cultivation, or college test scores.

In *Hunt, Gather, Parent: What Ancient Cultures Can Teach Us About The Lost Art Of Raising Happy Helpful Little Humans*, Michaeleen Doucleff, PhD, introduces us to three non-western cultures that are recognized for their unusually good parenting. They have preserved very different parenting traditions and are famous for producing calm, kind, helpful, and confident children. Doucleff bravely dragged her 3-year-old daughter to these communities in search of wisdom and advice. I have found looking outside our own culture to be extremely useful in finding parenthood that makes sense. *Hunt, Gather, Parent* is loaded with insight. She shares completely different attitudes towards the parent-child relationship, and fresh ways to nurture calmness, emotional regulation, executive function skills, kindness, helpfulness, internal motivation, autonomy, confidence and much more.

As you raise your toddler to childhood, you will find yourself surrounded by expectations, pressures, and assumptions about everything kid related. Take a deep breath and a second look at everything. Start looking twice *now*.

There are many other parenting books with their own perspectives. Remember to think about emotional, behavioral, inter-relational, developmental, even cultural influences on parenting issues. Don't get stuck on one theory, one book, or the latest parenting trend. When you read a parenting book, keep an open mind. Perhaps the perspective they preach needs to be balanced with some of your own. If things aren't running smoothly with your kids, ask yourself what might be the best angle from which to address this particular child and concern? What is giving *you* insight that seems to click for your situation? What feels right to you?

KID TIME OUTS? NO! MOMMY TIME OUTS? YES!

You know that whole "time out" routine we do with kids? You put your misbehaving child in a time out location and have them stay there a length of time equal to one minute per year of age. So, a 3-year-old would get a three minute time out and a 4-year-old a four minute time out. Well, according to Kazdin, our behavior fixing guru (see previous section) studies have shown that a three minute time out is no more effective than a one minute time out. In fact, a 10 minute time out is no more effective than a one minute time out, regardless of the child's age. Basically, time outs are minimally effective in changing behavior. They are best used to interrupt a behavior in process or to allow a child time and space to calm down enough to communicate their feelings. Once you get the hang of positive reinforcement, you may find you can just drop the whole "kid time out" from your parenting repertoire.

On the other hand, a "mommy time out" can be a very useful tool. I'm not talking about taking a break and going away for a refreshing solo beach trip or an artist's retreat. That's *definitely* worth it, but not my point here. No, I'm talking about giving yourself a cool down time out when you are about to explode. Or maybe you've already exploded and you say, "AAAAaaaargh! Mommy needs to calm down! Mommy is on calm down time out!" Breathe. Breathe. Breathe. "Don't talk to mommy. She's on time out." Big Deep Breath. And again. You may need three minutes. You may need 10 minutes. Wow, wouldn't it be awesome if we could take one minute for year of our age! Hee, hee! I'd get 57 minutes of calm down time! Oh, yeah, baby! That's enough time for a hot bath and, lying in bed and, and, and....pant, pant...I think I'm hyperventilating.

Calm down time really is good for you, and for your kids. They will see that when we are really upset, it helps to step away and cool off. So, you are modeling good behavior when you return calm and apologetic. It's another one of those humble pie moments of parenthood. "I'm sorry I lost my temper. I was very upset, and didn't handle it very well. I love you very much even when you do things that make me feel upset."

TODDLER DEFIANCE A.K.A. WILD BEASTIES!

At some point, your kids will hit a resistant stage. It will often be bold and in your face. My kids would look me straight in the eye and say, "NO!!!!" with great glee and defiance in their eyes. When they do, I try (this can be hard at times) to see this as healthy self-assertiveness. I'll also try to make a game out of it and yell "YES!!!" back with the same smile. We go back and forth for a loooong time, then I'll throw in a "NO" and a "MAYBE" and then "BOB'S YOUR UNCLE!" Finally, I'll start a pillow fight until we are all feeling silly. If you can do it wholeheartedly and long enough, you may win some compliance. Remember when our kids are teens and someone offers them a pill laced with Fentanyl, we want them to be able to say "No." Nurturing that self-assertion, that belief in one's own choices, and ability to think for themselves starts now. Which is hard because their brains are not yet fully developed, and we cannot allow them to "self-assert" themselves into the middle of traffic. But, it does help to remember the goal when the light of defiance hits their eyes, and you find yourself trying to out think rather than out battle a pair of preschoolers.

6 MONTH BEHAVIORAL OSCILLATIONS

If your kids are driving you crazy. If they won't sleep. If they only say "NO!" If they are having massive meltdowns. If they are still wetting their pants long after potty training. Remember, "this too shall pass." Young kids will swing back and forth from periods of smooth sailing to rough and bumpy patches about every six months. They master some set of developmental challenges, and things are good for six months or so. Then they run into a new set of challenges, and go all cranky, and ornery, and uppity for a while. If your 2.5-year-old is pushing your buttons, there's a good chance that by age 3 things will have calmed down. Ah, smooth sailing. Then, in about 6 months, you can expect it to get all rough and difficult again. This is not just my personal experience. Skim through a bunch of child development books, and you'll find this oscillation mentioned repeatedly. So, I guess those experts do get it right occasionally. There's nothing you can really do about this oscillation. But, sometimes it's just good to know what to expect.

BATH TIME CONFLICTS

Sometimes children develop a sudden and unexplainable refusal to engage in soap related activities. Parents tend to feel strongly that such activities *do* need to occur. Thus, the bath time conflict. So, what to do? First, try to give them as much control as possible. Let them pick a wash cloth from a stack. Let them squirt the soap onto the cloth and wash their own knees and legs. Kids love learning new skills that may seem trivial to us. If you normally bathe your kids together, then do them separately. Do a "shower-bath." Put a couple of inches of water in the tub, then turn on the shower. Or introduce them to the shower by itself. Pack up the old bath toys, and let them pick a waterproof regular toy for bath time. My son loved to bring hot wheels into the tub. Bring in a doll, action figure, or stuffie for them to wash. Give them a straw and let them blow bubbles in the bathtub. Put some swim goggles on yourself and leave a child size set nearby. Wait until they ask to try the kiddie goggles, then show them how you can hold your nose and look underwater. Of course, you can try telling them they *can't* have a bath. Tell them they can't have it, and they will insist on it. It's amazing, but that works for a very long time. Remember too, that most little kids don't need a bath every day so you may be able to cut back on how often you engage in the splash zone drama.

CLIMBING OUT OF CRIBS

At some point your little sweeties will grow big enough to climb out of their cribs. Even with the mattress in its lowest position they will manage it. This can, and usually does, result in one of the great parenting nightmares, nap and night-time pandemonium! You will have finally gotten your kiddos on a nice routine and then suddenly chaos... complete chaos will descend upon your life. This often occurs when the kids are around 15 to 24-months-old. You can also find yourself with two toddlers hitting this stage at the same time. With kids this young, impulse control or even simple hesitation is not high in their skill set. Once they discover they can get loose in the room rather than sleep, they will get into everything they can get their hands on. It could be their sister's hair or the contents of the diaper pail. If it's in the room, it will be fair game in their adrenalin fueled eyes.

There are no clear and easy answers to this rite of passage. Some parents will put the crib mattress on the floor and remove the crib. Others switch to toddler beds. Many parents strip the room completely of everything but the bed, and put a baby gate on the door. Then they hope the phase will pass. Some people will lie down in the room when the kids are napping or going to bed, and stay there until the kids are asleep. Some will leave the room, and watch the beasties on the monitor, then try to stop them before they get out of hand. It's basically a messy difficult time. The babies aren't getting enough sleep, so they are extra cranky. You'll be cranky too!

Just be aware that the jail break days will come, and that it's often disruptive and painful. But, you are not alone in enduring this crazy time. And, this too shall pass!

TANTRUMS/ BIG FEELINGS

All toddlers get big feelings. And some kids get big, Big, BIG feelings. Anger, frustration, exhaustion, fear. All of these feelings can come in overwhelming force to a small creature whose existence on this earth we still count in months. It is hardly reasonable to expect a 15-month-old to have the emotional maturity to handle such intense feelings in a socially acceptable way. And quite often they don't. What they do is melt down in a torrent of tears and screaming. All those feelings jumbled up, tumbling out and no way to understand them or explain them. Thus is born what some call a "temper tantrum." Personally, I don't like that term. It implies the child is "spoiled," not really upset, or trying to manipulate the adults. Those things do happen, but some kids are just completely overwhelmed by big feelings.

My son was one of those kids who would have massive meltdowns. He would be inconsolable. He rejected all attempts to comfort him, and just wailed and wailed in such deep wounded distress. He could go on for 45 minutes. An hour. Non-stop. It was exhausting and painful to watch. One book I read suggested leaving him alone in his room. The idea was to not give him any reinforcement of "bad" behavior. I tried it, but it didn't feel right. He was so young, and so lost in his distress. Wasn't it *my* job to help him find his way in the world of big feelings? Of course, when they are deep in a meltdown, they are not able to understand anything. Talking about things comes much later when they are calm. One article I read suggested just sitting with them.[7] Just being present for them when they are crying and so upset. It was never easy. Ultimately, it felt more right than anything else.

---

[7]   I don't remember who wrote this article or where I read it, but I'm very grateful!

You may get one of these kids with big feelings. My advice is to simply sit with them. If they have a lovey and will accept it, then give it to them. Sit as close as they will let you. Later, maybe the next day, you can tell them that you love them even when they are really upset. These meltdowns are very emotionally draining for parents. Remember it's just a phase they are going through. It's growing pains. Your child will grow out of it.

It can be helpful to spend extra effort teaching them to name their feelings. Look at books with different facial expressions, and talk about how a child across the playground might be feeling. This can help your child develop emotional literacy. You may also find they need more sleep, extra snacks, or free time in their schedule. Each child is different and figuring out their needs at this age can help head off some meltdowns. In the end, however, some kids just need time to grow and mature. My son's meltdowns waxed and waned from when he was 15-months to 2.5-years-old. Then they disappeared for a year. At age 3.5, the meltdowns briefly returned, but by then he was older and had more life skills. Thus, the phase didn't last as long.

One more point for you about big feelings. Remember that if one child is melting down, other children may be very upset by their sibling's distress. They will need some comforting as well.

AGGRESSION

Aggression in childhood is normal. Part of teaching your little beastie how to be civilized is teaching them how to handle their aggressive impulses. The trick is recognizing your little beastie's brain is immature. They don't learn in the logical rational way of adults. (okay *some* adults) Your toddler is going to need endless repetition of "No hit!" and "No pull hair!" and "No bite!!" If you're dealing with multiple young'uns, you'll have a pack of wild, unrestrained, impulsive critters wanting the same toy. There is no quick fix here. You're going to have to watch them closely and repeat yourself for a *long, long* time. It can be helpful to arrange spaces in the house where you can separate them when needed. Two pack-n-plays can become private playrooms. You can use plastic fencing to divide a room in half. If another adult is present, then you can divide and conquer. That gives children some parental one-on-one time without them having to compete with their sibling. Even a little of that goes a long way towards increased harmony. And don't forget to praise them when they do well. "Good job being gentle!"

If your kids are very different in size or temperament, you may need to work especially closely on handling aggression. The fluffy hair of a wobbly 1-year-old, may be incredibly enticing to a charging 2-year-old. They are going to reach for that soft tuft of head fur, and pull hard on it.

You may spend a lot of time saying, "No pull hair! Owie!" As children get older it can also become important to coach a less assertive child to speak up for themselves.

Sandbox aggression towards other kids can also be an issue. If your child is taking another kid's toys, then remove your kid from the sandbox. Help the injured kid get their toy back. No, you do not "let them work it out" at this age. A suburban sandbox full of toddlers is not the wild savannah. We are not here to practice kill or be killed. However, it is a great place to start teaching the basic social skills of community. If they act without social conscience, and they will, then teach them sharing and empathy. Over, and over, and over again. Be sure to notice and praise them for *not* taking something from another child even when they clearly want it. If a younger baby takes your child's toy, and your kid doesn't react aggressively, then praise them for "being gentle with the baby."

Biting or hitting at pre-school is another form of aggression that can become a parent's nightmare. It's common. It's normal. It can also be hard to handle. If you have a good pre-school, they should be familiar with how to address this behavior. They should have a plan in place for dealing with aggressors and victims. They should be able to work with you on a consistent at-home and at-school plan to help your child. Unfortunately, some pre-schools will simply tell you that your child is no longer welcome. If you are working, this can create quite a crisis. I never had to deal with biting, but a good friend struggled for a long time to get her son through this stage. (He's now a very nice, gentle, loving teenager.) As with other forms of aggression, lots of repetition will be required. It's also good to step back and ask yourself what else this child might need. More sleep? More one-on-one time? An extra snack at a certain time of day? A chance for quiet play time by themselves? A toy or two that just belongs to them? A mid-day break from having to interact with other kids? A positive reinforcement plan with rewards for good behavior? Perhaps a small in-home day care would be better than a pre-school environment for this child? Sometimes just finding ways to take a bit of stress out of certain times of day can reduce or stop acts of aggression.

You also need to expect that teaching your kids how to handle conflict and aggressive impulses is a long-term, on-going process. There will be improvements, and then backsliding. The sophistication of what you are teaching will evolve from "No hit! Ask for help!" to concepts of empathy. That spans a pretty large age range. As your kids become more verbal you can begin coaching them through the following statements:

When_____. I feel_____. Because_____. I need_____.

When there is a conflict, encourage both the aggressor and the victim to express themselves using this format. The more passive kids will learn to assert their feelings. The more assertive kids will learn to listen and recognize feelings. Eventually, they will learn how to better handle conflict. This is a valuable tool they can use throughout their lives. Just remember, you're gonna have to repeat yourself a thousand times before they truly get it.

Another technique for teaching acceptable conflict behavior, is for adults to role play while the kids watch. Mom and dad can pretend to be kids in conflict over a toy and go to a grown-up for help. If you do this nightly with different situations as a kind of "theater" then the concepts can be taught indirectly when they are calm. You're modeling the behavior you want to see. Kids learn a lot by simply watching what adults do.

Finally, this stage can become one in which a lot of parents are yelling "NO!" So, while you are doing all of the above, try to focus on noticing when they do *well*. Really, really focus on any good behavior and praise them when it occurs. If you see one child looking at another with a toy, but *not* grabbing for it, then praise them right away. When the kids are getting *praised* for *any* good behavior, it helps *all* behavior.

Don't worry that there's something wrong with your children. Aggressive behavior, while frustrating for you, is as normal as it gets for young kids. Share your challenges with other parents and you'll likely discover that they, too, are struggling to teach the skills of civilization to their own Neanderthals. Hang in there. Repetition, time, coaching, role modeling, books, and reinforcement of the positive will all work...with time.

POTTY TRAINING

Stress-free Potty Training: a Commonsense Guide to Finding the Right Approach for Your Child by Sara Au and Peter Stavinoha, PhD is my favorite resource for this stage. The wonderful thing about this book is its emphasis on different approaches based on each child's individual temperament. This is particularly vital for parents with multiple young kids.

You may think you can use the same potty training approach on all your children. Certainly, if you're training two preschoolers at the same time, the instinct is to do the same thing with each child. Or if potty training went smoothly with your first child, you may naturally start the same way with your second. However, one child may be relatively sensitive to new sensory input. They may willingly follow directions, but become very upset by noisy flushes, splashing water, cold seats, or air across their bottoms. Your other child may not care about any of that. However, they may have no intention of doing anything that isn't *their* idea first. You can see how each of these children will do best with different potty training approaches.

In *Stress-free Potty Training*, the authors present five different temperaments: the goal-directed child, the sensory-oriented child, the internalizer, the impulsive child, and the strong-willed child. With clear do's and don'ts for each temperament, the authors offer a lot of useful insight. It's a great book and will improve your chances of potty success.

In addition to working with your children's individual temperaments, be wary of defiant phases when starting potty training. Remember those six-month oscillating phases kids go through? It may have been smooth sailing with the kids, but suddenly there's frustration and resistance and general upset. Well, don't start potty training when your 2.5 year old is practicing saying, "No!" Okay, all 2-year-olds love to say, "No!" Nevertheless, there's a phase when they become really, truly resistant to everything. If that's where they are, just wait for smoother sailing.

I was all set to start potty training when my daughter *really* got into "self-assertion." So, I put out the potty seats, stocked up on supplies and waited. Five months later she ran to one of the potty seats we had strewn about the house, and insisted on using it. I'm sure the fact that it was *her* idea was very helpful. Fortunately, I had stocked up on "special pull-ups" and "big girl undies." These proved to be powerful motivators for both her *and* her brother.

For a whole week, my son watched his sister get extra attention and special pull-ups. He knew that I also had train pull-ups and boy undies in the closet. But, I never said anything to him about trying the potty. Finally, he couldn't stand it anymore and *asked* to use the potty. Once he got the "big boy pull-ups with trains," he rapidly lost interest in the potty. So, I explained they were only for training and we'd have to go back to diapers if he wasn't going to use the potty.

His sister was rapidly mastering her potty skills. So, lavishing *her* with praise inspired both kids. However, be aware that you may have one child who trains at 2-years-old, and another who isn't ready until they are *well* over 3-years-old.

Before your kids are actually ready to start training, you can set the stage. It takes practice for a toddler to learn to sit down on a potty seat. When they first try to sit, they often miss and land on their bottom. (Which is pretty funny!) So, get a potty chair or two, and let them get used to sitting on them with or without clothes. It's also a good idea to get them used to the sound of flushing toilets, and the sight of water and tissue swirling away. Try making it fun. "Ready? Wheeee!" Then flush and laugh. When they're interested, let them do the flushing. Practice this on a toilet at home, and be sure to warn them about loud flushes in public restrooms. "Ready? This is soo cool! It's really loud!!" Flush, laugh, yipee!

When you're actually potty training, be very wary of public toilets with automatic flushes! These can totally freak kids out as they often flush *while* your child is still sitting. You can take a strip of toilet paper and drape it over the sensor, use your hand to block it, or even use a sticky note. Just make sure your kid is off the toilet before you unblock the sensor to let it flush. Loud hand driers can also become the bane of your existence. Even if *you* don't use them someone else might turn them on unexpectedly and upset a sensitive child. I was unable to convince my kids that these sudden loud noises were fun and entertaining. My solution was to warn the kids to cover their ears whenever I suspected someone was about to use the hand drier.

Most public toilet seats are also too large for young children. You can buy portable potty seats that rest on top of the toilet seat making the opening smaller for kids. This prevents falling in or you having to hold the kid up while your back gives out. We also learned that some public toilets were too high for my son to stand and pee in front of. He was adamant that he didn't want to sit to pee. So, we found a little step stool in a baby store that was only 3 inches high, and carried it with us in a tote bag.

It's not just the kids who have new skills to learn with potty training. You will have a whole new set of routines to learn, too. You'll need to figure out where all the public restrooms are and which ones are clean. You'll still need to have emergency pull-ups in your diaper bag, but mostly you'll want extra clothes and wipes for accidents. We also carried around a bag with the toddler toilet seat, and the little step stool.

Many parents keep a potty chair, or two, in the back of their car. We had a full set up in the back of our mini-van with two potty chairs, and all the necessary supplies. If the park bathroom was too gross or the rest stop too far away, we'd just use our very own car-port-a-potty.

Line the bowl of the seat with a plastic bag, and then put a few pieces of toilet paper in the bottom. The toilet paper prevents splashing and makes closing the bag for disposal easier. DO NOT use the thinner plastic grocery bags as a seat liner! They always have small holes and will leak. (Yes, I learned that the hard way.) Instead, use bags made for diaper disposal, dog waste, or specifically for portable potties. I liked the biodegradable dog waste bags.

It's also a good idea to teach your kids to pee in the bushes. Boy or girl, this is an important skill. It's highly likely you'll find yourself looking for a bush while your kid bounces with legs crossed. Some kids will think peeing in the bushes is the coolest thing ever, and others may feel quite anxious about it. Just be aware that your kids may make unexpected generalizations. A friend was with her kids at the local upscale, open air mall. She turned around to find her kids with their pants down peeing in the planter box!

Child rearing is loaded with controversy, and potty training is no exception. Thus, the "pull-ups" debate. Useful tool or diabolically problematic consumer product!? Okay. Whatever. Just relax. Some people like to potty train using the "let them run naked all day" routine. If it works for you, and your kid is not sensory sensitive and freaked out by pee running down their leg, then fine. Do the naked routine, and skip the pull-ups if you can. If like me, you are *yourself* freaked out by the idea of random puddles of pee and poo being created and smeared around by little beasties, then you may prefer using pull-ups. Really, there is no right and wrong here. Do what works for you. If along the way it stops working... then change it up!

One final thought on the process of potty training. Remember that all new skills require a lot of practice to master. Whether it's learning how to pee in a potty or learning how to play ice hockey, we all take three steps forward, and then one back as we learn. Only Mozart could play the piano at age 4. The rest of us non-geniuses have to learn in sporadic bursts of success and failure with lots of repetition. Don't be surprised by episodes of potty training regression. These are common and often occur just before skills solidify.

MORE ON POTTY TRAINING: CONSTIPATION AND ENCOPRESIS THE SECRET SHAME

And now a topic near and dear to me: constipation. Childhood constipation, that is. It's another one of those dark secrets left unattended. Significant issues due to chronic or recurrent constipation are very, very common in childhood. Treating these problems is long, involved, and often highly distressing for families. What's really remarkable is that none of the numerous potty training books I read addressed this problem. Yet, the most common time for problems with constipation to develop is in the prime potty training years. Furthermore, if parents are armed with some simple knowledge and tools we could probably head off a great deal of trouble and anguish.

So, what is constipation? After infancy, it can be normal to have bowel movements as often as several times a day or as rarely as every few days. Stool should be smooth, normal diameter, and easy to pass. If your child is having pain with passing stools, the diameter is large and clogging the toilet, the stool has deep cracks or comes out as round hard balls, then you're dealing with constipation. In kids, constipation often leads to pain, which leads to the holding of stool, which leads to worse constipation. Now you're in a vicious cycle. Once a child is backed up and impacted, then soft liquid stool from farther up the colon begins to leak out around the impacted stool. This fecal leakage is called encopresis. The child will *not* feel the movement of this liquid stool because the chronic constipation desensitizes the rectum. As the stool remains impacted it stretches out the distal colon. That loose flabby colon can't fully empty with bowel movements. This leads to repeat impaction. Let's be clear. The child will not feel the leakage of stool, nor will they smell its presence no matter how ripe they become. Really. You will walk into your living room and your 5-year-old will be engaged in the most adorable game of stuffed animal tea, and they will smell like poop. When you look, you'll find feces smeared on their bottom. They will be completely unaware, and they truly can't control the leakage or stop it. This will be the first of many, many times you'll be dealing with this embarrassing and confounding situation. Healing this biological process requires an enormous amount of parental involvement, medical intervention, strict behavioral routines, and at least a year of intensive effort.

Sooooo, let's not go down this road. Instead, start your child on a potty sitting routine after meals. About 20 minutes after the start of a meal there is a normal colonic movement. If your child is sitting on the potty at this time, the chances are good they will have a bowel movement. If you keep this up as a routine after meals, you will help your child learn to recognize this colonic reflex, and become better tuned to their body's needs. You will be teaching them good basic body hygiene habits, and may well head off a great deal of trouble for both your child and yourself. Potty sits should not last more than 5 to 10 minutes to prevent straining the anal sphincter. I would avoid giving your child electronic devices during a potty sit. They tend to become obsessed with them, and will not even notice if they have a bowel movement. Instead, books, paper and marker, or music can help your child pass the time. Hopefully, these activities will still allow them to become aware of intestinal movement and the passage of stool.

It is important to make sure your child is getting enough fiber and water each day. To soften stools, look for more soluble fiber than insoluble fiber. There are a huge variety of fiber bars, cookies, cereals, and gummies that can help you fill out their fiber diet. You can take your child's age and add 5 to it for a good starting goal on daily fiber. For example, a 3-year-old would aim for 8 grams of fiber a day. Add in plenty of water and you've set the stage for your child to succeed at ongoing bowel control.

You may be thinking this whole topic seems a bit out of left field. Speaking as both a medical practitioner and a mother, I assure you this is a *common* problem. It occurs more frequently in boys than girls, and in the U.S. we see rates of 1-2% in kids under age 10. This means if your elementary school has 400 kids, then 4 to 8 kids and their families are quietly suffering with this chronic condition. This can bring enormous challenges and angst to families. When children are experiencing encopresis, they lose sensation and control. They won't know they have leaked, and smell like poop. They really don't know. It can take months to a year of regular stool softeners and laxatives before a baggy, stretched-out colon can shrink back to a normal diameter that allows the child to regain sensation and control. It is truly way, way more pain and trouble than you want. So, part of your early potty training can be a good bowel hygiene routine. Do the fiber. Do the water. Have them sit on the potty for 5 to 10 minutes after meals. Make it a routine. Much later, when your child is age 6 or so, you can assess whether your child has a regular bowel movement time. If they do, then consider reducing potty-sit times to match their normal pattern.

If you have a child who has already been diagnosed with encopresis, I recommend you get clarity on their diagnosis. What I have described above is the more common *constipation*-based encopresis. With treatment, this kind of encopresis usually will improve over six months to a year. However, there is another medical condition sometimes called functional or *non*-constipation based encopresis. These kids were initially successful in potty training, and do not have a history of constipation. When they have studies of their colon, it is *not* stretched out and flabby. Yet, they still experience uncontrolled fecal leakage. This group of children is much, much harder to treat. Unfortunately, the medical pathophysiology of functional encopresis is truly not understood. Sometimes kids are holding and releasing their anal sphincter muscle at the wrong times. These children do well with bio-feedback and pelvic floor exercises taught by a physical therapist. However, once you've ruled out the typical intestinal disorders there remains a group of kids who still struggle with fecal leakage. These kids and their families can continue to have difficulty well into teenage years and adulthood. After that, they often become lost to follow-up care. Many adults will hide their problems with fecal leakage even from their doctors.

If you have a child with true non-constipation based encopresis, and a normal colon is found on anal-rectal manometry, then make sure you have a good pediatric gastroenterologist. If they are dismissive or bad communicators, find someone else! You're going to need medical help from a supportive and trusted gastroenterologist who stays current with new research. There are also some medications that may help kids with this type of encopresis. These medications are often approached late in treatment, but are worth bringing up in discussion with your child's doctor. For some kids these medications can be very helpful. They are the opposite of what you would use with a child who has constipation based encopresis. So, you have to be clear on your child's diagnosis of *non*-constipation encopresis before you give them a try.

Finally, if you have a child with true non-constipation encopresis, then you have a child with a chronic medical condition. This is emotionally very hard for both child and parent. You will want to fix them. To find them treatment that makes them well again. It may feel like you are failing them over and over again. Furthermore, since the condition is poorly understood, you may find many medical providers will imply that *you* are indeed failing them. Or they may imply that your child's *medical* condition is actually a psychological or behavioral condition. This is actually a common mistake of medical providers. When there is a high rate of treatment failure for a condition, doctors often blame the patient for being "non-complaint." Certainly, that can be the cause of problems in some cases, but when a medical condition has a uniformly high rate of treatment failure regardless of where, when, or who is treated, then the problem is often a medical establishment that has poor or inaccurate understanding of this particular disease process. The treatment is failing because the doctors are failing to understand the disease. As a medical provider, I promise you that there are many, many diseases where a sudden change in understanding has led to a change in treatment. Suddenly, there's a huge improvement in treatment success. After which everyone forgets they had been telling patients it was an emotional problem.

I encourage you to have regular check-ups with a good pediatric gastroenterologist. Then focus on teaching your child the behaviors and management skills they need to live with this problem. Since most of these skills require a certain amount of maturity, you will likely need to help them for many more years than you'd like. Try to keep to regular meal times, track and supplement their fiber, stick to a potty-sitting routine after meals, develop routines for packing extra clothing in cars and school backpacks, work out codes for teachers and your child so they can be sent to change clothes discreetly. You can try using pads in underwear, and anti-friction gels or sticks, which are used by athletes can protect a raw bottom from chronic stool exposure.

Resources:

For constipation based encopresis:

1. WebMD has a good summary of encopresis
2. *The Ins and Outs Of Poop* by Thomas Duhamel, PhD. A great book as well as a support program for constipation-based encopresis.
3. *Softy the Poop: Helping Families Talk About Poop* by Thomas Duhamel.
4. *Everybody Poops* by Taro Gomi.

For encopresis without constipation, stool retention, or a stretched out colon:

1. Rajindrajith S, Devanarayana NM, Benninga MA, *Review Article: Faecal Incontinence In Children: Epidemiology, Pathophysiology, Clinical Evaluation And Management.* Alimentary Pharmacology & Therapeutics. 2013 Jan. [PubMed PMID: 23106105]
2. Ambartsumyan L, Nurko S, *Review Of Organic Causes Of Fecal Incontinence In Children: Evaluation And Treatment.* Expert Review Of Gastroenterology & Hepatology. 2013 Sep. [PubMed PMID: 24070156]

SEPARATION ANXIETY

Most parents must deal with some degree of separation anxiety in their young children. It will often wax and wane depending upon age, development, and family changes. The onset of toddler daycare, preschool, or a new nanny are especially challenging times. Here are a few thoughts to help with this issue.

The first thing to remember is to avoid letting your kids see *your* anxiety about leaving them. Keep your expressions loving and matter of fact or you'll just increase your child's fears. You can cry in the car later, just not in front of the kids. It can help *your* anxiety if you call your nanny or preschool 20 minutes after drop off to see how your child is doing. In most cases, your child will calm down shortly after you leave. Knowing this can help you get through the first days of separation, and the daily crying at departure. Many kids continue to cry at both drop off and pick up, despite playing happily throughout the day.

If your daycare provider or nanny is telling you that your child never adapts or stops crying, then Elizabeth Pantley's book, *The No Cry Separation Anxiety Solution*, may help. Her technique uses a gender neutral bracelet that often comes with the book. She teaches you steps that help your child associate the bracelet with you and your love. Once that association is in place, it becomes something the child can wear as a link to you when you're apart. Favorite loveys can also fill this role. I used to make a big deal about "loading up" my kid's loveys with love and kisses for them whenever we were separating. I'd tell them their lovey "has a thousand mommy kisses for you until I come back." Then hug and kiss the lovey for way, way too long while making a big deal out of it. Then you snuggle it into their arms.

You can also make a small photo book for your child to take to school or daycare. Fill it with pictures of family and any special friends. It doesn't have to be huge. We had a hand size book with about 8 to 10 photos in it. We tucked it into the kid's daycare diaper bag so they always had it. Once your child is established at daycare, take a few pictures of the daycare providers and add them to the book. This helps your child remember *them* at home. Ironically, many kids have more trouble adapting to pre-school or day care if they are going *less* often. Every other day may be okay, but young kids who are going 1 to 2 times per week just can't remember enough from one visit to the next. At one time my kids were in daycare 5 days a week and very happy. When they were about 3-years-old, I stopped working and cut daycare to one day a week. They had been going to the same place for over a year, and knew everyone well. But after a few weeks they started having trouble with the transition at drop off time. The daycare explained they often see this happen to kids who don't attend frequently enough to remember everyone. For a young child, one week is a very, very long time!

There are also a number of books you can read to your kids that can help with separation anxiety. Read them repeatedly. Here are a few of my kid's favorites.

For pre-school age separation anxiety:

1. *The Kissing Hand* by Audrey Penn
2. *Llama, Llama Misses Mama* by Anna Dewdney
3. *The Run Away Bunny* by Margaret Wise Brown. (baby bunny runs away, but mommy bunny always finds him)
4. *I Love You All Day Long* by Francesca Rusackas (piggy goes to pre-school and Mommy loves him all the day)
5. *Oh My Baby, Little One* by Kathi Appelt (mommy goes to work and baby is surrounded by her love throughout his day)
6. *Wherever You Are, My Love Will Find You* by Nancy Tillman. (a little less direct, but still lovely and loving)

For school age separation anxiety:

1. *The Kissing Hand* by Audrey Penn
2. *Miss Bindergarten Gets Ready for Kindergarten* by Joseph Slate
3. *Twas the Night Before Kindergarten* by Natasha Wing

Another place some moms encounter separation anxiety is when going to the gym. Getting out of the house with a few child-free moments to exercise can be a precious time for many moms. I joined the local YMCA specifically because they offered great childcare while I got a break. But all gym childcare is not the same. Here's where a bit of research on your part can help. The YMCA I attended really had it all figured out. You did not need to schedule care ahead of time. You could show up whenever you managed to get there. They had separate areas for infants, young children, and older children. They kept the areas well-staffed and had good safety procedures for drop off and pick up. Most importantly, if a young child was upset or new, they would carry and comfort that child for as long as needed even if it was for an hour! The staff quickly learned the names and preferences of children who came regularly. The minute we walked through the door, my son had a giant monster truck and my daughter had Elmo or a costume. All of these things meant that over several years of working out at the gym, I was only paged once to pick up the kids. (I think one of them started running a fever.) However, not all YMCAs have the same set up. It's well worth researching a gym's childcare service before you sign up.

Separation anxiety can be quite a challenge. You can wind up feeling really trapped when you can't get time free from your kids. Don't give up. Your needs matter too. It's a phase. They'll get through it, and so will you.

AVOID PATHOLOGIZING YOUR CHILD'S BEHAVIOR

We are a nation in love with a good diagnosis. Whether it's a vitamin deficiency, a personality disorder, or a behavioral variation, we want to label it and then treat it. It gives us a wonderful sense of control. And there are many very real issues kids face which can be vastly improved by recognition and intervention. For example, the importance of access to early intervention in autism spectrum disorders is *huge*. But, there are also many crazy, annoying, troubling, disruptive, stressful, and often worrying behaviors that kids engage in that are simply normal. In our culture parents, family, and childcare institutions can become inclined to read pathology into these challenging behaviors. This can be especially true if a child's normal development puts them in conflict with the structure and bureaucracy of school, childcare, or a family's scheduling needs.

Remember that for most of human evolution, children were raised in hunter-gatherer societies. In that kind of culture, children roamed in multi-age groups. They would live and learn in an environment that allowed tremendous behavioral latitude. They were free to grow at their own individual pace. Now we expect *all* kids to conform to the rules of childcare, school, and structured society. Then, when a child doesn't fit into these constructs, we may be inclined to pathologize *them* as opposed to asking what is wrong with a culture that can't give them the time and space to be young and immature. Perhaps sometimes the flaw is in a system that is unable to flex enough to embrace the needs and *talents* of these children. Perhaps the flaw is in the childcare or school. Perhaps the society we are expecting our kid to function in is antithetical to their strengths.

If your kid is kicked out of preschool because he's "too disruptive" or "too aggressive" or "too upset," it doesn't necessarily mean your kid has a "disorder." This is no small issue for some parents. You may really, really need your child to go to preschool so you can go to work! And if other kids can do it, why can't yours? Right? There must be something wrong with them? And your child's preschool teachers may encourage your concern by implying some sort of pathology for your kid. Just be aware that this can happen. Then seek out some help from a good *specialist* in *child development*. Your kid has no impulse control at age 5? Guess what. That's well within the normal developmental spectrum.

I'm a medical practitioner. I know the power of a good diagnosis. Still, misdiagnosis and over diagnosis can also be very damaging. Get some good knowledgeable advice before you give your kid a diagnosis that will follow them through their school years. A label that will shape the picture you have of him in your mind. A diagnosis that will shape the picture he has of himself within his own mind. You may need to look around for good resources in your community. Remember that most pre-school caregivers have little to no education in the growth and development of a child's brain.

Some young children don't do well in a preschool environment. Perhaps they are 3-years-old and have all the skills they need to run wild through the woods with older kids. They could do it for hours on end, and come home hungry, happy, and ready for more. *But*, they don't have good "sit in a circle for story time" skills or good emotional-social skills. They are very, *very* young! They may just not have developed these skills yet. So, which is broken? The child or the environment? Do we medicate the child to fit the pre-school or do we find a way to provide the environment that this child needs at this stage of their development? Personally, I believe that the U.S. needs to make major changes in the early childcare programs that are available. One size does not fit all when it comes to young children. In some countries, there are options for "outdoor preschools" or "forest kindergartens." Rain, snow, or sunshine, the kids spend most of the day outside in nature with an adult who facilitates their individually motivated explorations and activities. These adults are not simply chaperoning. They are teachers specializing in child development who are focused on the emotional, social, and language skills of their young students. For some kids, boys and girls alike, this outdoor freedom to learn is just what they need. For some, it's truly critical. It is what will allow them to grow without the constant condemnation and criticism by adults who want them to be developmentally ready for circle time.

WHAT IF YOUR CHILD DOES HAVE A BEHAVIOR DISORDER?

Autism Spectrum Disorder (ASD), Attention Deficit Disorder (ADD)[8] Attention Deficit – Hyperactivity Disorder (ADHD), Sensory Processing Disorders (SPD). These and many other behavior disorders are known

---

[8] Attention Deficit Disorder is now officially classified as a subset of ADHD. I think that's a mistake. I feel the older terms are more accurately descriptive. We currently have no neurobiological reason to describe ADD as a subset of ADHD. So, I use ADD.

or strongly suspected to be neurobiologically based. This means the neurological and chemical connections within the child's brain are different from what we might consider in the average brain. Sometimes those differences can cause profound difficulties in a child's ability to function in the world. Sometimes those differences come with profound *gifts* that allow a child's brain to understand things in unique ways. Certainly, from a scientific perspective, it can help to label and define these behavioral conditions. That process of definition can aid in identifying and helping these kids. However, as parents, I think it's important we recognize our child's brain has its own unique arrangement of neurons. We need to understand that behavior we may see as exasperatingly inappropriate may, to them, be neurologically reasonable. They may be living in a world which is antithetical to their own neurobiological self. When we see kids in this way, it opens our eyes to a more compassionate appreciation of who they are. I suspect there is little else that is *as* important to a child, a parent, or a family than finding the compassion, the love, and the appreciation of a child that allows you to build a space in the world that welcomes them. With this in mind, I try to shift back and forth between perspectives in my head. On the one hand, I focus on a scientific understanding of their "condition" and effective "interventions." On the other hand, I focus on the child as *perfectly* different so I can stretch my understanding to encompass their reality.

Autism Spectrum Disorders (ASD) are often improperly diagnosed in children who actually have other issues. Every symptom of autism can be found in other disorders, and this can make it challenging to diagnose correctly. The key to identifying autism is that *the first* and *primary* impairment *must* be in *social impairment*. Some of the early signs can be a child who does not pay any attention to nor have much awareness of other people. They may not make eye contact or smile while taking a bottle. A toddler may not look up when a parent enters a room. When lacking language skills, they will fail to use gestures to communicate. You may roll a ball to them, and they don't look at it or try to get it. They don't engage in reciprocal interactions. If you have a child who is showing these signs then I'd encourage you to have them evaluated by a developmental psychologist. Early intervention for children with ASD can have profound life changing benefits.

If your child *is* diagnosed with ASD, you're going to need to find yourself all the supports you can get. Fortunately, the parents of children with autism have become extremely active and organized in recent years. Many resources are now readily available for parents newly facing this challenge. One great place to start is Autism Speaks. You'll find a wide range of useful tools including "First 100 Day Kits for Families of Those Newly Diagnosed." Three different kits are available based on your child's age at diagnosis.

You can also find regional support groups on Facebook. These groups can provide guidance and insight into local services and specialists. I encourage you to tap into these communities. You no longer need to take this journey alone. Often these autism support groups can give you current information than you're unlikely to find elsewhere.

Other behavior disorders that you may hear about are Attention Deficit Disorder (ADD), Attention Deficit Hyperactivity Disorder (ADHD), and Sensory Processing Disorders. Up until puberty a child's brain is laying down more and more neural connections. Parts of their brains are literally thicker than an adult's brain. As puberty hits, this overly enmeshed brain is steadily pruned. The thickness of these brain areas decreases while cognitive abilities increase. Basically, the road map of fast, smoothly working neural connections is forming with the removal of extraneous routes that slow things down. This process goes on for many years. Furthermore, the frontal lobe that controls executive function is often one of the last areas to fully develop these superior and faster neural connections. The result is that kids don't act like little adults. They can't. They live in a brain that is a jumbled mess. Thus, some very normal kids exhibit behavior that does not function within the rules and constructs of daycare, preschool, or even early elementary school. These are *highly artificial environments* which may seem reasonable to adults, but they do not reflect the environments our species evolved to live in. It is only realistic to expect that *some* children simply will not fit within our adult rules. Unfortunately, our society doesn't provide many schooling options. We don't have the "outdoor pre-schools" and "forest kindergartens" of the Scandinavian countries. Nor do we pay parents to stay home and raise kids. Women have joined the work force outside the home. This means we adults *need* our kids to function within the constraints of daycare, preschool, and grade school, so *we* can go to *work*. This also means that if our child doesn't function well in preschool, then we are far more likely to seek an explanation that offers a hope of "treatment." In addition, other challenges can cause behavioral conflicts. Anxiety, depression, trauma, abuse, and family instability can all cause children to act out in strange ways. It can be challenging to tease out the difference between a child whose behavior is that of a typical child acting out in response to stressors vs. a child whose brain has an atypical neurobiological structure which leads them to behave differently.

Children with ADD and ADHD have brains that are literally wired differently. The neurotransmitters in their brain also work differently. Richard Branson, Simone Biles, Charles Schwabb, Bill Gates, and Micheal Phelps all have some form of ADHD. There is a huge list of highly productive and creative thinkers who struggled through school due to these neurobiological behavior "disorders." Perhaps we would do well to think of ADHD as a neurobiological variant. Normal, and one of many variants. Their "disability" may have more to do with how adults teach, manage, and guide these children.

So, how do you figure out if your child really does have a specific behavioral condition with a neurobiological basis? How do you figure out if she's not fitting in simply because she is young or needs a different environment? Well, it's not easy to sort these things out. You'll likely spend a good bit of time and energy looking for answers and solutions. You can start by gathering information and concerns from your child's school, teachers, coaches, and caregivers. Don't assume what you hear is all correct nor that it's all wrong. Just gather the input and weigh the value of the sources. These people may seem like child care "experts" to you, but most are *not* educated in the normal range of children's neurobiological development. Next, take a day and go and sit in your child's preschool or classroom for as long as they will allow. The longer you are there, the more you'll understand your child's environment. You may decide the *school* or *teacher* is the problem. If so, you can work to get your kids somewhere else. Or you may decide the school isn't the main problem. The next step is to get a really good assessment of your child by someone *educated* in *child development*. These are often child neuropsychologists who have experience in teasing out behavior issues caused by stress and emotions versus those that are neurobiologically based. Typically, an assessment for behavioral issues, such as ADD, ADHD, or Autism is done by a specialist referred through your child's pediatrician. This evaluation is for *behavioral* concerns. However, *learning* differences can also cause behavior issues, and can be overlooked if not evaluated. Thus, you may want to have your child assessed by their school system as well. They are required to evaluate all children age 3 or older if the parents have concerns. This involves a psychoeducational assessment which can tease out dyslexia or other learning differences that may be causing a child to act out even before they are challenged with learning to read. This evaluation is also useful if your child does have ADHD or other behavioral disorders. Many of those disorders come with delays or impairments in executive function. Some school systems will look at a diagnosis of ADD or ADHD and decide all the child needs is extra time. However, a psychoeducational evaluation may show other very specific areas where active intervention by the school can be very helpful. If it is not defined or diagnosed, then the school will not be forced to help.

So, if you're worried about a possible learning disorder, ask the school system for an evaluation. If you're worried about a behavioral diagnosis, I recommend a psychoeducational evaluation from the school system, and a behavioral assessment referral from your pediatrician.

Resources:

- *Autism and Insurance Coverage: State Laws.* National Conference Of State Legislatures, August 2018. https://www.ncsl.org/research/health/autism-and-insurance-coverage-state-laws.aspx
- Autism Speaks: https://www.autismspeaks.org

An excellent article on Sensory Processing Disorder/ Behaviors:
- *The Unbearable Sensation Of Being: Some Kids Find Everyday Stimuli Excruciating. Scientists Are Finally Figuring Out Why.* Clair Conway, UCSF Magazine, summer 2018. https://www.ucsf.edu/magazine/unbearable-sensation-being

PRESCHOOL or DAYCARE ISSUES

The first challenge in finding a daycare or preschool may be figuring out *where* you want it to be located. If your employer provides in-office childcare, then you may want to take advantage of that. However, if you have a long commute, consider selecting childcare located closer to home rather than to work. Long commutes are hard on kids even when they are well. If they are running a fever or throwing up, it's much worse. And you *will* get that call from daycare at some point. "Please come pick up Johnny. He has a fever and diarrhea, watery diarrhea." You'll be better off if you've only got 10 to 15 minutes in the car between daycare and home. In addition, if you have one sick child and one well child, then you can take the well one to daycare and keep the sick one at home. However, you won't want to drive an hour through commute traffic to do that. If both parents are working and their offices are in opposite directions, then it is even more critical to pick childcare closer to home.

Once you figure out where you want to look, you'll need to evaluate specific options. Larger pre-schools can be easily found with an Internet search. Smaller in-home daycares can be harder to locate. Cities and counties often have a list of authorized daycare providers, and can be a good place to start. There's also a lot to be said for "word of mouth" referrals. You can talk with friends, parents at the playground, or post your search on a mother's club web page. I recommend exploring both larger preschools and smaller in-home daycares. There is tremendous variation out there. The details will matter. You may like the feel of one more than others, and you may find locations offering a services that are highly helpful to you.

I found one in-home daycare around the corner from my house where all the caregivers were fluently bilingual. They had good outdoor space, so-so indoor space, offered "preschool" type activities every day, and had mostly kids under age 3. Unfortunately, they had no flexibility for the part-time daycare that I needed. Another in-home place had great outdoor space, but you couldn't see it from inside the house. This meant kids could only be outside when everyone was outside. The place we finally picked came with a strong reference from a mother whose child had gone there in the past. The daycare was set up so kids could go inside and out while being easily watched. They had both sunny and shaded play areas. It was run by a Russian grandma who made lunch for the kids every day. This was *hugely* helpful to us. Packing a daily lunch for toddlers involves an enormous investment in time and planning. The owner's daughter had advanced degrees in early childhood development. They offered child initiated preschool activities, and had a music teacher in once a week. They were gentle, loving, and had loads of experience. On school holidays, some of their older now "graduated" kids would spend the day and play with the younger children. It was not fancy. It was clean and happy, and my kids loved it. They also offered me the flexibility of starting part-time and moving to full-time once I returned to work. It's really worth looking around!

At some point, I mostly stopped working, and we dropped day care. Later, when I wanted the kids to attend some half-day childcare, we found our old daycare was full. This time I visited local preschools and pre-K programs for my now 4-year-old kids. Close to home, I found a city sponsored program that had good facilities, good hours, a director I liked, and two separate classes. That would allow me to put the twins in different classrooms which at the time I felt would be good for them. I was about to sign the kids up when I decided to spend a good hunk of time just sitting and watching the class. The first thing I noticed was that the kids did not *really* have the freedom for child-initiated activities. If the teacher was leading a craft at the table then *all* kids had to be at the table. They could sit and do nothing if they wanted, but they were not allowed to step three feet away to play with the dinosaurs or costumes. Obviously, this was not free play with child-initiated activities. As the morning progressed, one teacher got frustrated with a 4-year-old girl and walked her to time out. Then left her there. When 15 minutes went by and the girl was still in time out, I went to inform the director who put a stop to it. The rule for time outs, which don't really work anyway, is one minute per year of the child's age. Max time for a 4-year-old is four minutes. But this teacher had clearly been displacing her frustration on the girl who hadn't actually committed any kind of severe infraction. Until I'd witnessed this interaction, I'd felt pretty good about enrolling my kids. Remember, in this kind of situation your kids have absolutely no power, no way to speak for themselves. It can be hard to know what's going on in a daycare, a preschool, or with a nanny at home. Your best bet is to spend time there, and make unannounced visits. If your gut doesn't like it, then pull them out. It can be frustrating to give up on childcare you've finally found, but sometimes you find something even better.

After I gave up on the first preschool, I found a much less expensive and better pre-K nearby. It had great hours, and one of the best childcare teachers we've ever had. Freya was awesome and loving. She even helped me help my son when he was struggling with health issues. Freya, was quite comfortable with nurturing preschoolers in a free play environment. There might be seven kids listening to a story, while across the room one child would be lining up stuffies and another was playing with colored tiles. Freya learned each child's interests, facilitated emotional and social learning, and easily moved between offered crafts and following a child's lead. We love you, Freya!

Having your kids in school can create opportunities to make friends with other parents. It can also generate all sorts of parental politics. Maybe this father never follows the pick-up/drop-off parking rules, and that mom didn't realize her kid had hand-foot-mouth disease and brought them to school. Now half the class is sick. Another parent never bags her kid's hats despite the recent lice outbreak at the school. Masking and Covid-19 protocols have certainly led to many parental conflicts. The list goes on and on. A lot of these things you just have to let go. We can't control everyone or everything, and we all need to get along.

Even more difficult to manage are vague hints of concerning situations at school. Perhaps your child gets bitten by another kid at school or becomes the target of another child's aggression. You're going to be upset when your 3-year-old son shows you a bite mark and tells you, "Allison hits me every day." You ask, "What do the teachers do when Allison hits you?" Your son says, "Nothing." Now you're fuming! You ask, "How long has this been going on!" Your son says, "Allison's been hitting me every day from the beginning!"

Now is when you need to stay calm, and consider a careful approach. It's always hard to know what's really going on when your information is indirect or coming through a young child. I'd go to the teacher with an open mind and non-judgmental tone. Start your interaction with a positive statement of appreciation for their work. Remember these people really do care about your child. Then express your concern. "I'm worried because my son says that Allison is hitting him every day. He came home with a bite mark on his arm. Can you tell me what's going on? Is there something I can do to help?" Starting out in this respectful and non-judgmental manner will get you a more open and honest response. Then you'll have a chance to deal with issues in a positive way. And you may discover that "Allison hitting" is just her tapping kids a bit too hard in games of tag, and that the teachers had no idea your son was upset. And the bite mark actually came from your son's best friend when they were playing "vampire" and bit each other on the arm. Or maybe your son has been showing Allison how much he likes her by pushing her every day for a week, and Allison finally had enough and bit him. (Because they are young and neither kid knows how to express themselves appropriately!) Or it may be that there are kids with real aggression issues, and these teachers are clueless about how to handle it. Whatever is going on, an open minded non-judgmental approach will get you the best picture of what's happening.

Parents sometimes become concerned when their preschooler comes home with small injuries. As kids get older the bumps, bruises, and scrapes are an inevitable result of their growth and exploration. I could've wrapped my 4-year-olds in bubble wrap, and they'd still have managed to get a splinter, bruise, bonk on the head, scratch, or poke in the eye. And they'd get filthy dirty in the process! No matter how carefully someone is watching the kids, they will get more and more minor injuries as they push the boundaries of their skills. If the teacher is looking one way and something happens behind them, they may not know an accident even occurred. Try to recognize this is all pretty normal.

If, however, your kids are fearful of a teacher, do not seem to be adjusting, or if something has set off your alarm bells, then look into it and trust your "mommy instincts." It's very hard to leave established childcare and start your search over again. Still, sometimes that's what you have to do. In these situations, you are your child's only voice.

DEVELOPMENTAL VARIATIONS

In her first year of life, my daughter did the usual babbling and goo-gooing typical of babies. But my son didn't babble. He made long airy "raaa" and back of the throat "gaaar" sounds. I was worried that he would have a speech delay as this is more common in twins, especially boys. My daughter said her first word at 1-year-old. A week later my son said his first word. A couple months later he started combining words into short sentences, and his speech became amazingly clear even to strangers! On the other hand, it was my daughter whose speech was hard to understand for a long time. This generated great frustration for her.

In her first year of life, my daughter was definitely not interested in crawling. Really! She wasn't interested in exerting any effort to move from one area to another. She would sit happily like a sessile organism or insist on parental transportation services. My son was rolling, crawling, pulling up, climbing on the couch and then diving off head first. I figured my girl would be late to walk. Right? Wrong. At 12 months, they both started walking within a week of each other.

By 15-months my daughter could feed herself without dumping the contents of the spoon into her lap. My son couldn't do that until he was 2.5-years-old! I had to make all his food sticky so at least a small bit would cling to the spoon, and make it into his mouth. At 15-months we showed both kids how to do a somersault. My son practiced and practiced. After 20 minutes he could do it by himself. It took my daughter another year and a half to learn to somersault without help. At age 3 my girl could hold her pencil correctly. My boy couldn't do it until we nudged him at 4.5-years-old. He could do complex puzzles that stumped my girl. She could write letters long before him, yet he became the better speller. They both learned to read at the *end* of first grade and were *not* "early" readers. But, by second grade, they were both reading above grade level and loving it.

Every child grows and develops at their own rate. Even twins raised in the same environment. The range of normal for the development of any given skill can be huge. As long as your child is in that range, don't worry. If they are not "ahead" in one task, it's because they are busy learning some other skill that you haven't recognized. Try not to compare your kids to other people's kids or to each other. Try not to panic if all the other kids can tie their shoes and yours doesn't. One of my 8-year-olds decided it was too much trouble to learn to tie his shoes. However, Velcro and elastic laces were "for babies." So, he went everywhere with loose floppy laces. Sigh. Sometimes, if no one was looking, his sister tied his shoes for him! Of course, she can barely stay on the new pogo stick for one hop. Her brother practiced for hours and got up to 32 consecutive hops on the first day.

You can use these developmental differences as a lesson for your kids. As they get older they will compare themselves to each other and to classmates. "She can't do *this*!" and "He can't do *that*!" Here is a life lesson you can give them. My kids love to hear the stories of my son dumping his food in his lap, and my daughter upside down and unable to do a somersault. Told in a gentle loving way, it is a lesson in how we all have our talents, and we all learn at our own pace.

KINDERGARTEN READINESS

Kindergarten readiness can haunt the minds of many parents of toddlers. Sometimes people feel desperate to get their kids into "the right" pre-school to ensure they will be "ready" for kindergarten. If you're feeling anxiety and pressure about kindergarten, I encourage you to take a deep breath. Let's get some perspective. How are we supposed to enjoy our child's youngest years if we're obsessing about college prep when they are only 3? You may find that researching "kindergarten readiness" will ease your concerns.

Kindergarten Readiness Checklists:

- https://www.familyeducation.com/school/kindergarten-readiness/kindergarten-readiness-checklist
- https://www.understood.org/en/learning-thinking-differences/signs-symptoms/academic-readiness/skills-kids-need-going-into-kindergarten

Take a good look at kindergarten readiness check lists. The necessary skills do not include "reads chapter books" nor "algebra." They do include holding a crayon or pen well, using child safe scissors, and hopping on one foot. There are concepts like starting with two candies then taking away one candy. How many are left? Growing into an adult is a long, long, *long* process. If you don't have a child who is showing developmental delays or social-behavioral concerns, then you can relax. They will get there. You might as well enjoy the show as their lives unfold before you.

The *original* goals of kindergarten were to *nurture and prepare a young and immature beastie for the social, emotional, and moral rigors of social learning*. In many parts of the world this is still the main goal of kindergarten. Frankly, these are the developmentally appropriate tasks for this young age. Waiting turns, kindness, compassion, how to explore the world, how to manipulate objects, sounding out language. All this and much more are the developmental tasks of early childhood *play* and exploration. Later, when they have had the leisure to grow into these skills a bit, later…when they have had the chance to grow their brains a bit, later…like age 7…is what was once called the "Age of Reason." Reason? Okay, that's a bit of a stretch, *but* this is the age at which children were traditionally felt to be developmentally ready for academic learning. At age 15, kids in Finland score the highest on international tests year after year after year. They have fully play based "kindergarten" available (but not required) to all kids from *1 to 6 years old*. Children are not taught to read during their kindergarten years unless they show individual interest and readiness. They do play games that involve phonemic awareness in songs and chants. This helps them to hear the sounds and syllables they will need later. But, mostly they learn and grow through a mix of daily free and structured play times. At age 7, they start what we might call first grade. Much of the learning in first grade remains play-based. This is also when Finnish teachers start reading instruction. In Finland, joy is apparently considered critical to successful learning. It's part of the required curriculum. Hmmm, imagine that.

REAL KINDERGARTEN READINESS

How do you help your child prepare for the exciting and scary first day of kindergarten or a new preschool? If your school offers "kindergarten camp" that's a great way for the kids to get a gentle warm up while meeting a few kids. This "camp" is usually held at the end of the summer. For a few hours each day the kids meet in a kindergarten classroom with one of the school's teachers. They do play time, story time, and take walks around the school grounds to visit libraries, locate bathrooms and playgrounds. It gives a young child the chance to get familiar with everything before "the big day." In addition, the kids in the camp will be going to the same school. This gives you the chance to set up some play dates with the potential new friends. Even if they don't wind up in the same class as their new friends, it is a great relief to children if you can tell them they will have a friend to meet at recess. For our family, this was a big help in decreasing first week anxiety.

If there is no camp available, you might be able to meet some parents at the orientation or teacher assignment meetings. Then set up play dates with their kids. It doesn't matter if they become long term friends, it just helps if you can say, "Jimmie/Janie will be there at recess." Before the school year starts, you can visit the school playground or do a scavenger hunt around the school grounds. The more comfortable they are with the campus, the less anxious they will feel. Make sure to check out the bathrooms, and flush the toilets. They will probably have a single toilet in their classroom for TK and K. If there is an orientation day, take the time to check out the bathroom together as this is often an area of anxiety for kids. Visit the office, library, multipurpose room, and classroom a couple of times if possible.

Letting your kids pick out lunch boxes and backpacks gets you a bit of personal "buy in." You can put a special treat in their lunch boxes the first week. Let them know there's a surprise in there for them. Definitely get the kids used to waking up and to eating earlier. My kids have a hard time eating first thing in the morning. Some snack bars stashed in the car can be a good way to get a few morning calories in the little critters. Try to get to school ahead of time so they can play for 10 to 15 minutes before class. This lets them burn off energy, and have fun before school. It's a great morning transition trick that helps for many years. Promise them you'll stay for a bit after drop off on the first day. Once they are settled, you can ease out. If you have multiple young kids in different classes, then it will be *really* helpful if you can bring two adults on the first day of school.

In our family, we tend to have a long morning routine. However, many parents who have to work will by necessity have a short one. Remember that kids will adapt to whatever you set in place and can re-adapt if you need to change it later. Allow time in your mornings for going to the toilet. If your kids often poop in the morning, then you want time for them to wake up, get dressed, brush teeth and hair, eat, *and* sit on the toilet before leaving. If you can, have their lunch packed before they get up. It will help. It's good for the kids to learn to put their lunch box and water bottle into their backpacks, and then to carry it themselves. As the years go on, this will evolve into them making and packing their own lunches. So, start now with simple responsibilities.

If possible, allow some time at pick-up to stay and play on campus at the end of the day. Bring snacks to share, and meet a few other parents. Unfortunately, this after school time is not always allowed. Some districts close the playground at the end of the school day. However, if this is not an issue at your school, stay for an afternoon play date. I found I was able to develop a nice community of moms through these play dates. That "mom community" is reason enough that schools should keep playgrounds open. Anything that helps people build community in our fractured society is precious to us all.

Finally, be aware that the after school pick-up time has the potential to become an important time of the day. Whether you're walking home or driving, many children will suddenly open up and tell you about all the joys and tragedies of their day. All the bad and good they have kept inside for hours will suddenly start spilling out because they feel safe sharing these feelings with you. Often this avalanche of feelings will initially focus on all the slights, concerns, hurts, and fears from the day. Most likely, they have saved all their complaining for you! As a parent, it can feel overwhelming and concerning if you think you're supposed to fix all this for them. But you're not. You're supposed to let them vent. Share your sympathy. Help them understand their feelings. Talk through any issues they want to talk about. And help them find and talk about the positive parts of the day too. Some of the best conversations I have had with my kids have been in the car on the way to and from school. Sometimes it's about their day, and other times it's about homelessness, or politics, or empathy. Aim for open ended questions without a yes/no answer. "Tell me one thing that happened at school today?" If you get to do pick-up or drop off, then I encourage you to *avoid* routinely filling up the time with music, or phone calls. Instead let it grow into time for listening to and talking with your kids.

Here are a few good books to read with your kids in the week before starting school.

- *Miss Bindergarten's Kindergarten* by Joseph Slate and Ashely Wolff.
- *T'was the Night Before Kindergarten* by Natasha Wing and Julie Durell.
- *The Kissing Hand* by Audrey Penn and Ruth Harper.

READING ANXIETY

One of the most common parental fears these days seems to focus on early reading. So, what's the "normal" age for learning to read? Well, here's the thing. Our brains are wired to learn spoken language. They are *not* wired to learn written language. Yeah. Writing was a later invention on the evolutionary time line. This means that there is a wide age range at which children *build* the necessary neuro-circuitry and connections in their brain that allow for processing written language. (You might want to go back and read that sentence again!) Some parents will push their kids to learn reading early in the misguided hope it will give them a head start in school. Really. As I have said before, children's brains are not like adult brains. They are still growing and developing. Some kids will read between ages 4 and 5. Many more will learn between 6 and 7, some will get it closer to 8 or 9 years of age.

However, as early as kindergarten or first grade, many schools will apply enormous pressure on your kids to read. These children are just too young for this kind of pressure. Developmentally, some are ready to read and others are not. *Pushing* all children to read at this point is a mistake. It is not necessary, and can have very negative consequences on your child.

Studies have shown that regardless of when a child starts to read, by age 10 kids are typically reading at the same level. By age 15, kids who are pushed to read early are actually reading less hours per day than kids who learned later. Why? It's not clear. Likely it's because children who aren't pushed finding reading pleasurable. It may also have to do with being allowed to develop their own internal motivation to read when they were young. There are many child development experts who are pushing back against early academics. In high school academic testing, Finland routinely scores at the top. Yet, they don't start formally teaching children to read until age 7. In the U.S., poverty seems to be the main thing that lets kids fall behind and stay behind. Large, careful studies have shown that the best way to get sustained academic improvement is to help raise a family out of poverty. Unfortunately, many school systems are busy pushing early academics. Let me show you how this can present itself, and what you can do.

My kids started kindergarten at a fairly progressive public school. My daughter learned her letters quickly, and happily wrote me adorable phonetic notes. My son was slower to write letters, but still happily learning at his own pace. We moved, and they changed schools. My daughter's new teacher put enormous pressure on her to write *neatly*. My daughter quickly learned to hate writing, and refused to write sentences anymore! But, this was just the beginning of the reading and writing pressure.

Some schools will lay the pressure on thick. They will preach the importance of first grade reading to both parents and kids. My 6-year-old daughter was told that if her entire first grade class had memorized all the sight words by the end of the year, then the class would have an ice cream party. Hmm, 1 in 5 kids has dyslexia. So, with this plan, a child with a learning difference will feel like they are failing themselves *and* their classmates. You'd think an experienced teacher would recognize the problems in this so called "team" challenge. But it's not just the kids with learning differences who suffer in this pressure cooker. My daughter was doing great at school, but cried everyday due to stress and anxiety over expectations and homework.

Parents for this class of first graders were given a chart showing how reading for twenty minutes every day accumulated book time over the years. It did make a pretty bar graph. However, it had nothing to do with current or future reading *behavior* of children. Furthermore, a statement was attached that connected hours of reading time to standardized test scores. The date on the statement, and thus the testing in question, was twenty years old! Nevertheless, the "parent packet" looked good, and your average parent could easily miss the bullsh**!

My 6-year-old son was still working on his letters when his teacher told him he had to *read* for 20 minutes every night. Then they gave him these incredibly boring first readers. He was at the stage where every word was a struggle. They wanted him to do this for 20 minutes. Every day. That's crazy! At that stage, you help them read the words "Star Wars" on their Lego box. Or the name on their Beanie Boo tag. Or the sign that says "cupcakes" on the store. You make reading a word relevant and interesting and fun. Telling a 6-year-old boy that he needs to focus for 20 minutes on something insipidly boring and obscurely hard is sure to crush any possible interest that previously existed for the subject.

This is exactly what happened to us. My son, who had been intrigued by the idea of reading now wanted nothing to do with it. He was over-whelmed by the pressure, and completely turned off to all of school. He became depressed and began saying, "I hate school. I hate school." I told him he did not need to read to me, and I got some Star Wars and Lego early readers. I just left them around where he could flip through them without pressure. In the evening, I read to him whatever he wanted me to read. I volunteered in his classroom to see how I might help. What became clear was that I couldn't fix the environment that was crushing my children's love of learning.

So, two months into first grade we moved the kids to a private Montessori program. They had no homework at all. The teachers accurately assessed the different levels of each of my children and formulated child specific learning plans. Within a month they liked school again. By the end of first grade both my kids were up late reading in bed every night. By their own choice. I had to tell them to "stop reading and go to sleep!" By the end of second grade, I had to confiscate the books at bedtime or they'd stay up too late reading.

You want your child to love reading? Back the pressure off. It's not a race. If you child's school says they must read for 20 minutes every night then tell the teachers "No." Don't force this random magic number on all kids. The truth is that if you make reading miserable, then your kids won't want to do it. As a result, they will not be reading much as they get older. If on the other hand, reading is so wonderful that they are always looking for their next book well then your job is done!

So, relax. Read to your kids every day. Let them see you reading. Tempt them with books that touch on their interests. Take trips to the library and bookstore, and let *them* pick books regardless of whether you think it's at their level or not. Help them when they want help reading, and wait patiently when they want to struggle through alone. If they want to read the same thing over and over, don't worry. They are learning more and more every time they repeat it. They will move on eventually. Offer lots of praise. Keep reading *fun* and *stress free*. Let your child come to it when they are ready, and how they are ready. Let it be their choice. "Do you want to read to me tonight or should I read to you?" This is so, so, so important! If they are done at 10 minutes or 5 minutes…stop. Tomorrow is another day.

Make *sure* their school is using a *phonics based* approach to teaching reading. It is the only approach that is clearly proven to work. If your child is a late bloomer with reading, and you're concerned then get them an assessment. If you find they have dyslexia, you can intervene. If you don't find a learning difference, then give them the gift of time. Just follow their lead and go with the flow. Their reading will feel strained and slow at first. Then one day it will suddenly "click" for them. You'll be driving and the kids will start reading the signs on stores. Before you know it, you will no longer be able to "spell out" secrets.

Mom says to Dad, "Should we stop for I-C-E C-R-E-A-M?"

Kids scream, "YES! ice cream! ICE cream! ICE CREAM! YEAH!"

Here's a good article from Today's Parent magazine:

- *Learning to Read: What Age is the "Right" Age?* by Susan Goldberg, Today's Parent, 5/17/2016. https://www.todaysparent.com/family/activities/right-age-to-read/

LEARNING DIFFERENCES: DYSLEXIA, DYSGRAPHIA, DYSCALCULIA, SLOW PROCESSING

The first thing you need to know about learning differences is they are truly often *differences* and *not disabilities*. The list of brilliant people who struggled with these so called learning disabilities is huge. Really, really, HUGE! Steve Jobs, Michael Phelps, Whoopi Goldberg, Steven Spielberg, Jammie Oliver, Charles Schwab, Richard Branson, Anderson Cooper, Magic Johnson, Agatha Christie...on and on the list of great minds goes. Each of them labeled with dyslexia or dys-whatever-ia. Research has shown that people with dyslexia actually excel at certain kinds of reasoning. Unfortunately, our educational system remains in the dark ages. Most of your child's teachers, principals, and counselors generally have had very little instruction in how atypical kids learn. Many states do not require much, if any, course work in the science and neurobiological underpinnings of learning. Furthermore, our understanding of the neurobiology of learning is growing so fast that even the well informed may have very limited understanding of these developmental variations. Which is quite a bummer.

One in five kids has dyslexia! That's 20% of the population! If you have two kids and your best friend has three kids, then the chances are good that one of them may be dyslexic. If you or your partner had any trouble learning to read, then there's an even higher chance of dyslexia in your children. And that's *just* dyslexia. There's also dysgraphia, dyscalculia, slow processing, working memory impairments, executive function challenges, and many others. So *more,* much more, than one-fifth of the school age population has a *neurobiologically* different way of learning, and most of our teachers have *no training* in how to identify or teach these kids. Furthermore, our school boards are busy arguing over whether to include the contributions of minority groups in our history texts or to focus history books on a "pro-American" message. For much of our educational system, the politics of "what" to teach the masses takes priority over "how" to teach the huge diversity of different brains sitting in our classrooms.

What exactly is a *neurobiological* learning difference? Imagine your brain as a mass of interconnected train tracks. If you have a neurotypical brain then you have a smooth, well-used track that runs from New York City to Washington D.C.. It's easy, and fast for you to send a signal from one to the other. A child whose brain is *neurologically different* may not have *any* direct connection from NY to D.C.. If this child wants to convey a message from NY to D.C., they may need to send a train to Chicago! Once in the Chicago train yards, that train may get sent to D.C. or it may get rerouted to Seattle! If the neurons in your brain are laid down differently or connected differently, then you can only use them the way they are *currently* laid down. That's a neurobiological difference that affects *how* a child learns and thinks and behaves.

The neurobiological *science* on learning differences is steadily growing. And yet, our entire educational complex is so far behind as to be virtually unaware. This means that if your child has one of these learning differences, then you need to become a strong, informed, and vocal advocate for your child. This is challenging, time consuming, and often highly emotional. What I want to offer is a brief overview for parents of a few of the more common learning differences. I'll go over some early signs you might see in your child if they process things differently. This is not remotely comprehensive. I provide it as a launching off point for questions and investigation.

Dyslexia is one of the most common and most well studied of the learning differences. It is a language processing difference. In one type of dyslexia, children have trouble processing the component sounds of language such that it becomes hard for them to break apart words, and then label different sounds. In another type of dyslexia, kids have trouble in how a letter or word is perceived and processed in the language areas of the brain. In the third type, children have combined challenges with both the processing of visual and auditory input into the language areas of the brain.

Some possible early, early signs of dyslexia are:

- A language or speech delay.
- Difficulty with rhyming or noticing rhymes.
- Behavioral avoidance of reading or listening to the reading of stories.
- Trouble with rapid naming. This is when a child may know and be able to name what a bat or ball or circle is. However, when shown the object suddenly and out of context, they are not able to retrieve the word quickly.
- Avoidance of activities that require a crayon or pencil.
- Socially well adapted kids with dyslexia may develop severe emotional distress and avoidance around school.

Many of these clues can show up as early as age 3. However, it can be very hard to get school systems to recognize dyslexia in a child that is younger than the typical reading age. This is unfortunate as early speech and occupational therapy can significantly help kids with dyslexia. Most school systems are charged with the task of identifying and addressing learning disabilities. How well they address this task is highly variable. Nevertheless, you can ask your school system to do a psychoeducational assessment of your child as young as age 3.

If your child does show signs of dyslexia, then in all likelihood, you have to become a strong advocate for their needs regardless of their age. Our educational system was aware of dyslexia when I was a little kid. I remember being screened for it in elementary school along with hearing and vision screening. So, way, *way* back in ancient times, like the 1970's, we knew that some kids struggle with dyslexia. And yet…and yet! The California school systems have done such a poor job of responding to the needs of dyslexic kids that in 2017…2017! They had to pass a law specifically saying that schools *must identify* and *accommodate* the needs of dyslexic children. And still, *still* in 2020 many parents will give up on public schools, and instead seek out and fund their own intervention. Obviously, this is a privilege of the wealthy that leaves many low income dyslexic students behind. Perhaps this is part of why people with dyslexia make up 40% of the world's self-made millionaires *and* 48% of our prisoners.

Which brings us to what some have called the dyslexic advantage. In their paradigm shifting book, *The Dyslexic Advantage*, Fernette Eide MD and Brock Eide MD, MA present the long unrecognized strengths of dyslexic thinkers. They present evidence that people whose minds are wired for dyslexia are often gifted with enhanced abilities in *M*aterial reasoning (architecture and engineering), *I*nterconnected reasoning (science and design), *N*arrative reasoning (writing and law), and *D*ynamic reasoning (economy and entrepreneurship). So, dyslexic kids often have enriched reasoning of MIND. Which leads us to the question: are we dealing with *learning* disabilities in kids or *teaching* disabilities in adults?

Dyscalculia is similar to dyslexia in that a symbol (a written number) represents an amount (or magnitude) as opposed to a sound. Early on, kids with dyscalculia may have a hard time picking the larger pile of candy when encouraged to choose the biggest. Montessori math often works well for these thinkers because it's based in hands-on materials and meaning-based learning. Kids with dyscalculia will often have a much harder time with math that uses rote memorization learning. Dyscalculia is under studied, less well known, and often missed by teachers and family alike. You will probably need a good assessment by an educational psychologist to spot this in a child struggling with math.

Dysgraphia is a *group* of learning differences that can involve several different areas of written language processing. Like dyslexia it is a *language processing* challenge not a purely motor issue. We know this because we can now do functional MRI's on neuro-typical and non-neurotypical people as they write. When we do these tests, it is the language processing centers of the brain, not the motor areas, that light up when we write. Unfortunately, dysgraphia is much less studied and understood as compared to dyslexia. Because of this there is a great deal of misunderstanding of dysgraphia within the educational system and even in many learning disability advocacy groups. As of this writing, a simple Internet search will lead you to many articles using older terminology and criteria. The truth is this is an area that needs further study. Some people will tell you that you can't have dysgraphia with neat hand writing. Others will tell you that dysgraphia only comes as a paired condition with dyslexia. Both of these statements are incorrect. Here is a quick review of what I feel reflects the current state of our understanding of dysgraphia.

There are three major categories of dysgraphia.

1. **Graphomotor dysgraphia** – In these children the integration of language skills and motor skills is impaired resulting in extremely messy and disorganized penmanship. Often there is difficulty with organizing written material on the page as well. These kids may read well, but be unable to write. This is one of the most recognized forms of dysgraphia. You can see it on the page, and very young kids may struggle to hold a crayon or pencil correctly.
2. **Dyslexic dysgraphia** – These kids have extreme spelling challenges due to an inability to recognize and process the sounds of words while writing. It is more easily recognizable and has several subtypes. It can often be found in conjunction with dyslexias.
3. **Executive dysgraphia** – Kids with this learning difference can be the hardest to recognize. They may read and comprehend well. When copying or writing short sentences their handwriting may be completely age appropriate. However, as writing becomes more involved they run into other roadblocks. They may have trouble with verbal retrieval of the needed words or with the rules of grammar and syntax. They may struggle with poor working memory that limits their ability to hold all the components necessary for writing in the front of their thoughts. Or they may struggle with executive function skills that allow one to organize thoughts for longer writing. In practice, these kids will try to write, then may freeze up. Their mind is struggling to hold onto all the elements necessary to write, but they keep slipping away. Often these children are smart, may love to read,

and are motivated to express their ideas. Thus, their frustration level can be quite high when they can't write as other kids are doing. Since they may be doing well otherwise, they can easily be dismissed as lazy or not trying.

Another poorly recognized learning difference is in "**slow processing**." Processing speed has long been part of IQ assessment. However, it wasn't given much attention until recently. In *Bright Kids Who Can't Keep Up: Help Your Child Overcome Slow Processing Speed And Succeed In A Fast-Paced World,* PhDs Ellen Braaten and Brian Willoughby review both how to help, and what we know about children who struggle with slow processing speed. To simplify greatly, these kids may be very smart but slow, slow, sloooooow. Often at almost everything. It can have huge effects on home life, social life, family relationships as well as school life. If you think you might have one of these kids, then give *Bright Kids Who Can't Keep Up* a good look, and consider a full assessment for your child. It can also help to think of your child as a thoughtful, deep thinker, about everything.

There are many other learning differences and disabilities that I'll not go into here. But I do want to briefly address Executive Function Skills. As your kids get older you'll hear this phrase tossed around and it's worth knowing what it means.

From the Understood Team at Understood.org

> "**Executive function** is a set of mental skills that include working memory, flexible thinking, and self-control. We use these skills every day to learn, work, and manage daily life. Trouble with executive function can make it hard to focus, follow directions, and handle emotions, among other things."

These are functions of the frontal lobe of the brain which has been shown to be still maturing when people are in their *twenties*. Many, but *not all* kids, with learning differences have some difficulty with executive function skills. Perhaps you have more than one child. Perhaps you have noticed that one kid learned fairly quickly how to set the table for dinner. Perhaps your other child still needs coaching and micromanagement through the entire process. What you may be seeing is differences in executive function skills. One child can learn the task, hold all the steps together in their head, sequence them, modify for the addition of a dinner guest, develop better placement of dinnerware over time, and get it all done in a reasonable time frame...grumpily or not.

Child number two may start dancing with the utensils on the way to the table and forget what they are doing. Once reminded, they will decide to set the utensils in a special way. Creative? Yes, but slooow. And once done with the utensils, they will happily go upstairs to find a Lego creation they want to show you. They will not realize that the plates, napkins, and water cups are missing. This is a child who has made a genuine attempt at setting the table, but whose mind has difficulty holding onto and organizing all the elements of the task. Can this child learn to set the table? Yes, but they are going to need a lot more coaching and repetition before they master it. Can this child *use* all the dinnerware? Yes, even though they have trouble *setting* them all. This same child *might read* just fine, but have difficulty remembering all the rules of *writing* a sentence. Capitalization, punctuation, subject, verb, tense, between the lines, spacing on the page, content. (Yes, *I* know that is a fragment and not a complete sentence.) If you suspect that your child is a late bloomer in executive function skills, then make sure that any psycho-educational assessment they receive includes evaluation of these skills. It will help *you* understand your kid better. Furthermore, teaching interventions that addresses executive function skills can be important to your child's progress.

How to pursue school intervention services for your child could be a book in itself. While it's more than I can cover here, I will throw out a few bits of advice. You may find professional help and advocacy for your child at school. Or you may discover the school minimizes your child's learning challenges, fails to provide useful intervention, or tells you they are not required to help with your child's learning disabilities.

If you have the means, consider moving your child to a private school. Or seek disability specific help from private services outside the school system. Both of these options are clearly expensive, and often out of reach for many families. If the school refuses to authorize a "second opinion" assessment (an Independent Educational Evaluation or IEP), then you may wind up paying enormous sums for an independent educational assessment and a lawyer to *make* the school meet their obligations to your child. In fact, a whole network of consulting educational psychologists and lawyers specialize in these cases. If they find that your child does indeed have a learning challenge that the schools are required to address, then you can ask the court to order the reimbursement of the costs you've incurred in assessing, treating, and lawyering-up. This, of course, requires that you have the time and money to pay for the services up front and *hope* for reimbursement.

The complex child assessment process is one that parents generally have no experience with. The schools and the people who conduct these assessments, however, have been through them many times. They are familiar with the procedures, the meetings, and the implications of various conclusions. *At the same time, they may be grossly misinformed and uneducated about learning differences.* Really. Truly. Most principals and educators simply have not kept up with the neurobiological science of learning disabilities. You're expecting them to be experts. They may *sound* like experts while making *huge* errors. For this reason, it is very helpful if you can bring someone with you to the meetings. Preferably, someone who has been through the system before. You should record all meetings with the school on a cell phone. You're allowed to do this if you inform them in advance, so they can make their own recording. Research your legal rights, and the obligations of the schools. Look for local parenting support groups that can point you towards resources and seek out the most knowledgeable person you can find to help you advocate for you child.

A dear friend of mine is an educational psychologist. At some point she realized her children had dyslexia. Imagine her frustration when she had to *push* for her kids to get an assessment, and was unable to get the public school system…*that she worked for*…to provide the intervention her kids needed! Ultimately, she pulled her kids from public school and found outside dyslexia tutoring for them. Previously a strong advocate for public schooling, she now works the other side. Frankly, you could not ask for a fiercer advocate for children and families struggling with learning differences. When one of my children needed an assessment, my friend kindly went over the test results with me. She pointed out that one of the most important tests, based on our concerns, was administered incorrectly. It was truly invalid information due to how it was conducted. Nevertheless, the school presented this as evidence of lack of problems in this area. I have a master's degree in medical science, but I would *never* have known the specifics of *how* a particular psychoeducational test needed to be conducted. Furthermore, they presented a whole group of test results using the wrong scale! This artificially shifted some results from "low" to "average" and created a false impression of how my child was doing. When confronted, they clearly *knew* they were using the wrong scale, but refused to admit it created a false result. I promise you that virtually no one, other than an educational psychologist or school tester, is going to know what scale needs to be used on every test. Without my friend's informed review of the testing, my lawyer husband and I might have agreed with the school that things looked kind of okay. Most parents are not going to have an educational psychologist in their back pocket. So, be aware that you may be well out of your element. If you feel the school has missed something or is glossing over your concerns, then try to hire an expert to review test results with you.

Be aware, if your child has had and educational assessment through the school system, the educational psychologist who works for the schools will help define any learning differences your child has. Unfortunately, they often don't include recommendations for best interventions for your child. If they did then the school system would be obligated to purchase and provide those specific interventions. If your child has dyslexia, the school system may say they have a program for that. However, the program your school currently uses may not be the best one for your child's specific dyslexic challenges. This stuff is studied. There's data on what teaching systems work best for different kinds of learning differences. Your child doesn't need just any old something thrown at them. They need the correct specific intervention. Furthermore, many children have a mix of different learning differences, and some programs may combine approaches better than others. But, the school system may be strapped for money, and not want to invest in purchasing a new program for your child. If they can't prove that what they have fits your child's needs, then they are required to provide it in some way. They can purchase and learn a new intervention. They can pay to send your child to a specialized school or for outside specialty services. The big challenge here is that you won't know what interventions might be best. You can ask the school psychologist to make specific recommendations with links to what data show these will be best. Or, you can get an opinion from a consulting educational psychologist from outside the school system.

It's all just sooo easy for a parent to handle. All sooo cheap and affordable for struggling families. I am truly stunned by the obstacles some school systems will create to prevent a child from learning. Even free accommodations like extra time for children with slow processing, dyslexia, or dyscalculia can be refused despite overwhelming evidence that it's appropriate for a child. However, it does not have to be this way. I have also worked with schools who genuinely understand learning differences and variations in child development. Within the constraints of the public school system, they have set up environments that support the wide range of needs in a classroom. There are schools that listen to findings from educational assessments and work to address each child's needs. Finding these schools is extremely hard and rare in my experience. Certainly, school funding that was not based on local property taxes would even the playing field a bit. But, we also need teachers and administrators who have been educated in these issues and have the freedom to build a better way.

Finally, advocate for time limits on your child's homework. Kids have many developmental tasks and needs outside of school. Make sure they have time for them. If school remains difficult and unrewarding for your child, then it is even more imperative they have the opportunity to be involved in other activities that float their boat. We all need multiple things in life that we value. Family, friends, work, hobbies, gardens, people we help, favorite places to walk, simple pleasures. All these things add strength and depth to our lives. If disaster strikes one, then the others are there to provide balance. If your child doesn't click with school, then it is *extra* important they have other activities where they *do* click. It could be karate, or swimming, or Lego club, or video camp, or art classes. Whatever they love to do that taps into their skills and abilities. School, especially grade school, is not the only place that we learn the skills of life. You can help them find and validate their abilities. While you're at it, you can remind them that in college they can pick for themselves what to explore. That's much more fun than grade school!

SEPARATING TWINS IN SCHOOL OR NOT: EMOTIONALLY HEALTHY TWINS

Do you keep twins in the same class at school or separate them? This is a question with a lot of history behind it, and many diverse opinions. In the past it was the *school*'s choice. For a while, the twin bond was felt to be so special that twins would be kept in the same classroom. And in small schools, grade levels were often mixed anyway. So, it was not uncommon for non-twin siblings to be in the same class. Later, the psychological concept of individual self-actualization was believed to be of paramount value. This led to schools *forcing* the separation of twins into separate classes. The current movement across the country is to make the decision a parental choice. In many, but not all states, parents now have the legal right to make this choice. However, I know parents whose schools had strong opinions on the issue, and pushed hard to separate twins despite the parent's decision to keep them together.

What are the issues here? Some of this is addressed in an excellent book, *Emotionally Healthy Twins* by Joan Friedman, PhD. The author is herself a twin, had twins of her own, and is a psychologist who built a practice around twins and twin parenting. She also spent time interviewing adult twins about their experiences as children and how they felt about them then and now. Some twins were schooled together and were later forced to separate. Some of those twin sets found the separation traumatic and unnecessary. Others found it liberating and key to personal growth. The point here is that each set of twins and every family situation is different. What works best for some will not be the same for all. What works when the kids are 5-years-old may be different from what they need when they are 9 or 16-years-old.

Some young twins can become so emotionally enmeshed that it becomes problematic. One twin may go silent, and let the other speak for both of them. One may always lead, and the other always follow. One may monopolize an interest and not allow the other to explore it. In these kinds of situations, the simple act of giving the kids separate classrooms can allow them each to fully grow into themselves. This kind of dysfunctional interdependence, however, does not always occur. Some kids go their own way and mature healthily while sharing a classroom with their sibling.

Personally, I could not imagine having to share a classroom all day with one of my siblings. I think I would have hated it. With this in the back of my mind, I decided early that I would get my twins some time of their own by separating them in school from the beginning. But… the part-time pre-K that I really liked only had one class. So, I enrolled them together. And the teacher said they did great. Each developed and played with their own friends, and basically did their own thing. When kindergarten came along, my son was having some health issues. I decided they would both be fine together, so I put them in the same class. Again, the teacher did not see any emotional or developmental problems occurring between them.

For first grade, we again moved to a new school district. Finally, I put my kids in separate classes. My kids were nervous about this, but I figured it would be good for them to have time away from each other. Socially, they were fine. Unfortunately, the school was a mess and we wound up pulling them out. Fortunately, I found a fantastic Montessori K-8th grade school and moved them there. But my kids had been through so many changes and school troubles that I decided to ask them, now 6 years old, what they wanted. Together or separate? They both picked together.

Within a couple of months of adjusting to the new school they were both thriving. When they moved to second grade I asked them again if they wanted separate classrooms or not. They chose to stay together. So, despite my firm intentions to separate my kids early, I've in fact kept them together. And, they are doing great!

Some twins can have a very special relationship that can be a great strength and support through life. But it is also true that we all grow as individuals when pushed to rely on our own resources. Somewhere in there is a balance between the richness and strengths of human connection and the freedom and strengths of independence. Each family will have to find the balance that works for their children. Remember that *our* culture highly values independence and encourages self-discovery. Some other cultures highly value strong family bonds, inter-dependence, and duty to others. Keep an open mind and follow your instincts for what you feel will work for your kids. Don't let set beliefs of others or school systems push you around. Don't be afraid to try something new or change things if they are not working for your kids. Nothing is set in stone.

Another variable to consider is that separate classrooms can double parental workload when your kids are young. Little kids don't remember from one minute to the next what they need for school projects or homework. That will become *your* job. One week they may be told to wear specific fruit colored shirts each day as the class is learning fruits and veggies. The next week they wear shirts with buttons for counting. There is always something going on that parents have to keep on top of and guide the kids through. Frankly, it's a ridiculous burden to add to the parental load. Like parents don't have enough to juggle! If you have two *different* classrooms, then each child will be doing totally different things that *you* must now track. I couldn't keep up with one kindergarten class's worth of parental involvement. Two different agendas would surely be a chore! Remember, the stress load of parents directly affects quality of life for the whole family.

In addition, school is not the only place your twins can learn how to fly alone. Summer camps are a great way to let them experience the challenges and freedoms of doing an activity without their twin present. Like singletons of different ages they can solo walk into a class and meet new kids alone. I found that booking my kids into separate camps and classes really helped them develop their confidence and independence.

Keep these thoughts in mind as you consider all the pros and cons for your twins and your family. Remember that what you do now isn't written in concrete. You can always do something different later.

NIGHT TIME FEARS AND BED HOPPING KANGAROOS

As your children get older your sleep issues will *not* go away. But, they will change. And in general, you'll likely get a lot more sleep than you did in the first year. As I discussed earlier, some people will continue to have their children sleep in "the family bed" as they get older. Most, however, will work to transition their kids to a crib or bed in their own room. Perhaps you'll go through a period of time when your kids seem to be doing pretty well in that room across the hall. You've made it through the crazy time when wild toddlers are climbing out of cribs, and some small semblance of normalcy and routine has developed at night. Many siblings continue to share a room even when there is extra space. Or they may each have their "own" room but one child gets up and goes to sleep on the floor in the other's room. So, there will be some nighttime shenanigans.

You will be juggling these issues when you are hit with the Age of Nightmares. (Cue Twilight Zone music.) I know scary thought, right! Instead of a crying baby, you'll have an older child at your bedside shaking you from sleep. Afraid and still crying. Sigh. It's a phase. It is, however, one that comes and goes for quite a while. And it definitely gets worse just after Halloween! So, what to do?

Most sleep advisers will likely tell you to comfort your child and then walk them back to bed. You want them to feel safe in their rooms yada, yada, yada. However, that's not what I'm going to recommend. First, I have very clear memories of being young and afraid of the Giant Tarantula and King Kong and Godzilla and the sinking Titanic. (I had older siblings. Despite being banned from watching such movies, I somehow managed to sneak in and get good and scared!) And I also clearly remember feeling deeply, deeply grateful to my father for sitting in the hall while I fell asleep at night. It meant *so* much to me that he was just present.

I've also had a nightmare or two in my life. If I try to go back to sleep right afterwards, I will go back into the same nightmare. So, I get it when kids don't want to go back to their own bed. It's not always about "learning to sleep on their own." Sometimes it's about the overwhelming feelings that haunt us in nightmares, and can be hard to escape when we are still barely awake.

And then there's my friend Constance, a stay-at-home mom with four kids. She never knew where her family would be every morning. They might...might...all start off in their own beds. By morning, however, they could be anywhere. Hubby might be on the couch, one child in the parental bed, mom in the kid's room, and three kids in the guest room scattered over the double bed and floor. But basically, they all mostly slept. When my kids were little, I thought she was crazy. Later, I realized the wisdom of just tucking a wandering child in wherever they wanted to be so that everyone could just go back to sleep.

Now, when we hit a spell of nightmares, I do one of two things. If it's just my daughter who's awake, I let her climb in bed with us. If it's my son, he gets to sleeps on the floor in our room because he kicks in his sleep and migrates sideways taking up an entire king size bed. If both kids are up, then both go on the floor. They are almost always back to sleep very, very quickly. Me? Not so much. But then I'm peri-menopausal and can't blame *all* of my sleep issues on the kids!

I've heard you can teach your kids not to wake you up, and instead just crash out quietly in designated sleep nest on the floor. Thus far, I have had intermittent success with this concept. Sometimes my daughter is just too upset or my son too disoriented in his half-asleep state.

The moral of *this* parenting story? Sometimes we don't need experts, we need the wisdom of experienced moms. Sometimes kids don't need training, they just need our presence.

MULTI-AGE PLAYGROUPS

As I mentioned earlier, over most of human existence, we have lived in hunter-gatherer societies. In these cultures, children are not segregated by age. Instead, young kids of 3 and 4 run around with all the village kids. The tweeners and the just beyond toddlers are playing and learning and growing together. A lot of study has shown a great benefit from these multi-aged groups of kids. When a 5-year-old plays catch with a 10-year-old, the younger child benefits from watching the skill of the older child. And the older kid has to dive and work to catch the balls that the 5-year-old pitches wild. Thus, the older child benefits from the responsibility of being the teacher and from a challenging game of catch. In the recent past these multi-aged playgroups would still form within neighborhoods. Unfortunately, these groups are disappearing as the kids are funneled into age segregated activities.

Sometimes you can create a multi-aged play-group and simultaneously generate some good "mom time." You can start having Friday afternoon "play-date-and-mom-date" in your back yard. Have parents bring all the kids, and turn them loose outside. Adults can sit back and yack. As partners get off work, they can join you. This kind of casual gathering can be great for children and adults alike. If you can pull one together in your neck of the woods, you may find you've built a community!

PROS AND CONS OF DIFFERENT BIG KID BEDS

When you have multiple young children, finding room for them can become a challenge. Many people skip toddler beds, and instead go from crib to crib-mattress on the floor. This gives the child time to learn how to sleep on a small mattress without falling out of bed. For some kids this is a big issue! I think my daughter fell out once, but my son, whoa, a lot of thuds in the middle of the night. Usually the impact was followed by a visitor to mom and dad's room, but he did sleep through it on at least one occasion! You can roll up a blanket or towel and put it under the bottom sheet to make a barrier to keep your child from the old floor dive. Unfortunately for our son, it took us a while to learn that trick.

At some point, you may decide to switch to twin beds, a bunk bed, or loft beds. It is not recommended for children under age 6 to sleep in an upper bunk or loft. The risk of fall and broken bones is too high in this younger group. That said, you may find that even your older child is too klutzy, impulsive, or wild for an upper bunk. You also want to consider that changing the bedding in an upper bunk is not easy. If your child can't help you with changing the sheets or if they are still wetting the bed at night, then maybe give a pass on elevated sleeping. On the other hand, if these are not issues for you, then a bunk bed or loft bed system can offer much more floor space for the endless small plastic toys that are coming your way. In addition, a private play area under a loft can provide a child with a "space of their own." This can be important for kids who find themselves stuck with each other most of the time. If you have the space, then giving each child their own room can be helpful. However, they still may wind up wanting to sleep in same room. They can easily sleep on the floor with a blanket, and that may be where you find them in the morning!

TALKING ABOUT DEATH WITH YOUNG KIDS

Our culture tends to be very reticent about discussing death. But, I assure you, at some point your children will begin to explore this topic. You do them no service if you don't help them to understand death. My kids started asking questions about death when they were around 2-years-old. For us many of the teachable times occurred around bugs. My kids love crawly critters. We spent much time teaching them to be gentle. Inevitably, they would squash one or carry it so long in their hand that it died. This became a time to start explaining what that meant. We explained that the bug would not ever "wake up again." When they were 2-years-old and they asked about getting in a car crash, we would create a story in which everyone was okay. Like, "Good thing everyone was wearing seat belts and is okay." Because at 2-years-old they seemed to want re-assurance. Then between 3 and 5 years old, they began asking what would happen in imaginary scenarios that clearly would lead to death. They'd ask "what would happen if…someone fell into a giant pit of molten lava or our car crashed into a big hole, a truck fell on top of it, and then everything filled up with water?" So, then we'd tell them, "We'd all be dead." Because clearly, at that point, they wanted us to confirm for them what they already knew.

Death has also come up when they realized that the chicken they were eating was once a chicken like the one they saw at the farm. Our talk about eating chicken then led to discussions of carnivores, vegetarians, and omnivores. This led to the whole idea of eating things that once were alive, but are now dead. Discussing dinosaurs and what they ate can also be a way to broach the concept that we kill to eat. Teaching kids that pork is a pig and beef is a cow is also important. If you don't clarify this they won't make the connection.

All of these conversations become especially important if you have a family member or pet that is ill or aging. If you can talk about death before someone important dies, then you can help them prepare for their feelings of loss. It will be an evolving process of understanding. Start small with bugs, and let them lead you with their questions. Over time their understanding will evolve and you can expand your answers as they are ready.

For some people, this topic is so hard to discuss with their children that they freeze up. If that's the case for you then you can read books that deal with death or make one parent the designated talker on this topic. Remember that if they don't learn about death from you, they will get it somewhere. Probably from other kids and TV in the beginning or maybe a relative whom you may not want to be your child's source of information on this topic.

So, what exactly do you tell your kids about death? Well, that depends on what you believe.

25

"ADVANCED" PARENTING: SKILLS, TIPS, AND INSIGHTS

GIVING THE BEASTIES MORE CONTROL, MORE CHORES, MORE RESPONSIBILITIES

AS AN INFANT, MY DAUGHTER loved mealtime. She liked almost everything we spooned into her mouth. Suddenly at age 1, she started pushing everything away. It was strange. She seemed hungry, and until then meals had been going smoothly. We'd start with some easy finger food while grown-ups prepared the trays of baby food. We'd make a happy mess, and everyone left well fed and ready to move on. So, what had changed? Even my part-time nanny who'd had four kids of her own was puzzled as meals became difficult. Then one day I put the spoon in my daughter's hand. Her eyes lit up! I showed her how to scoop the food herself, and she was off to the races! What she had wanted those last weeks was control. As soon as I gave it to her, she happily mastered feeding herself, and meals again became fun for all.

There are two good reasons to give children as much control as possible. First, mastering the skills of life is a child's ultimate goal. Each time you give them control over an activity you give them a chance at growth and mastery. The other reason is that as they learn to do things on their own it really does make things easier for you. You have to invest the time up front to teach the skills, and allow them time to get it wrong and later right. But ultimately, it does pay off.

It's very easy to get stuck in the habits of "doing for" your kids rather than "teaching how." Instead, you want to be continually re-assessing. What's the next thing your kids are ready to learn? If you want your 12-year-old to cut his own meat, then you want to introduce him to a small butter knife at age 3, and perhaps a sharp knife with supervision at age 5 or 6. Why would you want to be responsible for dragging your 14-year-old out of bed for school when you can give an 8-year-old an alarm clock and start teaching her to get up on her own? I know. I know. It's much, much easier to put the laundry away yourself. But it's even more beneficial to teach your kids how to do it themselves.

In the beginning it requires parental supervision and pushing. Sometimes you'll keep it going and other times life will get in the way and chores will go undone. That's okay. Parenthood is not about perfection. But, make it a priority to be constantly teaching and expecting new skills and responsibilities from your kids. They need the skills. They need the sense of belonging and accomplishment that comes with participation in the family's daily routines. In addition, you will find yourself free to *enjoy* your children when your level of burden is eased by their competency. Are you raising the prince and princess of whatever-land who will have maids and butlers all their lives? No? Are you raising future commoners who will have to care for themselves and work for a living? Yes? Then your kids don't need you to be a maid. They need a parent who will teach them the skills of life.

In *Hunt, Gather, Parent: What Ancient Cultures Can Teach Us About the Lost Art of Raising Happy, Helpful Little Humans*, author Michaeleen Doucleff, PhD offers another interesting approach. She spent time in several communities known for their unusually good parenting styles.

Typically, children would be included in family chores from toddler-hood. It would start with an occasional request to "fetch that bowl" or "bring this to grandma." As kids get older they are invited to help wash dishes or put laundry away. They are never forced or pushed. They may fold one napkin and be done. Their contribution is acknowledged in a low key way. Since the chores are done together, voluntarily, and recognized, over time the children self-initiate chores without needing to be asked. Slowly over the years the parents invite them into more and more complex skills. They let them fumble and make a mess of it. They come home from work and ask questions such as, "What needs to be done around here?" These are designed to encourage the child to think and develop awareness of household needs. With time this leads to kids who notice what needs to be done and then pitch in to make the family run.

Whatever approach you take to teaching life skills there are, of course, a few caveats. Don't expect the process to go smoothly. Competencies will come and go in fits and starts. Sometimes you may need to look pretty far back in time to realize that forward progress has truly been made. You will also find that it's easier to teach these skills to some kids than to others. My daughter was highly, highly motivated to master self-care skills from a very young age. As she got older this drive extended to mastering all sorts of social and home skills. My son, on the other hand, has to be pushed to learn these skills. Putting on his socks, tying his shoelaces, hanging his shirts, or brushing his teeth are all a monumental waste of time in his busy mind. For my son, somersaults at 18-months or a new pogo stick at 8-years-old will warrant persistent practice until the skill is mastered. But when it comes to self-care, I gotta keep pushing him. Sometimes kids like my son will respond if you imply that they "can't" do something. Of course, one of the challenges of parenting is that you have different kids who often need different approaches.

To give you a glimpse of the future, I found that at age 8 my kids hit a stage where they were clearly ready to start internalizing skills and routines. It certainly helped that I tied some of their chores to things they want. After school, they'd each do dog and cat care chores, set the table for dinner, and take out the trash before getting TV time. On Saturday mornings, they'd clean a bathroom and start their laundry before getting computer time. On Sunday mornings, they'd sort and put away laundry while listening to music. Most week days they'd get up to their alarm clock, and get ready for school on their own.

The evolution of the morning routine, however, was rather amusing. It was quite hard for me to keep my mouth shut and avoid micromanaging. There was a lot of sleeping through the alarm, turning it off too soon, and last minute scrambles. We'd brainstorm in the car on the way home from school about what to try the next day. Tomorrow they want to try the "loud" setting on their alarm clocks. Brilliant! My daughter even noticed it was harder to remember everything without mom nagging her. Ah, so true. Yet, they made progress towards independence. To be clear, I certainly still have to intervene at times, but on the whole it's been a good process.

So, think of this future when you teach your little ones to sweep crumbs after dinner or set their cup for lunch. It's all headed somewhere good! For more in depth guidance on this topic, pick up a copy of Vickie Hoefler's book, *Duct Tape Parenting*. It's got a lot of great ideas on fostering independence at different ages. And definitely give *Hunt, Gather, Parent* a good read too.

ALLOWING MORE TIME

One sure fire way to make parenthood miserable is to try to live at an adult pace with young kids in tow. It's a guaranteed disaster. If they are infants, you'll have one blow out diaper after another delaying your plan to get out the door. Then they will spit-up on YOU as you put them back in their car seats. You'll manage a quick change, then juggle car seats, the stroller, and a giant diaper bag to the car. Just as you snap them into the car, they'll spit-up all over themselves. Sigh. You may have given yourself 15 minutes to get out of the house, but you're not going to get anywhere on time. You're better off giving yourself at least 30 minutes to get from house to car. Crazy? No, this is the new normal. And it won't go away for a long, long time.

You probably think that as they get older things will get faster. Nope. It will be different, but not faster. Once they are walking, kids will not always walk in the direction you desire. In fact, they often *run* in the opposite direction. This can slow your efforts down a quite a bit.

Then there's the "me do it!" phase. One child will insist on putting on their own shoes and socks. Great! But it's slooooow. Another child, will of course, prefer that their personal servant do the "shoes and socks thing" for them even when they are 6! There are the dawdlers. It's just who they are, and you will never speed them up very much. Or course, there's the easily distracted. For them every piece of fluff or toy on the floor offers a stream of ideas...none of which have anything to do with getting out that door. Finally, there are the "anti-transitioners." They can't bear to stop something not yet "done." It could be a stack of blocks, a train set session, a Lego creation, a video game, or a book. Whatever it is, they hate leaving it "unfinished." Thus, the transition to going out the door becomes full of frustration and resistance.

So, in order to minimize *your* frustration, allow a lot of time to get from the house to the car. Decide for yourself that it's just a new pace of life, and accept it.

There are a *few* things you can do to help move your kiddos along. You can have yourself fully ready before getting the kids moving. You can acclimate yourself to smelling like baby barf. You can pick and lay out kids clothes the day before. You can practice putting shoes on when you're not going out. When you really need to go, you can play "race to put your shoes on." You can give five minute warnings that it's time to go.

However, all of this is going to win you just a wee bit of speed. The reality is that these are beings whose brains are not even close to being fully developed. They will be constantly learning and developing for years and years to come. They need you to give them an allowance of time. A big allowance for a long time!

SCREEN TIME, NOT SCREAM TIME

When your kids are very young, screen time will not be an issue. The tiny kiddo's just don't have the attention span. In fact, you may find yourself relieved when they can be entertained by a cartoon long enough to give you a break. Road trips and airplane travel can also be eased with a bit of screen time. You just have to watch out for motion sickness. Car barf is not fun!

However, as the beasties get bigger the screen time issue may become quite a challenge. It's true that stepping away from a video or game is easy for some kids. Still, most of us have at least one child for whom screens become an insatiable draw. Of course, this is one more area in which there are many highly contradictory recommendations from "experts." I am not one of those experts. What I offer you is the consolidated insight of a parent who has struggled through screen time issues. I have read many of those contradictory expert recommendations. I also have discussed these challenges with many other struggling parents. I'm going to talk about the real world parenting issues of screens and some solutions. And I'm going to talk about several different kinds of screens because they are not all the same.

Television

One of the first screens your child may engage with is the TV. Maybe you put on Dora the Explorer or Bubble Guppies after lunch. Or your pre-K kid comes home from school and wants to watch Paw Patrol or Power Rangers. Frankly, I'm not bothered by TV shows that are basically simple entertainment. We all enjoy that sometimes. Provided it's not all your kids do, a little screen entertainment can be relaxing. However, I do turn off the TV at a specified time. One show. Thirty minutes. An hour. Whatever feels right to you, and appropriate for their age. I recommend you pay attention to how easy it is for them to transition away from the TV. If they are on too long they may become resistant and irritable when told to stop. Some kids are fine stopping after thirty minutes, but will meltdown and resist after given an hour. ***This is an important concept for all types of screen time use.*** Different kids, at different ages, will tolerate different *amounts* of screen time. Finding your child's sweet spot, with enough time for fun, but not so much that their behavior implodes, is really worthwhile.

In terms of TV content, I want to warn you about four potential issues. First, it may surprise you, but young kids can have a very hard time differentiating between reality and make believe on TV. Even cartoons can seem completely real to young children. If there are live actors, it becomes even more confusing to them. You may need to remind them that "this is make-believe" over and over even up to age 6 or 7! The more empathetic your child is the more they will identify with characters and potentially become confused. Don't forget to clarify this for them repeatedly. Second, even if kids are not "watching" adult news or TV, they can and will hear what's happening on the TV. They may not let you know in the moment, but their confusion or anxiety will show up later. If possible, avoid this kind of exposure when the kids are young. Adults can watch TV when the kids are asleep or listen with headsets.

Another area of concern occurs as the kids get older and have access to a greater variety of cartoons. Just because it's animated doesn't mean it's not potentially problematic. Some of the things you'll find are cartoons in which all the characters have some highly unrealistic body presentation. Girls with micro waists, curvy boobs, and ginormous eyes. Boys with massive shoulders, micro waists, and stony jaws. You can't police all of the shows your kids will watch. But, you can occasionally watch an episode with them and draw attention to areas of concern. Frankly, I was stunned when I realized halfway through "How to Train Your Dragon 2" that the only dark skinned person in the story was the arch villain with hair that was drawn a lot like dreadlocks. This led me to stop the movie briefly to bring it to my kid's attention. We discussed how a child of color might feel if there were no good guys who looked like him. You won't pick up on everything, and I surely couldn't stand to watch all the cartoons my kids watch. But do check in once in a while. Over the years, I've found that occasionally stopping a show and discussing it with my kids has helped them to learn how to analyze the content themselves. As they get older, they are seeing the implied and hidden assumptions within ads, videos, and even games. And, that is an absolutely vital life skill.

Finally, there's the scary content issue. The most benign thing can frighten young children, and as they get older some will be more sensitive than others. When my kids were 3, the grumpy troll on Dora the Explorer totally freaked them out! By the time the kids were 5 my son liked a little conflict in a show or film. My daughter, on the other hand, became very upset with the slightest hint of danger or conflict. Keep in mind scary scenes will come back and haunt your child at night! Which means they will also haunt *your* night time.

The Other Screen Time: Computer Games

This is one of the more challenging issues that you'll encounter as your child hits 4 to 5-years-old. It took me quite a while and much trial and error before I found an approach that worked for us. Current advice is highly variable regarding computer screen time. Some books I've read basically said, "This is the way of the modern era. Don't get in your kid's way. Just join in and participate." Others books have demonstrated how video games can put a kid into a constant "fight or flight" state with elevated adrenaline and other stress hormones. And others have presented statistics of increased depression and anxiety in kids and teens that corresponds with gaming hours or social media usage. Then there are studies that have tried to distinguish between different kinds of games to try and determine if some are "better" than others. All the ideas and opinions are out there, and there's no real consensus.

A friend with older kids offered this perspective. His two children had grown into lovely adults, and headed off to college. One of them had enjoyed video games, but turned them off without much difficulty when their allotted time was up. However, the other child would lie, break rules, and sneak around to turn on WiFi routers that parents had shut down to block access. Even in the middle of the night. Nevertheless, both kids grew into nice adults. The game obsessed child became less obsessed in late high school. My friend's advice? Stay on top of it. But, don't panic. They're just kids.

As it happens, I too seem to have one of each type of screen-time kiddo. My daughter enjoys many games, but will put them down without a fuss. My son on the other hand, gets deeply obsessed. Most of his lying behavior is related to video game issues, and there have been plenty of unpleasant battles getting him off a device. What to do?

The best decision I ever made on this issue came late. I bought a small home safe for about $40. If the kids are not using their screen-time, then the devices are "in the vault." It is fabulously freeing! I don't have to worry that the kids are sneaking a device or keep track of where they all are. The kids know they can't get at them so they *have* to shift mental gears and find something else to do. There's no point in hoping for a parent's vigilance to slip up because the screens are in the vault. Everything has gotten easier since I got the vault. Just make sure you research the size of your devices, and the size of the safe. Surprisingly, there's very little vault wise that's designed specifically for laptops or tablets. You can find single device safes designed for dorm rooms, but not a home safe designed for multiple devices. I wound up with a small safe designed for hand gun storage. The dimensions aren't perfect, but I can fit in several lap tops and tablets. For desktop computers, you can vault the key board and mouse. If one of your kids is screen obsessed, then get a vault and do it early!

You may be wondering about parental control software. I'm not especially technology nimble. I found the different controls that came with each device got very confusing. Sometimes I'd have all the controls set, and my kids couldn't get to a school site because it didn't accommodate the restrictions I'd added. Then I'd have to try to figure out new parameters and remember what each device was set for. This became a big confusing headache.

You can find independent software that lets you monitor a child's screen use from one of your own devices. Within this category there are many options. Some will work with only one kind of device. Others can handle multiple operating systems. Some offer location services. Some have detailed monitoring options. Wirecutter, the product review section of the New York Times, did an excellent review of current parental software. Give it a read and see what fits your family best. The combination of coordinating parental software and a vault can ease up the screen time conflicts.

With those two things in place you can address time limits and breaks. Even if you're allowing more time as kids get older, you may do well to break it up. Let's say you're good with an hour a day for your child. Consider allowing a 30-minute session then a require a 15-minute break with no screens. Then allow the next 30-minutes. Or you can split the time between morning and afternoon sessions. Timers are a great help with monitoring sessions. You may have different rules for school days and weekends. Another approach that works well on weekends is to have a screen time window. For example, computer time may be from 8 to 10 am on the weekend. You can require they be showered and dress before starting. This forces them to fill the rest of the day with other activities. Remember, your child's behavior when it's time to stop will let you know how long a session they can handle before needing a break.

We also need to consider the content of the game your child is playing. This I find even harder to supervise because I've never cared for video games. It's fine if you like them, but they just aren't my jam. I have found there are three levels on which content matters for kids. The first is simply what is the game about. Shooting and killing games get a "no" from me. But, how about the Nerf shooting game where the figures aren't realistic and no one dies? Is that okay? The next question is if it's a multiplayer game that's exclusive to invited friends or can outside players join? Kids really, really don't get it when you explain that the avatar who presents as a young girl may actually be a 50-year-old male predator. Even if they *seem* to understand when you explain it, they won't recognize the risk while playing a game. Furthermore, kids remain gullible to these ploys late into their teenage years. A friend's bright 15-year-old got taken in when he clicked on a pop up game that appeared while he was *at school on a shielded school computer*. It was several days before his parents learned who he was texting on his phone! So, even older kids get duped. For this reason, I try to make sure my kids don't play multiplayer games, or if they do, I've vetted everyone who's able to join the game. Mostly, I just say no to multiplayer games. It's much easier and there's tons of other material out there.

Games in which you build things, like Minecraft, can feel less problematic to parents. But you still need to be cautious. Often they are designed with no end to the game. This means there's no easy place to stop. For kids who are easily drawn into video games, this is kryptonite. They can't stop. Thus, even games with some social or educational virtue can become problematic.

Phones

I'm in favor of giving kids flip phones as early as age 7 or 8. As long as your kid won't lose the device it's an inexpensive convenience. You can buy ones that have limited access numbers and can't send photos. This lets your child learn how to make and receive phone calls to family and friends. Once they are old enough to start walking to a friend's house or riding around a neighborhood, they can bring a phone in case of flat tires and such. Lots of little conveniences and new skills come with a cheap flip phone.

Another option once they are older and have shown they won't lose a phone are the new browserless "smart phone like" phones. These are great for tweens because they look like a smart phone and have many useful features like maps, music, texting, and basic apps, but you can't access the internet even with WiFi. One current brand to look at is the Gabb.

With both flip phones and the newer browserless tech phones, what you *don't* get is social media, naked picture swapping, predator concerns, internet access, and a whole host of things that are way out of a child's league. Even young kids love taking pictures of naked body parts, toilets, or anything they find that's forbidden. You will need to police their devices as well as your own for any naked kid pictures they may have added to your photo albums. It is illegal for those pictures to even *be* on your phone *or theirs,* so delete them right away. And, of course, have a nice long talk with your kids. Plan on repeating this conversation for years and years!

I really, truly believe that smart phones and all the things that come with them should have an age requirement. Like 18 or 21! Teenagers really can't handle the social media craziness, and they get hammered with it. I encourage you to keep the smart phones out of their hands as loooooong as you can. Once they've got them you're gonna need to police them. Talk about content. Discuss what's happening on all social media accounts. If your child was going to be walking through a red light district several times a day, then you'd probably be monitoring and talking about what they are seeing. Well, a smart phone is a porn hub, a red light district, a bully tool, a torture device, and assorted other things all in your child's hand, and hidden beneath a veneer of other truly cool stuff. That is a bit much for a child or teenager to handle without guidance.

E-readers

One device that you can feel pretty good about with your kids is an e-reader like a Kindle Paperwhite or a Nook. Now you might be thinking to save money by getting a multi-use tablet instead of an e-reader. They could use one device to both read and play games. And you're right. However, that becomes a problem. Maybe video game time is over, but they want to read. So, are they actually reading or just gaming some more while you're busy? On the other hand, if you have a separate reading device, then you can vault all the other devices while giving them free reign over the e-reader. You may need to confiscate the e-reader at bedtime, but that's a good problem to have.

Overall, my philosophy for kids and electronic devices is to view them as chainsaws. You can do great work and create beautiful art with a chainsaw, but you do need an adult level of brain maturation to independently handle it in a safe way. Chainsaws do not make good birthday gifts for kids. You don't hand them one and say "have fun!" You teach. You supervise. You continue to supervise until adulthood. TV, video games, tablets, smart phones, and chainsaws…same, same.

I also firmly believe that good, healthy, emotional development requires a child to be present in the real world most of the time. Our brains are not fully mature until we are in our 20's! If half of that brain's development is spent in virtual land, then that child is not getting the life experience they need. Certainly, a bit of screen entertainment is lovely. It's one of the simple pleasures of life. And to be clear, I'm all for time spent in day dreaming. That's just time inside the real world of your own head. But the virtual world and the false reality of the social media world? These cut both ways. Chainsaws.

NORMAN ROCKWELL OR REALITY TV?

My friend's girls were 6 and 5. Bright and lively, they raced about the yard. White blonde hair trailing behind, bare feet skimming the grass as they chased Luna the bunny. "Daddyo thought it would be fun to get some good quality walkie talkies for playing hide and seek with the girls," my friend said. She'd been researching the radios when he got eager, and jumped in to order them with a two day arrival. "It sounded like such simple fun," she said, shaking her head in dismay. "I figured the girls would hide at opposite ends of the yard while secretly conferring about dad's location. And Daddyo would pretend he didn't know where they were and keep up a monologue over the walkie talkies. "I'm gonna get you! I'm gonna get you!" The girls would giggle and then run until caught, and everyone would fall down and laugh!"

Instead, the girls fought over them constantly from the minute the walkie talkies showed up. Whose turn was it to talk? Who was standing where? What channel was to be used? Which handset belonged to whom? And on and on. When mom and dad tried to teach the girls how to use the handsets, one girl would listen, but the other would get distracted and start fiddling with the dials generating static and feedback and loud bleeps. By dinner time the girls refused to let go of the handsets. Even dad, the strict one, couldn't muscle the energy to extract them. With the devices now so close together, and tinkered with by small hands throughout the meal, there was a near endless cacophony of high decibel whining feedback broken only by louder bleeps and static, and of course parental yelling. "Stop playing with the handsets!" "Just eat your dinner!"

Having detailed her ordeal, my friend shook her head. "It seemed like such a fun idea."

I promise, something like this will happen to you. It will happen a lot! You'll plan some simple fun activity. A trip to the pumpkin farm on the weekend, maybe. Your 3-year-old is excited about Halloween, so you look up the local farm. They have a bouncy house, hay rides, and pumpkin pie by the slice. You can just imagine your little guy with his arms wrapped around his "bestest" pumpkin as he tries to carry it to the car. The sun is warm and the air cool. It will be a perfect Fall family day.

But "little guy" takes one look at the bouncy house and declares it "too green!" He throws his shoes at it, and won't put them back on. He won't go in the bouncy house. He only wants to smash the pumpkins. He throws hay on everyone during the hay ride, then drops his pants and pees off the front of the wagon! He won't eat pumpkin pie. He has a fit and won't be consoled. You have no idea why.

You hoped for Norman Rockwell and what you got is the worst of reality TV! Believe it or not this is normal! Very, very normal. Very, very common. You are not alone. I don't think I've ever met a parent who did not have this reality TV experience. Lots and lots of this experience. It's just one of those roll with the punches moments. Pack it up. Call it a lesson. Cut your losses. I will offer a bit of hope for the future. As the kids get older this all does get better. Somewhere between 6 to 7-years-old my kid's capacity for adventure without excessive drama markedly increased. I didn't say, "no" drama. Just less excessive drama…slightly less.

BEING SILLY, KEEPING IT POSITIVE

You will win more flies *and* better behavior with honey than with vinegar. And silliness can be the "honey" that lubricates the dramas and conflicts of raising young children. Let's say one of your kids is not really interested in learning how to put on their own shoes and socks. You, on the other hand, are sick of putting shoes on little kids and want them to learn this skill. After all, their twin has been getting dressed for over a year. However, this other child is happy to have someone else do the work. You think, "Aargh! We are *not* leaving until they put shoes on without help!" This is called "butting heads with a toddler." *Not* a good idea. Instead, try putting the socks on their ears and the shoes on their hands. They will happily correct you. Then put the socks in their pocket and shoes on their head! At some point, they're going to gleefully show you how to do it right. Win, win. Repeat, repeat.

ENJOYING YOUR CHILD'S SENSE OF HUMOR

In my experience, humor in young kids is pretty basic. Actually, it remains pretty basic for a while. So, become goofy, silly, and confused. Channel your inner Groucho Marx or a non-violent version of the Three Stooges. You'll need to model this for them, so practice "silly walks" like John Cleese. Walk into the room with an extra pair of pants on your head and act like everything is normal. Carry a load of laundry in your arms and keep dropping and picking up things with exaggerated moves. Kids love it when adults bumble or goof up, so do it on purpose. Look high and low for the kid that's right behind you. You can set the table for dinner by putting the dishes on the chairs. Then mix things up when they try to fix it. Have fun! I've found watching my kids develop a sense of humor to be quite wonderful. And they enjoy the bumbling adult long, long after they're old enough to know it's a game.

Once they're reading a bit you can offer them some kid's joke books. Then your road trips can consist of never ending "knock, knock" jokes and silly kid riddles. It's actually better than listening to some cartoon playing on a tablet for the 500 millionth time. It's also fun to encourage puns. In the beginning, they won't get the humor, but if you keep it up they will gradually come to appreciate the verbal word play. Most of their early attempts to make a pun will simply not make sense. Then they'll hit one smack on, and your heart will swell with pride at their punny perfection.

But beware! Dangerous roads are ahead! Pretty much all kids will suddenly become obsessed with potty humor around age 5. I remember when my neighbor's girl hit this stage, and I thought "Wow, I'm glad *my* kids don't do that." Ha, ha! What a newbie I was! They *all* do it when they hit the right age. It will probably start with giggling over the word "butt" and become more scatological as time goes on. The word "fart" is a guaranteed side splitter for years to come. Some parents find this extremely vulgar and attempt to squash it. But I promise you that even if you are no longer hearing it, (unlikely) the potty humor continues behind your back. Other parents (probably a lot of dads) will embrace their younger selves, and join in with the more flatulent humor. Honestly, the potty humor and pratfall stage goes on for many years. In our home, parents generally join in on the fart jokes and slapstick. I do try to shut down the pee and poop jokes because if I don't…. they will go on, and on, and on, and on,….forever! Sigh.

But, mix a silly walk… with a fart sound… and a good pratfall… guaranteed hysterical giggles for years to come!

PARENTING A KID WHOSE PERSONALITY DOES NOT RESONATE WITH YOURS

With young children, we tend to be very focused on behavior. This is understandable. They are wild and can behave wildly! But, there is more to parenting than just behavior. The other side of the coin is developing a relationship with each child. And that means seeing what each child has to offer. Learning about who they are. Acknowledging their best qualities. Mirroring back to them the beauty you see in their soul. But what if one of your kids is, well, different?

One of the bigger challenges in parenting can be having a child whose temperament doesn't resonate with your own. It's easy to connect with, and positively reinforce, the temperament of a child who is like us. It can be much harder with a child who is very different. Perhaps you have one child who is very outgoing and bubbly, and another whom you see as quiet and withdrawn. Your instinct may be to encourage the quiet one to be more socially forward if you yourself are a gregarious extrovert. But that quiet child may not be "withdrawn." They may just be thoughtful, private, or prefer one or two carefully selected friends picked after much evaluation. We all tend to see the world and others through the filter of our own experiences, yet we are also capable of empathy. We can step back and imagine being, feeling, and experiencing the world as a different person. This is an important parental skill. Our children are not us. Even when they are like us, they are still not us. They are themselves. Learning to see them for who they are allows us to reflect some of this back to them. And that is one of the most validating and loving things you can offer your child. It says, "I see who you are, and I love who you are."

This is especially important when interacting with a child you don't easily understand. You will need to be very, very careful to avoid favoring an easier sibling. Resist the tendency to see the "different" kid through critical eyes. You may have to work to identify and nurture strengths that seem alien to you. Think of what Dr. Karp suggests in *Happiest Toddler on the Block*. You are an ambassador to this being from a strange land. You have the honor of being among the first people to get to know them. Who will this remarkable creature be? How will they surprise you? How can you make them comfortable on this planet? Let this child see your joy in discovering and knowing them.

If you're concerned that you're not doing this job well, then get some outside perspective and help. Trusted friends or family may be able to offer you key insights. Otherwise, look for guidance from child development experts, counselors, or family therapists. Even a few visits with a professional can help you see things from a fresh angle. This can help shift your relationship to a better place.

SASS, SNARK, AND MONOSYLLABLES LONG BEFORE THE TEENS!

We all expect a certain amount of sass from teenagers. What you may not realize is that this behavior often starts much younger, like around age 6 or 7. Some parents get quite upset when their kindergartener suddenly sounds like a disrespectful teen. You may find your spine going stiff, and an angry retort on your lips. Try to keep that shock and frustration in check. It's not really personal. If you do fly off the handle, you'll just be modeling "how to yell at family." That's not exactly the skill you want to foster. Believe me it will be very hard to avoid yelling sometimes. Kids are going to push your buttons with great accuracy. It's always worse at the end of the day when you're tired, of course. Sometimes pausing to think about the deeper layers of what's going on can help you find the patience to moderate your response.

I've found backtalk at young ages typically comes from one of two sources. One is simply that your child is developing their separate identity. In the process, they are pulling back while asserting themselves. It means they need a bit more space to learn with less micromanagement. They may need a bit longer leash paired with increased responsibility. They may even benefit from a new privilege. Perhaps all of the above interventions are in order. At one point when my son and I had been butting heads a lot, I realized he needed me to trust him more. So, I loosened the reins. I trusted him to take care of certain things on his own. And, I stop hovering. Then I gave him more chores. I also gave him a bigger allowance. This cluster of big kid freedom, responsibility, and privilege cut the sass, snark, and grunts way, way, *way* back. Did he flawlessly manage his new partial independence? Well, no. But he did better than I expected, and continues to improve as he practices and learns new skills. Better yet, our relationship grew stronger as he recognized my trust in him.

There is, however, another common reason some kids resort to snipes or monosyllabic whiny grunts. Sometimes they are angry or hurt, and don't know how to express their distress. This is especially common if they are upset with a parent. These kids need you to help them identify and verbalize what they are feeling. In doing so, you help them to develop emotional intelligence and literacy. You will also improve your relationship with them and keep the doors of communication open as they grow. You don't have to agree with their interpretation of events. You just need to help them put words to their feelings so they understand what they are feeling. They also need to know that *you* understand what they are feeling.

Let's say there is a conflict, and your child makes a snippy comment or an annoyed whinny grunt then walks away. Give them, and you, a chance to calm down for a minute and then seek them out. Sit sideways to them to avoid being too confrontational. Then try something like this:

Mom, "You seem pretty upset, Hon." "Are you upset with me or with Dad?"

Child, "Dad."

Mom, "What happened?"

Child, "He yelled at me for hurting Janie, but it wasn't my fault! She started wrestling with me, and I fell on her by accident. Then dad yelled at me!"

Mom, "That must have hurt your feelings that he assumed you did it on purpose. Huh?"

Child, "Yeah, it's not fair!"

Mom, "I'm sorry you're so upset. Let's go talk with Dad so he can understand."

Then you go with him to whomever he's had the conflict with and help him express his feelings to them. Your child may be far from innocent in the event in question, but a conversation becomes possible when you help him verbalize his feelings. It could be that the conversation ends with you helping your child realize they are upset because they know they behaved badly and now regret it! Or it could be that mom or dad apologizes for jumping to inaccurate conclusions and passing judgement without all the facts. Either way, the process will educate your child on how his own feelings work, how to put words to them, and how to communicate them to other people. These are vitally important life skills.

So, when your young child starts with the sass and back talk, try not to take it personally. I promise, you're not alone. Almost all kids hit this stage at a far younger age than you are prepared for. So, prepare for it. Expect it. Recognize it as a stage and not an invite to war! Then step back and look at the bigger picture so you can figure out what this behavior is telling you about your child's current needs. If you can do that, you might just buy yourself a few moments to cool off, and not react when they manage to push your most sensitive buttons! That cool off time will let you respond in a way that will strengthen your relationship.

Here are two articles which address other aspects and approaches to these issues:

1. *5 Ways to Help Young Kids Communicate Their Emotions* by Margarita Tartakovsky, M.S. https://psychcentral.com/blog/5-ways-to-help-young-kids-communicate-their-emotions/
2. *Back Talk* by Jane Nelson, Positive Discipline.com https://www.positivediscipline.com/articles/back-talk

RELATIVES

Gift or curse. It's all relative. (har, har!) All puniness aside, you may find yourself seeing family from a new perspective after you have kids. You may grow closer to some family members as you see them through new eyes and fresh challenges. Others may become the bane of your already chaotic life. Leave your heart open to those you trust and let them help. "It takes a village" and when you let the village "in" you will build connections and relationships that will enrich your years with children. But, and it's a big BUT, don't be afraid to protect your children from challenging relatives. Perhaps you have a parent or an in-law who believes in scaring children into good behavior. Perhaps they tell enormous, frightening lies to your 2-year-old that gives them months of nightmares. Well, don't leave that in-law alone with your kids. Ever. No matter how much they push. If they tell your kids a lie, then turn to your kids and say, "That's not true. Grammie Tia likes to make things up sometimes." Then they know not to trust everything Grammi Tia says, and also learn they *can* trust *you* to help them when their world is confusing.

You may have a relative who slaps hands or says cruel things. Whatever the behavior is, it's your job to protect your children. Young kids have absolutely no power within a family structure. They are defenseless and you must step up for them regardless of your relative's feelings. You can teach your children to be respectful of elders without condoning hurtful behavior by ignoring it. You wouldn't hesitate to protect your babies from an angry stranger or a cruel nanny. Yet, sometimes we get conflicted when the bad behavior is coming from within our own family. In particular, the fear of disrupting the established patterns of family relationships can leave us confused about how to handle situations that now include our children. Do you placate and protect the feelings of your relative out of a fear of disturbing family harmony? Perhaps you will become the new target of their critical behavior if you challenge the status quo? Well, you are the boss of your children's lives. You are responsible for them and *to* them. Protect your kids. Be as diplomatic as you can, but don't feel guilty. The grown-up is a grown-up...at least theoretically.

Some parents grew up in very dysfunctional family environments. And that dysfunction can try to insert itself into the non-dysfunctional family life you are trying to build with your spouse and kids. Sometimes the challenge is a sibling. More often, it's one or both parents who are now grandparents. One key to managing your relationship with a difficult parent is learning to forgive them for not being the parent you've wanted them to be. No parent is perfect. I'm sure our kids will remind us of that someday! But some adults have parents who so badly failed them that the heartbreak lasts well into adulthood. It gets carried around within us, then when confronted with family events, it surfaces again in old family patterns of behavior and relationship. On some unconscious level, we continue to want them to be who we needed them to be when we were younger. Of course, they never will fulfill those needs. Really, really letting go of those needs, forgiving your parent for not being able to offer these things, and truly accepting that loss is both hard and potentially liberating. Once you can let go of your old needs, you can see parents for who they really are *now*. All the good and bad becomes more clear. And that frees you up to manage your interactions and relationships in a way that is healthy for you and your family.

Let's take Thanksgiving. Perhaps every time you gather at your parent's home you find yourself skewered through the heart by a parent whose favoritism of one perfect sibling is nauseatingly obvious. If you're still locked into the old family dynamics, you may go to Thanksgiving with the news of a new accomplishment to share, only to feel hurt when that parent trivializes it. On the other hand, if you've really let go of wanting your parent to praise you like your sibling, then you can look at the invitation to Thanksgiving and ask yourself, "what would be good for me?" You may decide not to go to your parent's holiday meal. Instead, you may decide to start your own family traditions at home. Your parents may bring on the pressure, "We want to see our grandchildren! You have to come!" Instead, you can make plans to visit for breakfast the day after or some other interaction that feels more manageable. You have the right to do this. You can find a way to meet your duty and obligations to aging parents, and still extract yourself, your family, and your little kids from people who can be toxic.

How you find a balance with a difficult family can take many forms. People are never cut and dry, good or bad. My husband's parents could be very challenging people. Smart and capable of great integrity, they led difficult and courageous lives. But they were also capable of cruelty, insensitivity, favoritism, and selfishness. As they got older some of the worst characteristics seemed to flourish. I was impressed by how their adult children seemed to manage them. First, they stopped calling them "mom" and "dad." Instead, they called them by their first names. I think it helped them to see their parents as just a couple of adults with whom they had a relationship. This made it a bit easier to let go of the past.

Next, they banded together and discussed things on the phone. My husband was the "golden child" and capable of no wrong in his parent's eyes. So, after making a plan with his siblings, he would take the lead and smooth the way as much as possible for the planned event. As the wife of the golden child, I basked in his glow. Thus, I too could help with challenging situations like taking the car away when their driving was no longer safe. Or bringing all the food to gatherings. Thus, we headed off their mother's stern requirement to fully consume all the meat she had cooked into a rubbery mass or vegetables boiled into grey mush. In this way, my husband and his siblings cared for their aging parents while looking out for each other along the way.

If you have difficult parents, think about calling them by their first name. Think about setting up some boundaries for you and your family. Think about how to create your own non-dysfunctional family and traditions. Think about how to meet your obligations to your parents while maintaining a certain amount of safe reserve. A reserve that not only protects you, but also your very vulnerable children. Forgive your parents. They will never be all that you need them to be. Once you let go, you can build something new and better for your own family.

CHANNELING ANCESTORS

Have you ever seen that ad on TV showing a young couple at home, and one of them is slowly looking and acting more and more like their parent? The waistband of their pants gets higher and higher. They sit funny. The glasses slide down their nose and they start obsessing over strange and obscure things. All the while, the other person in the couple stands by and watches, helpless. This really does happen. Channeling our ancestors. Sometimes it's funny. "Don't run with scissors!" Wow, you think, did I really say that? Then you look across the room at a small boy who has already visited the ER twice in his short life. You've no doubt he will achieve ER "frequent flier" status before he's even 5. You think, "Yeah, I said it, and I'll say it again. Just like dad used to yell at me."

You'll reach up and feel the scars on your head from the old stitches and head injuries of your impulsive youth. You will feel for your parents in a new way, perhaps calling them up to apologize for all you put them through. Connecting with them on a different playing field than before. But, not all ancestor channeling is quite so benign.

Sometimes it's the darkest spirits who have the tightest hold on us. Usually it's those "ancestors" we'd least like to worship whose influence insinuates itself like a dark shadow into our relationship with our child. It's painful to watch it happening in your partner, and even more painful to find it occurring in yourself. We swear. SWEAR! We will not do certain things our parents did to us…and then aaaargh! We do them! Why? Why? Sigh. I don't know. I suppose we internalize many of the things from our youth that we most try to reject. It becomes the dialogue we know. If you pay attention, you can make yourself aware of when you are repeating your parent's voice with your own kids. This is, of course, the first step. The trouble is the mere promise to do things differently is generally not enough. You've lived with this parental voice in your head all your life. You can't wave some scented smoke at it and hope it will retreat to the dark nether regions never to venture forth again. (Sorry, I was a theater major in college. I lean to the dramatic.) But you *can* beat this. You've just got a little work to do. Once you've realized what you don't want to be doing, then you need to decide what you DO want to be doing. Then, you have to practice. (Hmm, sounds kinda like Kazdin for grown-ups.)

Let's say, your mother always criticized your hair, and you've found yourself making critical comments about your 4-year-old's tangled locks. How do you help yourself change your unwanted criticism? First, write down three nice things to say about her hair, and practice saying them every day for a month. Keep a log to make sure you remember to say them. At some point, you'll look at her hair, and there's a good chance the thoughts that come into your head will be kind instead of negative. You win and so does your daughter.

Let's look at a more difficult challenge. Your father competed with you over everything. As a result, your relationship was never about him knowing and loving you. It was about his dominating you. Now you find yourself not wanting to take any guff from an assertive toddler The child is just stretching his wings a bit, but to you it *feels* competitive. At this age, it's really good for kids to experience winning at games. So, you can decide to let him win *all* games and wrestling matches. This removes the question of competition, and allows you to enjoy watching your son have fun playing and winning. You still have to deal with the emotions of "losing," but think of it as a gift and not a loss. Next, set a daily alarm on your phone and make it a rule that every day you tell him at least one thing you love about him. No matter what.

Many of us have various "inherited" parental behaviors we'd like to exorcise from our repertoire. If you write out a plan of what positive behaviors you *will* do, sign it, and have your partner sign it as a witness, then you'll have a better chance of sticking to your commitments. Seemingly little things like these can help us shift our mindset. It's a bit of cognitive therapy, and a bit of self-designed positive reinforcement. These techniques can help us cast out unwanted ancestors, and embrace more of the life we imagined for our children. When you find yourself able to give that gift to your child, you should feel damn proud.

BREAKING THE ICE WITH VISITORS

Whether it's new nannies or relatives visiting from far away, kids can be very reserved around new people. My sister-in-law visits about once a year and is particularly good at getting my shy kids to warm up. She always arrives with a wrapped or colorfully bagged gift in hand. Shortly after the adults had said their hello's, she'd wave the gift around enticingly. At this point, my young kids would be either hiding behind a parent or buried under pillows and giggling shyly. Their aunt would hand them the gift or just put it on the floor. Once they start opening the gift, she'd slide over, and join them on the floor. Then she just started playing with them and the new toy. Now that they were playing, the ice was broken. If you have a relative who visits infrequently or is unsure with young kids, coach them ahead of time and hand them a new toy to share with your children. The toy need not be big or expensive. The kids will invent a way to play with almost any new curiosity.

Fortunately, our relatives seemed to recognize when our kids were feeling shy and were respectful of our children's personal space. But some guests can be overly intrusive with young children. I feel it's *my* job to protect my kids from adults who, while well-meaning, wind up intruding on a child's personal space. If a greeting wouldn't be appropriate for an adult to give to another adult, then it definitely isn't appropriate for them to force the behavior on a less powerful child. So, if a new person reaches out to touch a child's face or hair, then you can step between them to block the uninvited touch. If the adult asks why you stopped them, explain that it feels intrusive to your child, and you are protecting them from unexpected touching. Hopefully, the adult get the message! As for hugs and kisses, my kids seem to enjoy good-bye hugs so I *invite* them to give a hug. "Do you want to give auntie a hug good-bye?" If they back up, I reassure them that they don't have to hug. Maybe I'll suggest they blow a kiss or wave instead. By protecting and respecting a child's personal space, you teach them that it's okay and even appropriate for them to resist the approach or touch of an adult who makes them uncomfortable. It's not a guaranteed protection against abuse, but it's a start.

If you're concerned about teaching children to show respect or manners to adults, I recommend modeling the behavior you want them to learn. But don't expect them to do it for a long time to come. Just let them watch the different social interactions. When do *you* hug? When do *you* shake hands? When do *you* offer just a nod? Frankly, there is no need for a child to be anything other than distantly respectful until the power dynamic between the child and adults has equalized. If they've been watching, then your older child can decide for themselves how they wish to greet people.

ORGANIZING TOYS, TEACHING CLEAN UP

Okay, this topic is important for your sanity. Honestly, I did much of it all wrong. Start teaching clean-up really early. Toddlers want to do what their parents do. You may think they are too young to set the table, but this is when you *start*. At 18-months-old, they can carry their sippy cup to their high chair. At 2-years-old they can set their cup and plate on the table. At 3, they can clear their plate to the sink. Give them a dustpan with a brush, and sweep the floor together after dinner. An empty spray bottle and a rag can get a younger child in on the cleaning action. Use non-toxic wet wipes, and let them wipe floors, tables, and baseboards. It doesn't matter if they actually succeed in cleaning anything. It does matter that you pull them into these activities as everyday family time. Letting your kids help, can make the chores take longer in the beginning. But, it pays off in a BIG way down the road.

This is a vital part of parenting children. They *need* to contribute. Childhood in America is a very prolonged process. Not being expected to contribute to the family can leave older kids bereft of connection and a sense of value. You start nurturing that involvement and contribution when they are very young. Besides, you truly will need their help as time goes on. Start young. Start simple. Gradually increase the skills. Try to make it fun.

The other part of the whole clean up issue is dealing with clutter. This is where I kinda dropped the ball. If you can, teach your kids to clean up after each activity. This sounds easy, but it's actually not. The problem is that you are not a childcare worker whose job is to be present with the kids every moment. You are a parent who has to do laundry, get the car fixed, make lunch, call your parents, get some work done, check email, peek at the news. As your child drops their Legos and reaches for trains you will be happy that they remain engaged without needing your attention. You will be thinking, "Great! I got a few more minutes to get this strange sticky gunk off the floor." You will not be thinking, "I need to make them stop and clean up the Lego's before they play with the trains." And besides, they'll start combining the Legos and the trains in a new and inspired way. Why squash creativity by asking them to put all the inspirational toys away in a box! By the time lunch is ready, the entire floor will be covered with toys. Now the job of clean-up has become overwhelming.

Your kids will learn to clean-up after themselves at pre-school. But it will *not* naturally translate to home. You'll need to work hard at it. One of my big mistakes was failing to reliably include *kid's* clean-up time into my estimates of the kid's activity time. Again, this may sound straight forward, but for me it was hard. It was one more overwhelming thing to "get the kids to do" in a busy day. So, all the mess would build up till the end of the day when my husband and I would sweep it aside and collapse. If you can, try to incorporate clean up as a routine step in your kid's play.

I also recommend minimizing the sheer volume of "stuff" in your home. This, too, is easier said than done. If you have multiple kids, you have multiple interests in the house. My son builds elaborate Lego inventions. My daughter paints, draws, makes puppets. So, I can't get rid of the Legos or the craft supplies. Multiply this issue by many interests and you wind up with...stuff...a lot of stuff! Some of it may seem like "junk" to you, but to your kids these are "their special things." If you get too ruthless with the "throw it out" process, you can hurt feelings making them feel disrespected. Try to minimize the stuff brought into the house, and do frequent reviews of what can be given away. Neither of my kids cared about the platypus stuffy...bye, bye Plattie. *Mommy* will miss you! You can also sneak a few things out of the house when the kids aren't looking, but be careful. You might get caught!

Toys can be organized into easy, categorized cubbies. However, remember that your helpful husband will not understand the organizational pattern and will put everything into random bins...sigh. I suggest you learn to live with way, way more clutter than you could normally stand. Since it's hard to vacuum around the clutter, there will be way more dirt than you'd like too! Think of it as a phase in your life. The dirt and clutter, barf and poop phase. Someday they will leave home and you can again live in a clean, uncluttered, and perhaps even stylish home. Or at least you'll know who is responsible if your place is still a wreck!

LIVING IN A DISASTER ZONE

For Hera's sake, do not buy anything nice in this stage of life! Your kids will destroy everything, *everything* you own. They will barf and poop on your pretty rug, your fancy sofa, and your elegant work clothes. The stains will be permanent. You will buy only washable markers, but the kids will somehow find the one hidden Sharpie and tattoo themselves and your leather recliner! Your pretty wooden tables will sprout red and green flowers and scribbles and scratches. You will pick up your lovely pashmina shawl only to discover strange linear slits cut into it at random places. It was underneath the wrapping paper that your kids were cutting into confetti. Giant holes and markings will appear on walls when you have no plans for demolition. In their rampant, joyous enthusiasm, children will break it all. If you think this is an exaggeration, then you are clearly a newbie. It all happens when you're not looking. You'll be dumbfounded by what can be destroyed in those few moments when your hypervigilance lapses.

If you need a rug, buy a cheap remnant or some thin scraggly thing that you won't mind throwing out when it's stained and gross after years of spit up and baby poop. If you need furniture, go for very sturdy and well padded. Your 5-year-old will jump on the arm of the sofa breaking the wood within. They will innocently stash sharp items under the cushions that will poke jagged irregular holes in the fabric. Remember that dark solids show lint while light solids show dirt. You'll want the anti-stain coating on everything. Except *DON'T* get the anti-stain coating, because it has PFC's in it and those are nasty, nasties! (See chapter on toxins.) Now is the time to be practical with your home furnishings. This has been challenging for me. I have an artsy designer soul, and I'm easily swayed by bright colors and inner visions of exotic and eclectic style. I have to keep repeating to myself, "They are going to trash it. They are going to trash it." When I forget, I go look at the broken sofa and the "decorated" wooden table. Think practical. Think sturdy. Think, "I won't care when they trash it." Fancy days will come later…much, much, later.

TOO MUCH STUFF

I'm not the Scroogey sort who thinks we should pare our lives down to the bare minimum. I enjoy buying gifts for people, and have a strange affinity for buying funky used chairs...usually bright orange ones. I especially like *cheap*, funky, used, orange chairs! Oh, be still my designer heart! Nevertheless, the extraordinary volume of stuff that comes with kids in this country is mind boggling. And it kinda sneaks up on you. It starts with cute infant clothes and double sets of everything for siblings. Then comes the toy explosion. The strollers in the garage begin to reproduce. Shoulda gotten them "fixed" sooner! (har, har!) There will be sit-and-scoot toys, tricycles, scoot bikes, three-wheel-scooters, bicycles with training wheels, two-wheel-scooters, skateboards, roller blades, hockey skates and on and on. The big items you can usually pass on to another child. But then there's the junk! Stickers, stickers, stickers! Sheets and sheets of stickers! Little plastic things from goodie bags that break, are thrown in the trash, and end up in a landfill or floating about the Great Pacific Ocean Garbage Patch. Wooden toys will be left outdoors to grow mold in the rain. Kiddie pools that sprout leaks by the end of summer, and get replaced every year. Plastic water slides that are too moldy to use the next summer. By the time your kids are school age you may be stunned by the number of "things" your family has gone through in just a few years.

But there's another category of baby purchases that pose a great cluttering danger. These are the "it will make life easier" items. I confess I was very vulnerable to this type of promise. "Buy this item and life will be easier!" Parenthooding can be tough in the early years, and anything that might, might, *maybe* might make things easier will feel like a must have. For example, is a Boppy pillow really so much better than the ones you already have? Do women around the world raise infants without Boppy pillows? Yes. Yet, it seems like such a necessary item to have before your baby arrives. (I bought two!) Finnish infants often sleep in cardboard boxes provided by the government. So, you may not even need a crib in the first few months. A quick cruise of the Internet led to this list of items many feel are not needed for infants:
- Wipe warmer
- Shopping cart cover
- Disposable placemats

- Pacifier wipes
- Pacifier case
- Baby food maker
- Bumper pads for crib
- Bumbo seats
- Baby shoes
- Infant socks
- Infant towels
- Baby laundry detergent
- Changing table
- Bathtub thermometer
- Baby oil
- Baby powder
- Formula maker
- Baby movement monitors
- Play gym floor mat
- Bouncy seat *and* swing (one is enough)
- Activity saucer
- Bottle drying racks
- Dishwasher baskets
- Crib rocker
- Baby soother
- Diaper genie with inserts

This list only covers the newborn stage. As kids get older, more categories of "needed" items begin to haunt your awareness. Alphabet speaking toys. Phonics tech. Developmental toys. Toddler home playgrounds. Water tables. Sand tables. Sand and water tables. Sticker charts. Stickers. Wheeled toys. Ride on toys. More ride on toys. Bigger ride on toys. Soccer ball. Soccer shoes. Soccer socks. Soccer shin guards. T-ball uniform, bat, ball, glove. And the occasional dirt bike. All along the way, there will be something to buy for "developing" and gearing up your kids. I'm not saying you can't get a Boppy pillow if you want one. Maybe it's exactly what you want. But do think twice before you buy stuff. It may *feel* like a crib rocker will save you from a fussy baby, but no item is going to rescue you from the challenges of early parenthood. Most likely, it will just become one more piece of accumulated junk in your home.

I have no magic or key wisdom for you on how to avoid this over consumption. Perhaps if you are more conscious of where all this heads, then you'll be able to negotiate the flood waters better than I did. Avoid all small plastic junk toys. Don't give them as rewards. Don't put them in birthday goodie bags. Go to second hand stores for as much as you can. Really, you can find great stuff at thrift stores. If you can find someone whose kids are a little smaller or younger than yours, then pass down outgrown clothes. At some point, someone will start passing things down to your kids and then everyone benefits. You'll be going through your kid's clothes every 4 to 6 months to weed out what doesn't fit anymore. I also recommend going through toys frequently to lighten the household load. I know it sounds Scroogey, but the less you have the easier it is to keep it clean. Not that *I* ever managed to *not* buy my kids that super cute dress or that platypus stuffy or that plastic construction truck that makes too many sounds. Sigh. Kids get cool stuff! That platypus stuffy was awesome! Personally, if I could find shoes in my size that had flashing lights in the heels, I'd snatch them right up! And maybe that's half the challenge. Toys for kids tickle our inner child and whisper "Get me! I'm so cool!" Just try to remember that you've got a pile of junk at home already.

PARENTING MICHELANGELO

Childhood activities tend to produce copious works of art. Up on the refrigerator they go. What magnificent splats and squiggles! A budding Jackson Pollock? Best to save these early works for future art historians. In the interim, there becomes the question of gallery space. As you fill the fridge's surface, you may begin stacking these master works two or three deep. By then, the magnets aren't strong enough to hold all the layers. Time to resort to tape and a nearby wall. Steadily, your space fills with baby scribbles. I mean, infantile art. Um, juvenile master pieces?

With time you may wonder if those early works of genius are actually noteworthy? At first, the extraordinary talent had been so evident. Now? That talent seems faded and washed out. Actually, if you look with a discerning eye, you may realize the construction paper *has* faded. So, has the magic marker. The paint and stickers are peeling off. And, this stuff if everywhere in your once stylish home! The horizontal surfaces of the house are overrun with baby toys in plastic primary colors, and now your vertical surfaces are covered in art work with rolled edges, scotch tape, and indecipherable content.

At this point, you may find yourself losing a bit of that sentimental edge. It will dawn on you that not *everything* your child creates is precious and worthy of preservation. Unfortunately, the full avalanche of "not worthy" creations is still ahead. They do come in fast and furious in pre-school, but the truly apocryphal flood of your little Michelangelo's art comes with kindergarten.

What to do with your 5-year-old's "self-portrait" as a firefighter? That's special, right? Hmmm, let's see. There's the one he did in day care, and the four from pre-school, and two from day camp, and one from grandma's house. He'll probably be coached through 500 more before kindergarten is over. You will also get rocks painted in splats of jarring colors, weird things made of popsicle sticks, twisted clay objects, papier mache things, and on and on. Better set up a display case for sculpture next to those gallery walls.

By now, you may feel the need to get rid of a few pieces of art. You could try auctioning them, but chances are you're not going to make big bucks. You could donate them, but most likely the grandparents will only take a few pieces off your hands. That will still leave you with a rather large inventory of, well, trash. Trash that your kids think is precious! A priceless work they want preserved for all time! Aaaargh! Deep breath. Deep breath. There is an answer to your predicament. Others have been there before you. We know the path well.

Start small. When the children are at school or asleep, you sneak one masterpiece into the trash. Be sure to bury it deeeep. Otherwise, your child who's never noticed a trash can in her life will suddenly hone in on the bin, and screech with wounded alarm that her *gift* to you is in the *trash*! You must be careful! You must use all the stealth of a Power Ranger, the speed of Rainbow Dash, and the cunning of Dora the Explorer. Little by little you can slowly reduce the volume of kid craft in your home. However, if you go *too* slowly, then the incoming tide of art will overwhelm. If you go *too* fast, the kids will notice!

It's true some people line up their kid's art each week and take a photo of the whole wall. With everything now preserved, their kids will let them throw it away without protest. But, my kids won't go for that. You may still wish to pull aside an occasional item that touches your remaining shred of sentimentalism. By now, however, you'll find few masterpieces with that much emotional pull. So, when you run out of wall space, you can stack the stuff in boxes. Once a year, when they have hopefully forgotten about last year's projects, you ditch the whole box. But, only if the kids are not home!

Oh, man! Even as I write this my 8-year-old daughter was taking out the trash when she spotted some of her brother's "art." I kid you not! This masterpiece is a stunning Halloween-style hand-turkey. Yes, a hand turkey with cotton ear swabs glued down to black construction paper for the skeletal hand bones or turkey feathers or whatever.

"Mom! Jimmy's turkey is in the trash!"

"Uh, er, he didn't want it anymore?"

Deep, people. When you put the art work in the trash put it down *deep*!

BUYING CLOTHES FOR NEWBIES

This seems silly, but I was so annoyed when I first ran up against it. Like, why didn't anyone tell me? Do all moms have to stumble on this without warning or just me? So, here's your heads up. You know how all the Halloween candy comes out three months before Halloween? Then when Halloween is still a month away, all the Thanksgiving stuff comes out? Then before the first of October hits, the *Christmas* candy is out!? Well, with kid's clothes it's even crazier. Half way through summer your girl will outgrow all the shorts you bought her two months ago. You'll go to the store to buy shorts. And all you'll find is long fleece pants! Store after store will be full of puffy winter coats and fleece lined boots even though it's 95 degrees outside! In January you'll wade through the snow looking for fleecy footed PJ's. Nope. Tank tops and sundresses will fill the racks. You may have slightly better success online, but often sizes are running out. You have to buy your kids clothes a season in advance while trying to *guess* what size they will need six months from now. It's really crazy. But now you know so you don't have to look like a total newbie parent, and wander into a kid's store looking for a winter coat…in the winter! I mean, really! What were you thinking?!

Frankly, thrift stores will often have in-season clothes. If you have one nearby, it's worth regular browsing. In the beginning, you may have sentimental attachment to some of your kid's clothes. Before long, however, you'll become accustomed to throwing out or passing on whole wardrobes every season. I always buy my kids clothes on the big side. Yet, they truly outgrow a season's clothes before the season is over. So, buy used. Go thrift. Pass it on.

Oh, and consider having your kids change out of their school clothes, and into play clothes when they get home. I know that's an old-fashioned idea, but kids can really trash their clothes. You want to send them to school in clothes they can really get dirty, but you'll also be hoping for them to *start* the day looking cared for and kinda clean. This is much harder to do when they have stained and trashed every single piece of clothing they have. That's why you see all those little "urchin" kids running around. Those are kids like mine who did *not* change clothes when they got home from school. Instead they went straight into the pond to "play diving for frogs." Yeah, learn from my mistake. Establish a rule that you change into "play clothes and play shoes" after school. If you manage it, you'll thank me for that bit of wisdom one day.

OWNING vs. SHARING TOYS AND THE STRANGE POWER OF KITCHEN TIMERS

Many parenting books will tell you to make sure each child has toys that belong specifically to them. I found this was important when the kids were a bit older, but not before age 5. With the exception of each child's favorite lovey, we kept all toys as "share toys." Learning to share toys is something that twins must learn at a very young age, and I have never found any down side to this rule. It may be harder if you're adding a new baby to a family with an older child. I'd encourage you to raise your first child with the idea that the toys belong to mom and dad, not the child. This doesn't need to be harsh. Try, "Do you want to play with mommy's train set?" or "Time to put daddy's toys away." As they get older and a bit more mature, you can allow them the privilege of "owning" and item or two. It will help with sharing when other children come along as they will have seen you modeling "sharing" your toys. This doesn't mean your kids will truly appreciate the toys you so generously provide nor miraculously enjoy sharing with grace and patience. You are still going to have to teach them "how" to share.

One of the most useful tools for teaching kids how to share is the kitchen timer. I like the digital ones that continue to beep until you turn them off. When your kids are fighting over a toy you say, "We'll do turns. I'll get the timer." Then you start with a very short play time for the first turns. We'd usually do 30 seconds to one minute for the first few turns, and increase to 2 minutes and later to 5 minutes...if needed. Often after the first few turns they lose interest in the toy, and you're done! But here's the big secret. The timer has strange magical power. No, really, it does! If you time 30 seconds on a clock or phone, and tell the child it's time to switch, you will get protestations and a toddler fit. If you set the timer and let it keep beeping while you tell them it's time to trade, they just hand over the toy and wait! Yes, you could probably use your phone for this. But you don't want to introduce competition for your phone into the toy issue. I recommend you keep that tucked out of their line of vision for as long as possible. Get yourself a simple beeping timer. You will find it has power in a wide range of situations. Time to go home, time to sit on the potty, time to get shoes on. An older child can use a timer to learn how to regulate their computer time. A kitchen timer is a truly powerful tool.

USING REWARDS WITH TWINS OR SIBLINGS

Sticker charts and rewards are a useful form of positive reinforcement. In *The Kazdin Method for Parenting the Defiant Child,* the author details how to use them effectively. I'd like to highlight a few sibling specific issues that occur when implementing a reward based program. If you have two children who are working on the same behavioral task, then you provide them each the same rewards for successful behaviors. If, however, you have one child working on a task that the other has already mastered, then it helps if the working child earns rewards for *both* kids. Otherwise your non-working child will say it's not fair that they don't get to earn stickers or prizes. Sometimes you just don't have anything for the other kid to work on. If the working child earns rewards for both kids then siblings can support and encourage each other. Everyone is happy and celebrating when the working child succeeds.

Remember that what each child considers a worthwhile reward can be different. My daughter was easily motivated by a sticker on a chart. However, this was uninspiring for my son. He needed something a bit more substantial like a Hot Wheel. Fortunately, I did find they were both equally motivated by three chocolate chips. If you can't find something mutually exciting, then you're going to need to bump the sticker prize kid to something more substantial. Or you can have a reward bag they can pick from.

When using a reward, whether it's a sticker, a toy, or praise you want to give the reward as soon after the good behavior as possible. The younger the child the harder it is for them to appreciate a delayed reward. So, give it right away with praise. You can also have stages of rewards. They might get three chocolate chips right away along with praise for putting on their own shoes. Then when they have gotten rewards for five days they get an additional bigger prize and praise. You don't need to keep this up forever, but do continue long enough for them to solidify the skill. Then you can switch to just verbal praise.

DOLPHIN TRAINING

You can pick up parenting tips from all kinds of places. The zoo. The aquarium. Both are loaded with insights. Dolphins spend their lives zipping around in three dimensional space while pursuing one bright shiny object after another. Sound kinda familiar? Yet, these aquatic mammals need regular check-ups by supervising vets who must somehow convince an intelligent creature to swing by for a needle poke in the flipper, some goop in the eye, or a scope in the throat. So how do you convince a dolphin to participate in such an unpleasant visit? With treats, of course! Yummy fishy treats! Guess what. It works for kiddos too. Okay, not the fishy part, but chocolate works almost as well.

As soon as my kids were old enough to chew and swallow, I made it a point to bring small treats to all doctor's visits. Chocolate chips in a little plastic container were always at hand. Before the doctor came into the room, I'd place the container on the counter. The kids were told they'd get three chocolate chips when the doctor was finished with the exam. As soon as the doctor was done, they immediately got those chips. They would get three more if they needed a throat swab or a shot. When we had unfortunate occasions for a blood draw and an I.V., they earned ice cream. By this time, we had a well-established and trusted routine of rewards for difficult medical visits. Did they cry? Well, yes, of course. It's still hard for a child to go through these procedures. It's hard for many adults to go through them. They also walked in on their own and fought hard to cooperate despite their fear and pain. That's a *lot* of brave from a little one's heart! It's not just the candy that gets you there, of course. It's the promise and consistent follow through of a lovingly given treat that can be a gentle balm to a tired and stressed little soul. The small gift and the time you take in sharing it with them can become an expression of your love and comfort. Or you could just think of it as dolphin training.

P.S. Always bring their loveys to the doctor visits!

FEEDING KIDS AND INFANTS, FAMILY MEALS

The goddess of all things related to feeding kids is Ellyn Satter, nutritionist and author of *Child of Mine: Feeding with Love and Good Sense*. This is probably one of the *very* best parenting books you'll find. In our world of crazy food anxiety, her book is truly a "must read." I also find that her basic parenting approach also applies to other aspects of raising kids. Satter speaks of the division of responsibilities. It is the adult's job to pick *what* food will be offered, *where* it will be offered, and *when* it is offered. It is the child's job to decide *if* and *how much* of any given food they will eat. This division of duties is ultimately very respectful of appropriate emotional boundaries between parents and children. It is the parent's job to provide the food and structure that will give the child the opportunity to learn to eat a variety of foods. It is the child's job to learn to eat at their *own pace*. It is not the parent's job to short order cook or cater to their kids. It is not a child's job to eat when not hungry or learn to eat at someone else's pace. It is not a parent's job to "make" a kid try something nor is it a child's job to try something when they are not ready. It may surprise you, but learning to eat can take a long, long time!

Think about it. Newborns need time to learn *how* to breastfeed or take a bottle. There are hundreds of muscles in the mouth and throat that need to work in a coordinated way to bite, chew, and swallow. Just think of all the completely new and hugely different tastes, textures, and smells a child must become accustomed to while learning foods. Not that long ago your child, whom you may now want to be a gourmet foodie, was just a wiggly half blind lump! Furthermore, we are born with an instinct to be leery of strange foods in our mouths. Look at it from an evolutionary perspective. If you're a toddler wandering in the woods with your pals and sticking random leaves in your mouth, then you run the risk of being poisoned. Better to chew a bit, and spit it out. On the other hand, if famine strikes your hunter-gatherer clan, then a child who will eat anything may have a better chance at survival. Thus, we might expect humans to have a pretty wide range of food acceptance. So, don't be surprised if you've got one kid who loves everything they eat and another who's too suspicious to try most offerings.

"But, but, but!" you sputter. Isn't it a parent's job to teach them to eat their vegetables!? They *must* have them to grow their brain. We're talking vital nutrients here! And what about when they have to go to a business meeting with the boss, and all they'll eat is french fries! EEeeeeeeek! Must. Make. Them. Eat. Broccoli!

Easy, there. Deep breath. Let's go back to Satter's division of responsibilities. You provide the choices of *what* food is offered, *where* it is offered, and *when* it is offered. Your child decides *if* they will eat it at all, and *how much* they will eat. There are three other parental tasks to make this work. First, with regard to when food is offered, it's important that you are providing regular consistent meals and snacks. That way if a child refuses to eat a meal, you can both be assured that another opportunity to eat will be coming soon. Between meals and snacks, you do not allow grazing or sipping calorie filled drinks. Then they will be ready and eager by the next meal. The second point has to do with *what* you offer your children to eat. Make sure that there is something appealing to them at each meal or snack. Yes, you heard that right. There may be new or challenging foods that you're presenting, but you must also have an easy food on offer. So, if you have a starchaholic child, then a snack might be - carrots, dip, and *crackers*. They may only eat the crackers. That is OK. You can make dinners to adult tastes, but have bread and milk on the table for everyone. Or maybe in your home it's rice and milk or pasta and cheese. I like to also have fruit on the table at dinner. Something easy for the child to eat when they don't want to experiment.

"But, but, but!" you sputter. "Then they will never eat anything else!" Actually, if you truly, *truly* don't push or pressure them, eventually they will make the task *their own* and start to experiment. In the beginning, it will be slow going. Maybe they will start by just looking at the other foods on the table. Maybe they will smell something as they pass the serving bowl. Maybe they will dip a finger in something. One day they may chew something and then spit it out. That's okay! Some kids are chewers and spitters for a long, long time.

Try to imagine this. You're a seventh generation American, born and raised on hamburgers, fries, and corn dogs. You find yourself on a year-long sojourn to a small town in remote China. All day long you are learning the language and customs and local etiquette. By the end of the day you're exhausted, and you find yourself looking for a meal in the town's night market. Are you going to go for the nice, safe, easy noodles and broth? Maybe the fried dough? Or will you try skewers of roasted chicken uterus and scorpions? Most likely, you'll pick something easy the first few months. Slowly, as the sights and smells of the market become more familiar you might decide the meat on a stick does smell kinda good. Knowing full well that the noodle soup is nearby if needed, you may gradually begin to explore new foods. A child lives their life like a tourist in a foreign land. Everything is new. They are constantly making mistakes and being corrected. If food is not an area where they feel naturally comfortable, then who can blame them for not wanting to try your miso-glazed salmon on a bed of black lentils? And just because your *other* child likes everything doesn't mean there is anything wrong with your refuse-nick.

I personally am a foodie. I love a huge variety of tastes and flavors. I love to experiment with new foods, and have been an adventurous eater from a very young age. I was the kind of kid who was easy and very satisfying to feed. It feels good as a parent when our children enjoy the nourishment we provide. However, I am one of four kids. Not all of us were quite so excited about foods.

This brings us to one of the other common parental fears about what their children are eating. "They must eat a variety of foods to get the nutrients for good growth." Right. Well, here's the thing. We are not living in a time or place of famine. In fact, we live in a time and place of great excess of calories. Children with medical conditions or severe behavioral disorders will certainly benefit from a consultation with a nutritionist. But, most picky eater kids in the U.S. are going to get adequate calories and nutrients to grow just fine. I personally am well acquainted with two individuals whose childhood food repertoire was extremely limited. Yet, they grew just fine into their high IQ's and PhDs. And...and! As adults, they slowly expanded their food palate all on their own!

So, if you have a picky eater, decide that they're actually a *careful* eater, a *discerning* eater, a *supertaster*, or maybe a *thoughtful* eater. Then back way, way off on the pressure and let *them* own the process of learning to eat. If you keep this as a battle, you will ultimately lose. Stop worrying, and let it go. Stick to the rules. Make sure something is accessible to your children at meals, but do not cater to them or cook them separate meals. You provide the *what*, *when*, and *where* of meals. They do the *if* they eat and the *how much*. I strongly encourage parents to read Ellyn Satter's book, *Child of Mine: Feeding with Love and Good Sense*. Her advice starts with feeding infants and offers guidance through early childhood. She covers so much more in her book, and it's just brilliant.

ADVANCED PRACTICAL TIPS FOR PARENTS OF "PICKY EATERS"

While keeping Ellyn Satter's guidelines firmly in the front of your mind, and only after you've been practicing them for a long time, you might find a few of the following ideas useful. For some kids, their "pickiness" might have to do with texture or the way in which a particular food is presented. When my son was nine, his only vegetables were the very, very tips of asparagus dipped in ranch dressing or the very, very tips of broccoli if covered in melted cheese. Sometimes, *sometimes* he would eat these veggie bits. Both vegetables he ate spontaneously, by his own choice, despite having refused them for years. However, my veggie discerning son loves pureed soups. This has become a way for me to introduce new flavors to him through a door that's already partly open. I see it not as "getting vegetables into him," but rather as giving him opportunities to experience the world. It's the same as taking him ice skating or hiking or giving him paints. He may wind up loving art or not caring about it. It's his choice. In addition, if I know he likes ice skating, then I might introduce him to roller skating. I know he likes pureed soup, so I offer soup sometimes. For example, I'll sauté onions in butter, then add thin sliced celery, and chicken broth. Puree it in a blender, call it "butter soup," and offer it as an appetizer. You don't need to hide what's in it, but giving it an appealing name works at any fine restaurant. In this way, the range of flavors that my son enjoys is expanded by simply noticing he likes pureed soups and capitalizing on this fact. In the process, I've also added a whole assortment of soups and broths to *my* culinary repertoire. When you don't have time to cook, grab a can of vegetable soup, and put it in the blender! Adding a dash of seasoned rice wine vinegar and a favorite spice makes all soup better.

HOME MADE BABY FOOD OR FROM THE JAR?

I suspect that the babies who eat homemade baby food are mostly first-born singletons with a stay-at-home mom or a full-time nanny. By the time the second kid comes around or if you have twins the time dynamic shifts, and homemade baby food becomes complicated. If your baby is eating at the same time as the grown-ups, then perhaps you can just grind up some of the adult food. Right? However, it's generally not possible to spoon feed a baby, and eat your own meal at the same time. So, babies often get fed their solids at different times from the family meal. That means someone would have to separately cook and grind food for baby's every meal. This may be possible with just one kid, but the demands of twins or an older child with their own schedule could make this very hard. Yes, some parents do manage this. But, please don't feel that you are failing your child if you feed them from a jar or a squeeze bag of beets and pears. The hyper-perfectionism and endless demands expected of mothers these days is beyond ridiculous. Really. Is a single working mom with twins who works three jobs "failing" her babies if she feeds them jar food? No?

Well, then, neither are you. A little perspective is good here. Is it easier to reduce your child's exposure to bisphenols if you make your own food? Yes. Is this the sole determinant of their lifelong health and well-being? No. If *not* making baby food gives you more time to interact with your baby or take a minute for yourself, then that is time well spent!

PERSPECTIVE ON THE DIRECTIVE: FAMILY MEALS, QUICK DINNERS

We need to keep some perspective on the directive to have family meals. Gathering the family on a regular basis to sit together for a meal is a valuable investment. If you keep mealtime low stress and open, then just being together can create a solid touchstone in a child's day. So, I work hard to have sit down dinners. But, *BUT*, I don't have my kids involved in evening activities. I don't have older children with conflicting time needs. My husband and I don't have evening obligations. I'm currently a stay-at-home mom. All of these things make it possible to have those family dinners. When I was working and the kids were younger, it was very, very hard to swing the family dinner. If we'd had the benefit of a nanny at that time, we would have had her feed the kids before we got home from work. Maybe you can manage family meals on the weekends or certain nights of the week. That is good enough! If you are working, please don't feel you need to race around and cook some elaborate dinner every night. There's cooking a meal, and there's assembling a meal and they are both just fine. The point is to gather and connect.

If you *are* rushing home and pulling together a meal every day, then it can help to make a list of easy to stock and assemble meals you can pull together in 10 minutes. This may not be "cooking" the way it used to be, but it gets everyone to the table. It's okay to included foods that are easy for your kids. You can bump up the adult interest by adding a bag salad. I build my lists around my families current favorites. Generally, I put fruit out at every meal too. To give you an idea, here's the list from when my kids were 2-years-old.

QUICK DINNERS:

Bag salad, fruit, milk, a starch, plus…

1. Hummus or cheese, pickles, olives, crackers. Over time we varied the cheeses. Now my kids eat Brie with fig jam, Manchego with quince, Pepper Jack, and aged Gouda.
2. Grilled cheese sandwiches with tomato soup and coleslaw.
3. Meat loaf, roasted carrots, toast. Make and eat it on the weekend, then warm the leftovers.
4. Hot dogs/brats/meatballs/fish sticks with Tater Tots and peas.
5. Lentil soup or canned chili with cheese "sprinkles" and honey toast or leftover rice.
6. Yogurt, cereal, and fruit.
7. French toast with sausage, and fruit.
8. Eggs w/ cheese (maybe some spinach) and Kashi frozen waffles.
9. Pot stickers (pre-made and frozen) with dip and peas.
10. Quiche (from store or weekend leftover) with fruit.
11. Cream cheese and crackers w/ fruit.
12. Nachos w/ beans, salsa, and cheese sprinkles.
13. Spaghetti and jar sauce, with fruit.
14. Dinosaur chicken nuggets, peas, and pasta with garlic oil and parmesan cheese.

I also look for ready-made sauces to dump over chicken or other leftover meats, and pair it with rice/toast/noodle and fruit. I usually add a veggie to the sauce. You can easily find Mexican, Thai, and Indian simmer sauces, as well as gravies.

Dessert:

Chocolate yogurt, pudding, ice cream, rice pudding, pumpkin pie, custard pie. The last two are make or buy on the weekend, of course.

Appetizers:

Chex mix, raspberries, a small slice of pumpkin pie, a few chips, 1 or 2 crackers with jelly. Basically, whatever is on hand that is fun to eat.

When my kids were little they liked this idea of "appetizers." A small bowl of something enticing would lure them happily to the table giving me a few more minutes to pull things together.

These were weekday meals that worked for my family as long as we added a salad and fruit. My kids are older now, and as their meat chewing skills improved, our menu steadily expanded. But, you can still keep fish sticks and frozen tilapia around for nights when the chef is on strike!

THE DRUDGERY FACTOR OF THE DAILY DINNER

Before I had kids, I would have told you that I loved to cook. Now I speak with much more ambivalence and many more qualifiers. Making family meals, of any kind, day after day, night after night, year after year...wheeww. It's a lot of work! It's important work. Feeding the family. Bringing everyone together to talk. Creating that consistent pause in the day. Still, some days everyone is like, "Wow! This is yummy!" Other days you make favorite foods, and all you hear, "I'm not hungry" or "I don't like it." Tomorrow, of course, you've gotta do it all over again. Typically, families aim to gather for dinner, which is when everyone is exhausted from a busy day. It can be quite challenging to keep up this routine day, after day.

Parenting advice columns offer a wonderful solution to this difficult time. It goes like this: Every Saturday morning, Mom, it's always a mom, heads off to the grocery store and gathers supplies for a cooking extravaganza. Then she goes home and spends half her Saturday madly cooking, and packaging, and freezing multiple gourmet homemade nutritious and delicious dinners for the whole week. Then for good measure she pre-makes everyone's fiber packed, high protein, gluten free breakfast muffins and freezes them too! I'm sure she sings prettily while she cleans up the gargantuan mess in her kitchen. I mean, really. This junk just makes me mad! There are so many families racing frantically through their days, and then we put this ridiculously unrealistic expectation out there like it's a reasonable solution. You have no free time during the week? Well, then, give up your little bit of free time on the weekend to spend hours laboring in the kitchen! And why is it always the moms who are making a week's worth of dinners? The articles never have mom *and* dad chopping away in the kitchen preparing the family meals?! Look, if you enjoy spending a lazy morning stirring a pot, by all means have fun cooking for your family. But please, *please*, do not feel like you need to spend your precious free weekend time cooking if you'd rather sit and read, take the kids for a walk, or really do anything else! There are a million ways to feed a family. The purists just have too much time on their hands.

Maybe you've been doing the daily dinner thing…FOREVER and are just dying to turn in your apron and call it quits. Here are a few ideas to reduce the drudgery factor a wee bit. Make one night a week "cereal night" and another could be "frozen food night." Really, whether it's Indian from Whole Foods, Amy's Mac and Cheese, or Stouffers spaghetti and meatballs, you can probably find something to satisfy everyone without the hassle of cooking and clean up! Another night could be "cheap eats out night." Divide up the remaining nights between two partners, and you've eased everyone's burden. If, *if,* you are also following my instructions and continuing to teach your kids life skills, then you can slowly start them with cooking dinner once a month and build up to once a week. Now, you're really gettin' the team spirit!

PROPER BEHAVIOR AT THE TABLE…OR JUST GETTING THERE!?

It used to be that in rich and poor families alike, children under 6 or 7 were fed before the rest of the family. The belief was they were too young for the adult table. They would sit in the kitchen snarfing down their food, then be sent off to play. They were not expected to sit around using proper table manners while the grown-ups droned on.

You should also realize that when you call a young child to the table for dinner, you are interrupting them. It doesn't matter how many warnings you've given them. You are interrupting something. Their brains are flitting from one thing to another following a barrage of intriguing sights and sounds. And they want to react to all of them. They are living in their own "here and now." Telling them to leave their own exciting moment to come to the boring old table, is not likely to get an adult style prompt response. They are BUSY with much more important stuff. Like going through all the kitchen cabinet doors to see which ones have working safety latches and which ones are broken...and what's inside... hmmm, cool, glass bowls!...wonder what they sound like when you bash 'em together?!

This is why I like the appetizer trick. Because you can call them to something exciting that's happening right now. Just don't do it too early or you'll lose them once they've finished their first course! It's important that you don't expect too much of a 2-year-old when it comes to table manners. Don't expect them to be able to hang around very long once they are done eating. It is, however, reasonable to not allow the throwing of food. If they throw food say, "Oh, I see you're done." Remove their plate, and send them from the table. Stick to your guns on that one.

Praise any child who keeps their food on the table or high chair. Slowly, slowly as they mature, introduce manners like not licking the serving spoon, and using a napkin instead of their shirt (some never learn that one). Pick your battles and don't expect too much conformity to adult norms. Better to have happy, pleasant meals than ones full of stress and criticism. You want these kids coming back to the family table when they hit their tweens and teens.

AIR TRAVEL WITH TWINS OR 2 TODDLERS

How do you take a plane ride with young twins or a mess of toddlers? Scream in terror and run the other way! Har, har! Okay, let's get real.

This topic generates much anxiety, and is one that came up again and again on our parent's website. In this section, I'll review important points and tips for making air travel doable. You can do this!

First, some airline rules. If you are traveling with a child under age 2, you may be asked to show a birth certificate so bring a copy. Second, there is only one extra oxygen mask per section of seats. This means only one "infant in arms" is allowed in each section. If you have two children under age 2, and don't want to buy a seat for either of them, then the adults holding the kids will have to be seated in different sections. Otherwise, there wouldn't be enough oxygen masks for everyone. Two adults with lap children can be seated across the aisle or in different rows. If you buy one plane seat and put in an infant car seat, it will have to be in the seat next to the window. Otherwise, the car seat would block movement in that row. If you are going to use two infant car seats, then they will have to either be in the window and middle positions or in the windows of two different sections. Some airlines will not allow one parent to fly solo with two infants, so check the rules beforehand. (Frankly, I wouldn't recommend traveling solo with two infants.) Generally, children over a certain age (usually age 2) are required to have a purchased seat. International flights can have different rules. So, check with your airline before you book your flight.

BABES ON A PLANE

Alright, you've got some of the airline the rules down. Let's say you are traveling with infant twins. First, decide if you want to buy seats for them or not. Consider five factors. First, how long is the flight? Is it one hour, or six hours, or 16 hours? Second, will you be in the air at nap-time? Third, do you have easy to calm, laid back babies or colicky, fussy, hard to soothe babies? Maybe you have one of each? Fourth, how heavy are your babies? Can you hold a one ton babe in your arms for the entire flight? Fifth, in general, are you stressed out and wacko about parenting right now or more calm and relaxed? (ha, ha!)

My husband and I took our twins on a plane trip when they were 9-months-old. It was a short flight of 1.5 hours. We decided to buy a seat for my son, who was huge and heavy. Then we brought a strap on baby carrier for my daughter. Most airlines require you to take infants *out* of strap on baby carriers during take-off and landing. (I don't really get this, but that's the rule.) My son slept in his car seat for the whole flight. My husband slept in his plane seat for the whole flight. I walked up and down, up and down the aisle with my fussy daughter for most of the flight. At the end, I managed to sit in an awkward slouched position with her asleep on my chest. My back hurt and my bladder was full, but I didn't dare move! Would it have been easier if we'd bought seats for both kids? Maybe. Maybe not.

Be aware that changing diapers in an airplane bathroom is quite a challenge. Some parents suggest giving your nearby passengers a quick heads-up, then changing the diaper on the floor in the aisle or on your seat. I have no idea what the airlines think about that, but it is certainly easier than using that cupboard they call a bathroom. Either way, you'll want to have a small packet for each kid with just the basics: two diapers, small pack of wipes, changing pad, bag for dirty diaper disposal, cream, and hand sanitizer. Keep the clothing changes in a bigger diaper bag with back-ups of everything.

You may also want to pack some premixed formula. It can help your babies equalize their ear pressure if they are sucking on a bottle during take-off and landing. A certain amount of formula or bottled breast milk is allowed through security. However, the security officers may ask you to open the bottles, then wave a test strip over the open container. You may also find that at one airport they don't test anything, and at another they make you open every container even sealed infant Tylenol. It's probably a good idea to check the most current list of allowable items and requirements before you pack for the flight.

Most airlines continue to allow families with young kids to board first. However, much to my surprise some airlines no longer offer this simple accommodation. It makes a big difference if you have that extra time and space to board the plane. You are going to be hauling two kids, maybe two car seats, a bag for each parent, and diaper gear. You may also be gate checking a double or two single strollers. That's a lot of juggling! Flight attendants cannot help you belt in your child's car seat. So, someone is going to need to hold two babies while the other person sets up the seats. It's hit or miss as to whether the attendant will hold a baby for you or not. If your kid is in a stranger anxiety stage then you may not *want* them to help!

So, how do you get the stroller, the car seats, the kids, and the carry-ons from your car to the gate, down the boarding ramp, through the aisle, and to your seats? There are several options. You can buy a folding set of wheels that is designed to carry a car seat like a rolling piece of luggage. (Go-Go Kidz or Go-Go Babyz Travelmate or Brica Smart Move or Britax Travel Cart) Put the child in the car seat with the wheels attached, and use it as a stroller in the airport. You will probably have to detach and reattach the wheels from the car seat for security checks and again when boarding the plane. You will either have to do this one handed while you hold a baby or hold both kids in a double carry-up while someone else handles the bags. With this set up, you either pull another bag for carry-on supplies or use a backpack. If you also want to bring a stroller to your destination, put it through with checked bags. Strollers are a free allowance separate from other checked baggage.

Another option is to purchase a small set of straps that attach a car seat to a regular rolling carry-on bag. Again, you will find you have to attach and detach the car seat from the luggage when going through security and when boarding the plane. You may find yourself at the plane door with two kids, two roll-on bags, two car seats, a diaper bag, a purse, a computer bag, and two adults. That equals nine items and four hands. So, think it through. If you do find yourself in this situation, try leaving one parent holding both kids while waiting on the boarding ramp. The other parent can then ferry in and install both car seats, and stow the carry-on bags. Once you have everything settled, then both parents can take a child to a prepared seat.

Another option and my preferred technique works as follows. One parent takes the kids down the entrance ramp in a double stroller with the diaper gear stored in the stroller. The other parent takes the car seats down the entrance ramp. At the door to the plane, one parent prepares the car seats, takes them onto the plane, and does the install. Meanwhile, the other parent can wait outside the airplane door with the kids in their stroller. Once the car seats are installed on the plane, both parents can take the kids and diaper bag out of the stroller and gate check it right there. Having the stroller at the end of the entrance ramp means you don't have to double-carry-up two infants or toddlers while everyone waits impatiently for the car seat set up.

Another advantage to this plan is that the kids are in a familiar stroller while you are killing time in airports. They are also in familiar car seats on the plane. Remember, that regardless of the number of car seats you take *on* the plane, you will need two car seats at the end of your flight for a rental car or a family car. So, if you don't bring car seats on the plane, then be sure to check them as baggage, reserve them with your car rental, or arrange for family to have them ready for you at pick up.

AT YOUR DESTINATION

You'll want to plan sleeping arrangements for your destination. Any family you're visiting may be able to borrow, rent, or buy pack-n-plays for infants or toddlers. These can also serve as play areas if the home you're visiting is not baby-proofed. A safe place to put your babies down can make a trip much more relaxing! Our kids were pulling up and cruising on furniture when we took our first trip to visit my bachelor brother. His house had tile floors, sharp cornered tables, loose rugs, and a million fragile, antique, and first edition books right at toddler eye level. My husband and I *never* relaxed the whole time! When your kids are young, try to go places where you'll find helpful baby holders and childproof homes. It will be much more relaxing for everyone. If there are no such places for you to visit, well, the trip may be a refreshing change of scenery, but don't think of it as a vacation. You can bring tape and use it to wrap sharp corners in napkins or washcloths. It can also be worth packing a small bag of outlet covers. Remember to check for risks just outside hotel rooms as well. Beaches, rivers, decorative fountains, and busy streets can be just one step away from your small, giddy, and impulsive little beasties.

FLYING TODDLERS - 15 months to age 3

Young kids need to be prepared for what to expect on "airport day." Many things will be strange and new for the little tykes. They will pick up on tension from stressed out adults standing in long security lines or TSA officers barking orders near the X-ray machines. And of course, the loud rumble and shaking of the plane on take-off and landing can be very scary. I recommend reading books about flying to your kids in the week before traveling. I'd also play act going through security. This can vary at different airports and will also depend on whether your kids can walk through the scanner or will need to be carried. Show the kids videos of the different arrangements. Sometimes they can walk through the metal detector on their own. Typically, you send one parent through first. Then the child leaves the other parent and walks through the gate. They can also be carried through the metal detector and then wanded by security. Have them watch a video of parents going through the X-ray scanner too.

Some security personal will be very patient and helpful when children are involved, others are curt, tense, and most unhelpful. The best thing you can do is to keep yourself calm and relaxed so your kids can, hopefully, take their cue from you. Remember you'll also be juggling your gear through security. You may find that the TSA officers are barking impatient orders at *you* as you try to juggle the kids and all that stuff. Take a deep breath and stay calm. In a few minutes, this particular chaos will be behind you.

Toddlers are generally very mobile. You can use their car seats on the plane to contain them. You can use the airplane seat belt. Or you can use a "Cares Harness." These straps attach to the plane's seat belt and wrap around the seat back to make a harness. We tried these, but ultimately preferred the kid's car seats when they were younger, and the plane's seat belt when they were a bit bigger. There's no right answer here. Consider your kid's temperaments, the length of the flight, if they will sleep or not, and how mobile you will allow them to be on the plane.

In most cases, kids this age will only have a brief attention span for watching videos. Plan ahead and pack some new things for each kid. Consider new small toys, art supplies like paper, crayons, colored tape, and craft kits. Look for ones that have self-adhesive parts, and don't need scissors or glue. Also bring preferred snacks, a small blanket, and a favorite stuffie or lovey. Different kids will engage with different things. My daughter has spent most of a five hour flight making foam Christmas ornaments with stick on parts. My son spent most of another flight playing trains with a child in the row behind us. With this age range, you'll you need to become involved in keeping them engaged in an activity. It will help if you can trade off duties with another adult. Don't expect to nap or read a book. Unless, of course, you load children's books on your tablet and wind up reading "Hop On Pop" to your kids about a gazillion times! Don't forget to bring a sippy cup for your kids to suck on or something to chew during take-off and landing to help ease ear pressure.

FLYING KIDS - 3 to 5-year-olds

By this age, your kids will have developed more attention span for electronic entertainment. This can be a great boon for air travel. You'll have to decide if your kids can share one device or if you need one for each. We use two devices with volume limiting headphones that are designed to protect kid's hearing. However, even with fully loaded tablets, some kids need other distractions on longer flights. When she was three, my daughter would get tired of screen time and would shift to arts and craft activities. Don't forget to pack a bunch of favorite snacks. We now have a routine in which each child has two small containers with about 10-15 little jelly beans. They are only allowed to start eating them at take-off and landing to help with ear equalization. The anticipation of this jelly bean event creates much excitement!

I recommend getting each child a kid size rolling suitcase for their carry-on items. Get the really small ones (try big box stores) that can fit under the plane seats. This gives them easy access to their supplies without needing you to reach into the overhead bins. Since they roll, they are fun which means you won't wind up carrying them through the airport. Although, adults will still need to carry the bags on escalators.

My best "flying with kids" trick is to save a bag of Dum-Dum lollipops for after the plane ride. Exit the plane. Use the restroom. Break out the lollipops! At this point, everyone is tired and you still have a long way to go before you're settled. You have to walk to baggage claim, wait for suitcases, maybe take a shuttle to the rental car pick up, wait in line there, find your car, install car seats, drive to wher-ever you're going, unload everything, yada, yada, yada! Start passing out those lollipops with wild abandon! It just makes everyone happy and more patient if they can wax poetic about the relative virtues of butterscotch vs. root beer vs. fruit punch. Don't stress out about the sugar. We're not doing this every day. As adults, we can anticipate the more difficult part of a long day, and make it fun for everyone! My kids are now 12-years-old and still get excited about the jelly bean and lollipop travel traditions.

A WORD ABOUT AIRPORT SHUTTLES

Most airport shuttles don't have seat belts. Even a casual turn taken at low speed can send a child flying out of the seat. On three occasions, I've had to grab a kid mid-flight. So, hold those kids tight, and keep them close to you on shuttle buses.

BIRTHDAY PARTIES

Some people like to party big, while others like to party small. Either way if you're never thrown a kid's birthday party here are some suggestions.

1-YEAR-OLD

The first birthday party is really for the adults. If you've been through fertility treatment it may feel truly momentous to celebrate your child turning 1 year old. Invite your friends and family, especially the ones with their own kids. Have some champagne and gourmet goodies or beer and barbecue. Make accommodations for your friend's older kids, and just have fun.

2-YEARS-OLD

Two-year-olds are into the simple pleasures: bubbles, playgrounds, kicking balls in the grass, stacking towers and knocking them down. A backyard, playground, or basement can all work depending on weather, and the number of guests. You will most likely be inviting your adult friends and their kids. If your children go to daycare, they may want to invite a child or two from school. But, 2-year-olds are more into parallel play than interactive play, so they won't really care much about who is at the party or what is served.

3 AND UP

Here is where you can keep it modest or go all out. Which you pick is purely personal preference, but remember it can be harder to back down from big parties to small than the other way around.

THE THEME PARTY

Some parents like a big celebration. You may pick a theme for each child or a joint theme if it's a twin birthday. This can get harder if you have two very different twins. But it's not impossible. The children won't care if half the kids come as princesses, and the other half as Star Wars characters. Just make sure you have the same *amount* of decorations for each theme. Otherwise, it won't be "fair," and you'll never hear the end of it! You can do theme parties at home, at parks, or in rental spaces. You can rent bouncy houses, hire clowns, face painters, magicians, and taco trucks. Don't forget the goodie bags for the guests to take home. Obviously, this can all get pretty expensive. But for some families this is a way to share in their joy and celebrate with their community.

THE VENUE PARTY

There are an endless variety of kid's amusement venues for birthday parties. There are vast gaming arcades with adjacent rooms for parties. There are indoor bouncy houses, trampoline parks, and jungle gyms. Gymnastic and karate studios will do parties as will children's art schools. Most of these venues fall into a couple of categories. The big arcades typically provide a room with tables for the party and, perhaps, food. Usually the family brings the cake. Guests eat and then the child opens presents. After that, all the kids and parents are turned loose in the game area. There will be lots of other people in the arcade at the same time. The sports venues may have coaches who take the kids through activities in the gymnastic or martial arts studio. They provide table space and parents can have pizza delivered and provide a cake.

One of the biggest advantages of a venue party is that it's easy. Some places will have party assistants who will serve the pizza, drinks, and cake. Sometimes they will even orchestrate present opening and record who gave what gift in a list for you! Then they clean up. All you are left to do is invitations, cake, pizza, and goodie bags. The disadvantage of these places is that the big gaming ones can be impersonal, and some are basically gambling for kids. I don't like the arcade places, but I'm okay with the more sports or activity based venues. However, some adults love arcades, and the kids will surely love any of these places.

AT HOME OR FAMILY PARTY

A good friend gave me this "kids birthday party formula," which has worked well for us: pizza (frozen or ordered), juice, water, bowl of fruit, salad for adults, cake or cupcakes, goodie bags. That is entirely sufficient. The kids will just play. If you choose, you can add games - sack race, pin the tail on the donkey, chalk art on driveway, squirt guns, craft tables, or a piñata. Some people add entertainment: magicians, science shows (mix your own goo!). My favorite is the animal people who bring critters to show and hold. If it's a twin party you can let each child pick a theme for decorations, select a neutral festive design, or skip decorations entirely. Believe me, the kids will still run around and have fun. With this formula, you can make the party family only, just a couple of friends, or the whole kindergarten class. Some people like to say that a child can invite a number of kids equal to their age. With twins that can quickly add up to the whole class. Keep it small or go big. It's up to you.

OPEN GIFTS AT THE PARTY OR LATER?

How do you handle presents? When the kids were under age 4, a friend advised us not to open gifts at the party to avoid creating conflict with the other kids. And we went to other parties where this was the norm. Presents were left in an unopened pile, and guests took home a party favor. However, we also found that some people wanted to see the kids open their gifts. Once the kids turned 6, we opened presents at the party. There are important life lessons and skills to be learned during gift opening, so don't give this an automatic pass. Just before the party, coach your kids about showing enthusiasm and gratitude for all gifts even if they are actually disappointed. Talk with them about how to make eye contact, and give a genuine thank you to each of their friends and guests. Tell them they are responsible for making all their guests feel welcome and comfortable. It's highly unlikely your children will ever show these gentle manners to YOU, but you may be amazed to see how well behaved they can be with others!

GIFTS AND TWIN ETIQUETTE

When children come to a twin birthday, they will likely bring a toy for each child. The standard reciprocation is that when you go to that child's birthday, you bring a gift from each of your children. Once they're older and have distinct friend groups, this can change.

A NOTE ON GOODIE BAGS

Goodie bags can generate huge amounts of garbage. Many items marketed for this purpose are plastic pieces of junk. Please avoid this environmental insult. Instead, use a recyclable bag made of paper. Give candy, markers, pencils, Hot Wheels, a mini-stuffie, or a packet of seeds. Sometimes you can find small craft kits with biodegradable materials. Just remember to give your choices a second look. If it looks like junk that will never biodegrade, then give it a pass. Oh, and balloons are massively hazardous to animals. If you must have them, get the newer biodegradable ones.

26

LET'S TALK SERIOUS SAFETY

LEARNING TO SWIM

LEARNING TO SWIM IS AN important life skill. Here are a few useful tips for that endeavor. True swimming is a skill that requires a certain level of physical coordination and brain maturity. As a result, kids cannot truly learn to swim until around age 5. Prior to that, you can work with your child on a variety of pre-swimming and water safety skills. I think one of the best places to start is in the bathtub. A fun playful bath time is the first step in getting a child comfortable with water. We started with paper straws. We showed the kiddos how to blow bubbles into the tub. Each day we cut the straw shorter until their face was quite close to the water. Then we showed them how to hold their nose, and put their face in the water. Then we added blowing bubbles with their face in the water. Be sure to keep it all a game and follow their lead on the pace of change.

The tub is also a good place to introduce goggles. Realize that goggles will feel quite weird and perhaps tight on their face. You want your child to buy into wearing them from the beginning. One way to approach this is for the adults to start wearing them around the house. Don't say anything about them until your kids *ask* about the strange things on your face. Tell them that if they want to try them, you'll get some in their size later. Do this off and on for a day or two until they *really* want to try them. When you first put goggles on your child, just let them hold them to their eyes. Later you can get the strap over their heads. Be careful with the strap as this is a moment of potential hair pulling, which can lead to future resistance. Once they have goggles on start playing. Use the bath tub or a very large bowl of water. Put something fun at the bottom for them to find. Gradually, add in blowing bubbles, and you've brought your kids a long way into pre-swimming skills.

You'll also want to get them comfortable with swimming pools. Community swimming pools, a friend's pool, as well as gym and hotel pools can give you a chance to expand your child's comfort and skills. Make sure your child has a good flotation device on, then just play in the water while holding them. Be aware that inflatable "water wings" can pop, and are not allowed in some pools. Life vests, foam water wings, or the wings-plus-chest piece type of floatation all come in a range of sizes for little kids.

Some kids will be quite fearful of the pool. They recognize that it's deep, and that they are outside their skill range. They see danger and they are *right*. This is their natural protective instinct kicking in to keep them safe. They don't want to go into deep water the same way they don't want to step off a cliff. For these kids, go slow and start in shallow water. As they realize the life vest will keep them floating, and that *you* will stay with them, they will usually gain confidence and play. They are trusting you to keep them safe. So, don't fail them, and don't push them. Later, much later, they can start stretching their skills. Right now, just have fun. Play this way as often as you can with your young child. Once they see the pool as fun, you can bring in the goggles and bubble blowing.

When they have developed the above skills, and are 3 to 4-years-old, start working on the next two water safety skills. First, it's important that your child learns how to climb out of a pool without the steps. Take them to the side, let them pull themselves up, swing a leg over the side, and roll out of the pool onto the concrete. This is a very important safety skill, so repeat, repeat, repeat. Make it into a game if need be. Another important skill is "kangaroo hopping." This is when the child pushes off the bottom with their feet to get to the surface for a breath. You can start this by jumping in a shallow kiddie pool, and gradually move to deeper water as the child gets older and more comfortable with their face underwater. You'll need to be right there with them as they learn this. If they become frightened, just stop for a while. Swimming lessons for 5-year-olds will focus on these water safety skills before moving onto actual swimming.

If you have neither the time nor the facilities to help your child with pool comfort, then by all means, sign them up for swimming lessons. Just be aware that before age 5 your child will gain many valuable pre-swimming and water safety skills. However, actual swimming is not likely to occur until they are closer to 5 or 6-years-old.

PROTECTING YOUR CHILD FROM DROWNING: PARENTAL SKILLS

Drowning is the second most common cause of accidental death for kids under age 15. (Number one cause is car accidents.) Once the summer heat arrives in full force, all that water is going to be calling to you and your youngsters. If you want to protect you child from drowning, then you have some parental skills to learn.

First, remember that crazy stuff happens! Accidents occur because we can't predict them. So, here's the deal. Things are going to happen that you would never in a million years predict. Some of them will be dangerous. A few years ago, I was swimming at a local lake. The day-use area was full of families, and people of all ages were splashing around in floats and kayaks. I was standing in about three feet of water, and looked up towards the shore. Right at the water's edge, in about six inches of water, was a boy about 4-years-old. He had a fairly large round float ring about three feet across. He had fallen forward, face first into the donut hole. His face was underwater. His feet were in the air and kicking furiously. But his arms were wedged inside the ring, and he couldn't push himself out.

He was drowning in six inches of water while surrounded by people and right at the shoreline! I raced towards him. Just before I reached him, he managed to roll out. He came up coughing and sputtering with eyes wide in fear. The boy's grandfather was putting gear in the car, and left two older kids to watch him. They were playing nearby, but never realized what was happening. In fact, no one, other than I, had seen that he was in trouble. He was just a kid with a float ring goofing at the edge of the water where no one would expect a 4-year-old to drown. Crazy stuff happens! So, watch your kids, really *watch* them around water. Sitting nearby and looking at your cell phone *does not count* when your kids are young.

It's also very important to realize that drowning does not look like what we expect from TV. Many people drown *silently* and often *very close* to other people who *never recognize* that they are *drowning*! Maybe read that last line again. If someone is waving and yelling for help, they are in "aquatic distress." These people can grab a float if it's thrown to them. However, someone who is *drowning* will be caught in "the drowning reflex." These people cannot help rescue themselves.

If you throw them a life ring, they *can't* reach for it. They will be upright in the water with their head tilted back and mouth dipping above and below the water. They will be desperately trying to catch a breath, and unable to make any sound before slipping back under water. They will be *silent*. Their arms will be out at their sides as they try to keep their head above water. Generally, they will manage this for 20 to 60 seconds before they go fully under. You could easily miss this while reading your email.

Please, go to the link below and read this article by Mario Vittone, a former Coast Guard rescue swimmer. His widely praised article about what drowning really looks like is truly eye opening. It may save your child's life.

https://www.soundingsonline.com/voices/
drowning-doesnt-look-like-drowning

If your child has a *near* drowning episode, then be aware of a potentially life-threatening complication. Secondary drowning and a similar condition called dry drowning can occur after a child has taken even small amounts of water into their upper airway or lungs. Symptoms can develop shortly after the event or can be delayed by 24 to 48 hours.

In both cases a chain reaction of irritation causes the child's lungs to fill with fluid secretions. This can lead to severe respiratory distress and death. If your child has a near drowning event, get them medically checked out. If they start coughing, wheezing, have fever, weakness, shortness of breath or generally are feeling poorly, don't dismiss it, get them emergency care right away.

Home pools and ponds can also put children at risk. There are many different devices for minimizing the hazard. You can find sensors that strap to your child's ankle, and will alarm if submerged. But they'll have to keep the device on and it will have to be loud enough for you to hear. There are motion sensors that sit in a pool, and alarm if the water is disturbed. These can give false alarms if ducks land. But maybe they will be a good duck deterrent. Pool covers that can be walked on come in both automatic and manual varieties.

Many areas require either an automatic pool cover or five-foot-tall, non-climbable fencing around pools. Australia was able to dramatically reduce drowning deaths just by implementing and enforcing laws requiring pool fences. However, that pool fencing must *fully* surround the pool. If it attaches to your home, such that the pool can be accessed from a door in the house, then it will not protect your kids. Many children have wandered off from a party of attentive adults, fallen in a pool, and drowned. So, make sure that fence around your pool fully encloses the pool, is not climbable, is at least five-feet-tall, and has a childproof gate.

You can also get sensors for your home's doors and windows that will alert you if they are opened. If you live near a dangerous stream or lake, then door alarms may be well worth it. I personally know of a case in which a young child walked out of an apartment, and drown in a three foot deep decorative pond. The parents had been caring for a sick sibling. They were severely sleep deprived, and never knew the other child had gotten out of bed.

If you have a pool, a pond, or live on water of any kind, be aware these are real dangers for kids. I recommend you carefully assess those risks and work to reduce them.

Remember while you're planning, even older good swimmers can drown. Teach your kids to never swim alone whether in a home pool or open water. Teach your children about the dangers of moving water. Fast moving streams and rivers, drainage sloughs, steep sided irrigation canals, waves and rip tides all need to be pointed out with the risks explained to children. Don't forget that kids continue to take unexpected, impulsive risks long after you'd think they'd out grown such mistakes!!

Pool parties should have at least one designated adult on lifeguard duty. Switch them out, so they don't get fatigued. Give them a "do not disturb" sign, so they can pay attention to the pool. When pool play is over, close the fence or pool cover. If you can't completely secure it, keep someone on duty.

Finally, one of the best ways to keep children safe around water is to have them wear a life vest. Even strong swimmers *drown*. A life vest is truly a *life saver*.

Water play is sooo much fun, and a great way to deal with the summer heat. But it does have its risks. So, update your parental skills, your safety gear, your water rules, and pay close attention to your kids while they splash their way through the summer sizzle.

CAR SEATS AND CAR SAFETY

The only memories I have from when I was 4-years-old are from the night of the car crash. This happened before seat belts were standard in cars. As the driver, my father was wearing the only belt in the car. Mom was at home. We kids were all young, my sister was 8, and my brothers 3 and 10-years-old. My older brother was in the front passenger seat. My little brother and I were in the back seats. My sister was lying on the shelf under the rear window behind the back seats. It was dark, raining, and a twisty country road. On a blind turn a truck pulled out from a side street. Our car, an on-coming car, and the truck all collided. My 10-year-old brother slid under the front dash and cut his eyelid on something sharp. It just missed his eye. He got stitches in his eyelid. My 3-year-old brother was thrown into the back side of the front seat, and split his forehead open. He got stiches. I was also thrown against the front seat and floor hitting my head. My 8-year-old sister went flying. She flew from the rear shelf, over the back seats over the front seats, and smashed her face on the windshield. She severely lacerated her lower lip, broke teeth, and damaged her still developing adult teeth. My seat belted father took most of the impact but was uninjured.

I remember the blood on my father's shirt. I remember my sister crying. I remember the ambulance workers holding me while I vomited on the side of the road. I remember the ambulance ride, my sister and I sharing one gurney. I remember mixed screaming of both the sirens and my sister. I remember the white calm of the hospital. I remember the kindness and gentleness of an enormous nurse in her white uniform. For years and years afterwards, I'd tell people I wanted to grow up to be "a big fat nurse!" She was *so* kind to me. I also remember they were worried that my vomiting could mean I had internal injuries. They kept trying to get me to hold still for X-rays of my abdomen. They finally gave up and decided I was too wiggly to have internal injuries. I don't know what my siblings remember from this night. I imagine it involves shots and stitches and X-rays. My father would have been moving from one child to the other frantic and fearful for his young children. My mom must have gotten an awful call in the dark of the night. It was my sister who got the worst of it. She would wind up enduring years of orthodontic work to straighten the teeth that had been shoved around and then grew in at wild angles. Her lip was permanently scarred, and she went through later surgeries to revise and reduce the scarring.

Infant and child car seats did not exist when I was a child. So, after the accident my parents found children's harnesses that buckled into the back seats. They had seat belts installed throughout the car. And the new rule was, "The engine doesn't start until all the seat belts are buckled." That night, that seminal moment, shapes all my thoughts around driving and car safety.

Of all the things you can invest money in for your kids, I firmly believe that good car seats are the most important. Get a cheap stroller, but research your car seats and get a quality one. That doesn't mean you necessarily need the most expensive one. All car seats must pass extensive crash testing. But, ease of use, ease of installation, and comfort are as important. Because the most important thing is that you use them, and use them properly. This sounds easier than it actually is. Improperly installed car seats are very common. Many police and fire departments offer car seat installation inspections. I highly recommend attending one of these events. If you can, bring along nannies or grandparents who may drive your kids around.

The Current California Law: 2022

- Children under 2 years of age shall ride in a rear-facing car seat unless the child weighs 40 or more pounds OR is 40 or more inches tall. The child shall be secured in a manner that complies with the height and weight limits specified by the manufacturer of the car seat. (California Vehicle Code Section 27360.)
- Children under the age of 8 must be secured in a car seat or booster seat in the back seat.
- Children who are 8 years of age OR have reached 4'9" in height may be secured by a booster seat, but at a minimum must be secured by a safety belt. (California Vehicle Code Section 27363.)
- Passengers who are 16 years of age and over are subject to California's Mandatory Seat Belt law.

When can a child graduate to a booster seat?

- California law does not address graduation time from a five point harness to a booster seat. *In the interest of safety, do not rush to move a child into a booster seat before they're ready. Each time you "graduate" your child to the next seat, there's a reduction in the level of protection for your child. Keep your child in each stage for as long as possible.* (emphasis mine)
- A child is ready for a booster seat when they have outgrown the weight or height limit of their forward-facing harnesses, which is typically between 40 and 65 pounds. Read the forward-facing car seat's owner's manual to determine height and weight limits, and keep your child in a harnessed seat for as long as possible.
- Children at this stage are not yet ready for adult safety belts and should use belt-positioning booster seats until they are at least 4'9" and between 8 and 12 years old. Safety belts are designed for 165-pound male adults, so it's no wonder that *research shows poorly fitting adult belts can injure children.* (emphasis mine)

Infant Car Seats:

For newborns and younger infants, you have "infant" seats. The base of the seat stays strapped onto the car and the infant carrier easily clicks in and out. They are always rear-facing. If you're looking for an infant seat and expecting twins, then remember, twins are often premature so make sure it's rated for a 4 to 5 pound infant.

Convertible Car Seats:

For older infants and toddlers, there are "convertible" seats. You start them in a rear-facing position. Later, when the child is 2-years-old and over 40 pounds, these seats can convert to forward-facing. When they have out grown the weight or height limits of their forward facing convertible seat, you can move them to a booster seat with the car's regular seat belt.

Booster Seats:

It's very important to remember that a 6-year-old child is not developmentally ready for the freedom of a regular booster seat. They will discover the new freedom of the decreased restraint and will be reaching and leaning and goofing around such that they are not really safe. So, when your kids reach the weight and age at which booster seats are allowed, I'd recommend you look into one of the new "combination" seats. These are booster seats with a 5-point harness option you can use until they are more mature. These are relatively new products, and not yet required. However, I believe they are a very a good idea. Some are rated up to 120 pounds. If you family runs tall, then look for higher weight and height capacity in these seats.

All car seats must meet federal safety standards. However, ease of use and weight/ heights limits do vary. Here's a great website for comparing options:

National Highway Traffic Safety Administration
Child Safety Seat Ease of Use Ratings
https://one.nhtsa.gov/nhtsa_eou/info.jsp?type=infant

Car seat width at the base and top of the seat also varies. If you need to have three seats in one row, then measure both your car and the car seats to be sure they will all fit. We also found that some seats with the side impact protection limit the size of who can sit comfortably between two forward facing seats. My husband's butt fit easily when sitting in the middle between our convertible seats, but his shoulders did not. For me, it was the other way around!

Invest some energy in this decision if you can. Look into the latest information, and get some advice. Make sure your seat is installed correctly. Keep your kids in the highest level of restraint you can based on their size and weight. Don't rush to switch to booster seats unless you can get the five-point harness "combination" type.

Remember: The engine doesn't start until everyone is belted in. Put the phone down. Your kids will be distracting enough!

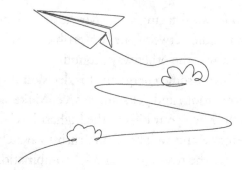

27

TOXINS, FEAR, AND EVALUATING RISKS

IT'S ONE THING TO MAKE decisions about organic vs. non-organic fruit for yourself. It's a whole different consideration when you're thinking about the accumulation of chemicals in your child's little body. This leads to one of the unique challenges of modern parenting. You will be hit by a barrage of information regarding the endless chemicals to which your children are being exposed. And, it will be *your* job to try and figure out which, if any, to worry about and what to DO about them.

If you live in a house with old paint, old water pipes, or old Venetian blinds, then you DO want to have them tested for lead. In my area, a branch of the health department sends out paint, dirt, and surface lead testing kits upon request. You take the samples, mail them back, and they contact you with results. You can also buy lead test swabs at many hardware stores. They are extremely easy to use, and will identify surface lead.

But, what about your water? Do you need to have it tested for anything? Do you want to filter it? Some trace arsenic in rice is normal. But U.S. rice has been found to have rather high levels even in organic rice. What about your baby's rice cereal? Is it safe? Balsamic vinegar from Italy has been found to have high lead levels. Are you only going to cook with U.S. balsamic vinegar? Are you going to research the latest findings before you buy? Do you use it so little it doesn't matter? How do you figure that out? Tuna, especially albacore, is high in mercury. How much of what kind of tuna is safe at each age? What about fire retardant chemicals? They can be on your kid's mattresses, pajamas, and sofas. Do you need to pay a premium to find products without fire retardants or are there economical options? How much time do you have to do all this research? What about phthalates in room fresheners, shampoos, and a million other products. They are endocrine disrupters. Did you know that most cash register receipts in the U.S. have bisphenol-a in the inkless paper? Bisphenol-a was originally developed to be an estrogen in a birth control pill! It wasn't quite strong enough for birth control so other uses were found for the chemical. It is still a synthetic estrogen! How much of that do you want your child absorbing? (Don't let your kids play with register receipts! And thank you Home Goods in Rocklin, CA for using BPA free receipts!)

All of this can be intensely anxiety provoking. It's also very, very time consuming to try to research the endless list of concerns. Even trying to figure out if you need to be concerned or not is often quite hard. There are no easy answers here. You'll have to figure out for yourself how much time, energy, and money you want or can put into these issues. I have various levels of concern about all the issues I listed above. And, there are many more substances about which others have raised concerns.

But, for all of that, it's much more important that your baby's car seat is properly installed! A statistics teacher once told me that people are not good at evaluating relative risk. We can obsess over scary things that have a very low chance of occurring while ignoring common and significant dangers. Falls from the changing table, car crashes, drownings (even in older good swimmers!), poisonings, choking...these risks need serious attention and appropriate actions to reduce dangers. Do your best on the more obscure and less defined hazards, but try to keep them in perspective. I still take the kids in the car. I just mitigate the risk with a good car seat, and I try to drive safely. So, I take the same approach with chemicals in the environment. Mitigate the risk, and then let it go and live life as fully and with as much joy as possible. As for mitigating the risks of chemical exposures, I'm going to help you with that in the next chapter!

Aside from the fact that chemical hypervigilance is one more "modern mom" responsibility, why does this issue shake us up so much? For me the issue is twofold. The first is the heart stopping, soul shaking love that I feel for my kids. I now truly understand how a parent would give their life for a child. News stories of injured children that would have been disturbing before I had kids will now make me physically sick. And this extraordinary deep love makes us want to protect our children from any harm, and to protect ourselves from the fear of any harm coming to them.

The second issue for me is control. We want to believe we can control our destiny. That we can protect ourselves from bad things happening if only we do the right thing. We certainly have the ability to influence how our lives unfold. But, healthy men with good cholesterol go out for their regular run and drop dead from a heart attack. Moms out riding their bike get hit and killed by cars. And meticulous health nuts still get cancer despite a life time of "living right." In fact, when I've read biographies of people who lived into healthy old age they often emphasize living life with joy. Studies show the main thing that confers longevity is having genetics from parents who lived into old age! Hard to control our own genetics.

For me, parenting has been a lesson in…okay, *many* things, but mostly in learning to let go a bit. Learning to not try to control everything. Don't get me wrong, I'm still a huge plan ahead, read ahead, wear the life vest, pack the safety gear kinda person. But I try to balance this with a bit of letting go. Frankly, my husband is better at this than I am, though it may be easier for him to not worry since I take care of that job! But, I have learned, and relaxed some, by watching his more "go with the flow" style. After a while, I realized if you give kids the basics, they really are programed to learn and grow. Still, I really don't like not having control over all these chemicals attacking my children! Sigh.

Alright, I guess there's a third issue. The fact that all these chemical concerns are vague and often hidden makes them feel all the more nefarious. We have these potentially very harmful substances about which the science is more and more suggestive of harm. Then we have the "modern mom" who is charged with making sure her toddler is learning advanced coding in time for kindergarten, which will undoubtedly set the stage for *all* future success. At the same time, she's confronted on a daily basis by how much is beyond her control. And all of this revolves around these little people we love beyond compare.

It's no wonder we're a bit wacko.

12 TOXINS TO CONSIDER AND WHAT YOU CAN DO FOR YOUR FAMILY

From the time I started writing this book until now, we have gained far more information and scientific evidence regarding many of these environmental toxins. As a result, I found I needed to completely rewrite this section. I also got very, very angry at what we have allowed to seep into our children's bodies and brains. Some historical perspective offers chilling insight into everyday chemical exposures.

The Romans, yes the *Romans,* knew that lead was poisonous. Miners, smelters, anyone who handled lead suffered well described lead toxicity. And, they knew it was from the lead. Yet, still they added it to wine and foods, used lead pipes, and wore lead armor. Medieval aristocrats used lead powder to slowly poison family members in order to obtain their title. We've known that lead causes acute and chronic illness or death for a very long time. Nevertheless, in the early 1900's the automotive industry encouraged adding it to gasoline. It was in our paint, our ceramics, and tableware. Lead was all over the place. After all, it was very useful. The Environmental Protection Agency fought against the use of lead starting in the early 1900s. No one listened. Today we are shocked when we find lead in our children's environment. However, people were screaming about lead poisoning for a long time before the public managed to win basic protections from lead. In the U.S. you have to prove that a substance is dangerous before it can be blocked from use in products. In Europe they flip this idea around. You have to prove that it is safe before you can put it in a product.

Unfortunately, in America we can't assume that the chemical additives in everyday products are safe.

These days it seems our government is protecting corporations and not the people. Our constitution says, "…in order to protect these rights, governments are instituted among men." In other words, governments *exist* to protect individual rights not company rights. I feel a rant coming on, so I'll stop there and move on to the nitty gritty of these stupid, vile toxins.

Okay, here we go, in no particular order:

BISPHENOL-A…and bisphenol-S, and "P" etc.

Need to Know About Bisphenols (BPA):

These are primarily synthetic estrogens which seem to have obesogenic (obesity promoting) effects. They make fat cells bigger and counteract adiponectin. (An important cardio protective hormone.)

BPA was originally developed as an estrogen to be used in a birth control pill. It wasn't quite strong enough so the developer went looking for other uses of the compound?! It found its way into plastics, (those with the #7 recycle number on them) onto the paper of "inkless" cash register receipts, into the lining of steel and aluminum cans. Yes, as in soda cans. Does it need to be in these things? No. Are there alternatives? Yes. Is it absorbed through the skin and gut? Yes. Yes! Does it have estrogenic affects in your body? Yes! It also has effects on thyroid receptors. Are you getting dosed with this? Yes!

Don't let babies or kids play with cash register receipts. Limit your own handling of them. Store them in a bag or pouch not loose in your purse where the dust will contaminate everything. Go for an email receipt whenever possible. Check this link:

https://www.marketwatch.com/story/your-receipts-
could-be-making-you-sick-2018-01-17

It is now becoming easier to find canned food with linings that are BPA free. Yippee??? Unfortunately, some are now using BPS instead or BPxyz. There's an alphabet of variations. BPS appears to have a stronger estrogenic affect and longer half-life. Which cans still have some form of bisphenol in their lining? Who knows?! The plastics companies claim their "formula" is proprietary, so they don't have to disclose what chemicals they are adding to plastics.

That may be why many plastics that are BPA free *still* leach estrogen active chemicals. This was confirmed in the study noted below and published in Environmental Health Perspectives in March 2011. This study took plastic samples from a wide variety of everyday products including many labeled "BPA" free. They made sure to sample plastics from all recycling categories 1 through 7. The plastics were subjected to normal use type of exposures, then the plastics were tested to see if they would leach chemicals that bind to estrogen receptors. *Every* sample tested positive for chemicals that had estrogen receptor binding. Let's say that again. EVERY TYPE OF PLASTIC TESTED WAS POSITIVE FOR ESTROGEN RECEPTOR BINDING CHEMICALS. Unfortunately, this means that you cannot trust any plastic with food products. Yeah. Not any of them. Not until the companies are required to fully disclose their plastics formulas, and they are all tested. Can plastics be made without estrogenically active leaching molecules? YES! Heated, scratched, and damaged plastic storage containers, plates, cups, etc. are probably leaching chemicals at a much higher rate. Don't microwave them *and* don't put them in the dishwasher.

The study below is long but there's a lot of info in the abstract alone. Worth a view:

Most Plastic Products Release Estrogenic Chemicals: A Potential Health Problem That Can Be Solved. Chung Zang et al., Environmental Health Perspectives, July 2011.
https://www.ncbi.nlm.nih.gov/pmc/articles/PMC3222987/

Where We Find Bisphenols:

1. Cash register receipts
2. Soda cans / aluminum can linings
3. Aluminum water bottle linings, steel are okay
4. Food cans linings both steel and aluminum may have some form of an estrogen activating lining even if labeled BPA free.
5. Plastics – ALL categories of plastics have tested positive for endocrine active chemicals.
6. Heated or damaged plastics are especially concerning for leaching these compounds.

What to Do About Bisphenols:

1. When possible look for food in glass rather than cans or plastic.
2. Get your soda and beer from a glass. Avoid plastic bottles and aluminum cans.
3. Avoid cash register receipts and sequester the ones you do get. Keep them away from kids. If you work as a cashier, wear gloves! Receipts are a major source of BPA and S exposure.
4. Cardboard drink, broth, or soup boxes that say "Tetra" or "Sims" on the bottom are reportedly free of endocrine disrupters.
5. Store food and pack lunches in metal, glass, or silicone containers. Use wax paper, plastic free parchment paper, or newer untreated paper sandwich bags.
6. Throw out all broken plastic.
7. Don't put plastic in the dishwasher or microwave.
8. Aluminum water bottles have a plastic lining. Don't use them.
9. Use a steel water bottle and make sure it does not have a lining.
10. Throw out most of your plastic storage containers. This one is tricky. You'll find it's fairly easy to stop using plastic storage in your home and fridge. What gets harder is packing school lunches. I have found it difficult to find non-plastic containers that don't leak in a lunch box. Stainless steel can be expensive and will usually leak

juice from packed berries. Glass is heavy and fragile. Sometimes I will pack fruit in a paper bag and put that inside a plastic container.

11. Throw out your plastic cooking utensils such as large plastic spoons, spatula's etc.
12. Use cooking utensils that are wooden, silicone, or steel
13. Avoid plastic spoons, straws, cups
14. You can order silicone or stainless steel straws on line. I like the silicone ones best.
15. Order silicone container covers in place of plastic wrap. They stretch to fit over bowls and work great.
16. Get rid of plastic mixing bowls. Go for glass or stainless steel.
17. Avoid buying plastic products of any kind. Look for an alternative. Metal buckets, metal beach toys, wooden blocks, etc.

GLYPHOSATE/ ROUND-UP

What to Know About Glyphosate:

1. Glyphosate by itself, with no other additives, has been found by the World Health Organization to be a "probable carcinogen" with specific risk for Non-Hodgkin's Lymphoma.
2. Round-Up weed killer states that glyphosate is its only "active" ingredient. "Non-active" ingredients are proprietary, and do not have to be reported. Toxicity tests for Round-Up show markedly more toxicity towards human embryonic cells than tests done on pure glyphosate.

Where Glyphosate is Found:

1. Virtually all non-organic grain products, regardless of whether they are GMO or not, are sprayed with Round Up just prior to harvest. It is used to "desiccate" or kill and dry up the crop so that mechanical harvesting is easier. It is commonly used

on wheat, oats, lentils, peas, potatoes, soybeans, corn, flax, rye, triticale, buckwheat, millet, canola, sugar beets, green beans, sunflowers. If these are GMO versions of the crop, then they likely got sprayed with Round Up more than once.

What to Do About Glyphosate:

1. Alternatives to using Round Up at home:
   a. Vinegar, and other weed control alternatives look up *10 Alternatives to Roundup*, Moms Across America, Updated July 16, 2019. https://www.momsacrossamerica. com/10_alternatives_to_roundup
2. Getting Round Up out of your family food chain:
   a. Focus on buying only **organic grain products**: breads, cereals, snack bars, corn, lentils, green beans, potatoes, etc.
   b. Looking for non-GMO is not enough. Go organic to avoid Round Up.

ATRAZINE

What to Know About Atrazine:

1. Atrazine is the second most commonly used herbicide in the U.S. Most often used in the Midwest to kill weeds growing between corn rows.
2. Atrazine in humans will turn on an enzyme in your cells called aromatase. This aromatase converts testosterone to estrogen in the human body.
3. Health implications: estrogen based cancers, infertility, abnormal male fetal development if exposure is at certain times in development, low birth weight, abnormal neurological development
4. Many water supplies in the U.S. are contaminated with Atrazine, especially in the Midwest. This contamination can have HUGE

seasonal variation. If tested during non-spray times, the water
may appear to have low levels. However, when tested during
peak pesticide spraying season the water sources for millions of
Americans are found to have levels much higher than guidelines
would allow. Check out the following link:

From the Environmental Working Group (EWG):

- *Hormone-Disrupting Weed Killer Taints Drinking Water
  For Millions Of Americans,* EWG, Nov. 2018. https://
  www.ewg.org/research/hormone-disrupting-weed-kille
  r-taints-drinking-water-millions-americans
- This analysis shows that many water municipalities will
  test the water for atrazine at non-peak times and then
  report that the water levels of atrazine meet EPA standards. In fact, testing by the EPA at peak times often
  shows levels of atrazine that far exceeded safe EPA levels.
  This information is being under reported in many, but not
  all water municipalities.
5. Additional information:
   - Article from Scientific American: Atrazine in Water
     Tied to Hormonal Irregularities, Lindsey Konkel,
     Nov. 2011. https://www.scientificamerican.com/article/
     atrazine-water-tied-hormonal-irregularities/
   - Article from CDC Agency for Toxic Substances and
     Disease Registry: Toxicological Resources Listing.
   - https://www.atsdr.cdc.gov/phs/phs.asp?id=336&tid=59

Where is Atrazine Found:

1. Contaminated water supplies through municipalities and ground
   or well water, especially in the Midwest.
2. Particularly where corn is planted.

What to Do About Atrazine:

1. If your home relies on well water, have it tested.
2. Use a water filter on your tap. See the EWG review of filters (link at the end of this chapter) to be sure that you pick one that removes atrazine.
3. Insist that municipalities test and report during peak seasons.
4. Buy organic to encourage reduced use of herbicides.
5. If you live in corn country or the Midwest, have your water tested regardless of its source.

PFC's — Polyflouro chemicals; aka PFAS's or poly flouro alkyl substances

What to Know About PFC's:

This is a group of non-stick, stain-resistant, grease-resistant chemicals that have been around since the 1950's. Teflon and Scotch guard are two PFC's that have been partially banned due to health effects. They are very long lasting persistent chemicals that accumulate in people and animals. Studies by the CDC in 2005 show that virtually all Americans have PFC's in their bodies. Other studies have shown that it is passed through the placenta and breast milk to fetus and infant.

Per the Centers for Disease Control (CDC):
Although more research is needed, some studies in people have shown that certain PFAS may:
- affect growth, learning, and behavior of infants and older children
- lower a woman's chance of getting pregnant
- interfere with the body's natural hormones
- increase cholesterol levels
- affect the immune system

- increase the risk of cancer
  At this time, scientists are still studying the health effects of exposures to mixtures of PFAS's.

Where PFC's are Found:

1. Grease proof food wrappers, boxes, and packaging: fluorochemical paper additives have been found to migrate to food during actual package use. Grease and oil in the foods can significantly increase the contamination of the food with PFC's.
2. Recycled paper products: The PFC's in paper products have been found to persist in recycled materials. Thus, a restaurant may use materials without PFC coatings, but if it is made with recycled paper, it may well still contain PFC's.
3. Waterproof fabrics – coats, 'shoes, outdoor wear
4. Gore-tex, Polartec, Stainmaster, Scotch Guard, and many other waterproof fabric coatings,
5. Upholstery – any "stain resistant furniture fabric probably has been treated with a PFC based product
6. Carpet stain protection
7. Some sneakers and waterproof shoes
8. Non-stick kitchen ware.
9. Microwave popcorn in the US is still produced in bags with PFC's.
10. Dental floss!
11. Contaminated drinking water: maybe check water before mixing infant formula
12. Cleaning products
13. Paints, varnishes, and sealants
14. Firefighting foam
15. Some cosmetics
16. Fish and seafood can bio accumulate PFC's

What to Do About PFC's:

1. Avoid all restaurant food packaging and wrappers. Ask for a plate.
2. Bring your own stainless steel coffee cup or mug.
3. When possible, ask for warmed food in cafes to be placed on a plate for heating and not on packaging or paper.
4. Avoid all waterproofed, stain proofed clothing and fabrics.
5. Don't use non-stick pans, pots, or cook ware. Use stainless steel or cast iron.
6. Research your cosmetics prior to use. Check the Environmental Working Group's (EWG) cosmetic guides.
7. Use organic cleaning products or make your own.
8. Filter your water, especially if mixing formula. Use the EWG's water filter guide.
9. Switch to wax-coated silk dental floss. This is actually easy to find online. I also found one in a metal (not plastic) reusable dispenser. Here are two I like:
   - Wowe Natural Biodegradable Silk Dental Floss with Mint Flavored Wax, Refillable Stainless Steel Container
   - Dental Lace Silk Dental Floss with Natural Mint Flavoring Includes 1 Refillable Recyclable Blue Dispenser Glass
10. Don't use microwave popcorn. It's very easy and fun to make it the old fashioned way!
11. Research paints, varnishes, and finishes.
12. Don't recycle paper you think might have PFC's on them.
13. Be wary of fish or seafood that may have bio-accumulated PFC's if farther up the food chain.
14. Use paper lunch bags. Look for grease proof ones without wax or other coating.
    - If You Care
    - Lunchskins products.
    - Or a reusable silicone bag.

- Fully compostable sandwich and storage bags, like Matter brand.

See article below from testing by the Environmental Working Group.
- *Many Fast Food Wrappers Still Coated in PFCs, Kin to Carcinogenic Teflon Chemical,* EWG, Feb 2017. https://www.ewg.org/research/many-fast-food-wrappers-still-coated-pfcs-kin-carcinogenic-teflon-chemical

CADMIUM

What to Know About Cadmium:

This is a heavy metal that can be found in some artist paints. It's also present in some glazes and paints used on dishes and pottery. It is a known carcinogen and should be avoided. Cadmium is especially found in red, orange, and yellow colored glazes and can leach from dishes. Even dishes made in the U.S. may have some cadmium in their glazes. Dishes from China and Mexico should be highly suspect, especially if it has a painted decoration or red/orange/yellow colors.

Where is Cadmium Found:

Artist paints:
1. The cadmium in acrylic artist paints has low solubility and is felt to be of lower risk.
2. Some acrylic paints now have a fully cadmium free formulation.
3. Oil paints with cadmium have a higher risk of toxicity and should be handled with gloves and precautions.
4. Airbrushing or sanding cadmium paints markedly increases exposure and should be avoided.
5. Kid's paints are generally made without cadmium.

Dishes, pottery, ceramics:
1. Cadmium is often added to red, yellow, and orange glazes.
2. Cadmium can leach from the dishes regardless of whether the outer glaze is intact, cracked, or chipped.
3. Fiestaware can send you a list of which of their current glazes contain cadmium and which do not. OLD dishes are a gamble as they may have been made before regulations were in place.

What to Do About Cadmium:

1. Most new all white dishes are both cadmium and lead free.
2. Corelle's current all-white dishes, both flat and embossed should be cadmium free and have tested lead free too. (See next section). This is not necessarily true of any with painted designs.
3. Trash your old plates or put special ones out for display only.
4. You can consider using some larger colorful plates as "chargers" and put a safer plate on top for the food. This is what I will be doing with my "good" dishes that I bought before I was aware of the issues.
5. Fiestaware does have numerous colors of dishes that are cadmium free and test with only barely detectable trace lead that, per the company, is a naturally occurring contaminate and not an additive to their glazes. I like the colors, but they are out of my price range.
6. Don't use any old dishes or glasses for serving food or drink.
7. Stainless steel plates and cups are fine and great for kids, pool side, or other places where you want to avoid using breakable table ware.
8. Bamboo plates are often made from bamboo "dust" mixed with a resin. Who knows what's in the resin? Avoid until we know more.
9. Melamine plates: I don't trust them. Melamine in other forms caused renal toxicity in dogs. Most are made in china with unknown paints.
10. Plastic plates: Plastic companies do not have to disclose their formulas, and we now know that all types of plastic have tested positive for estrogen binding compounds. So, I no longer trust any plastic, even if made in the U.S.A.

LEAD

What to Know About Lead:

Lead continues to be a significant poisoning risk in the U.S. ACROSS ALL SOCIO-ECONOMIC GROUPS. *Very small levels of lead poisoning will cause permanent, irreversible cognitive impairment in children.* Lead was used in multiple products in the past. Its use is now supposed to be controlled in the U.S., but many old sources continue to cause concerning exposure. In addition, lead continues to be used in products, paints, and gasoline produced in other countries, especially ceramics from Mexico and China.

1. What are the FDA guidelines for safe levels of lead in food?
   - Kids: max 3 ug per day (ug is micrograms)
   - Adults: 12.5 ug per day
   - Pregnant women: probably better on the low side.
2. Where do these numbers come from?
   - "The FDA assesses whether the amount of lead in a food product is high enough to raise a person's blood lead level to a point of concern. To do this, the agency calculated a maximum daily intake for lead from food, called the Interim Reference Level (IRL). In determining the IRL, the FDA takes into account the amount of a particular food a person would need to consume daily, as well as other factors, that would result in blood lead levels of 5 ug/dL, the level at which the CDC recommends clinical monitoring of lead exposure in children. The FDA calculated the current IRL at 3 µg per day for children and 12.5 µg per day for adults. These levels allow for differences across human populations and *are set nearly ten-times less than the actual amount of lead intake from food that would be required to reach the CDC's blood reference level.* The adult level is particularly important for women of childbearing age to protect against possible

fetal exposure in women who are unaware that they are pregnant, and against infant exposure during nursing. The FDA will continue to research and evaluate the health effects and dietary exposure to lead and will update the IRL as appropriate."

From the California Dept. of Health. Childhood Lead Poisoning Prevention Branch

If a dish contains lead then using the dishwasher can damage the glazed surface. This can make it more likely to leach lead into food the next time it is used. In addition, in some cases, lead may contaminate other dishes in the dishwasher.

- *Will the lead leach only if there are cracks or chips in the surface?*
  No. The lead-leaching can still occur even if the surface is not broken or worn. However, if the surface is chipped, cracked, or worn there may be a greater exposure to lead.

- *Will the level of lead I am exposed to from my dishes increase or decrease over time?*
  The answer is not the same for all dishes. Under some circumstances, as dishes get older, they may leach more lead into food or drink.

- *What's the difference between lead-free and lead-safe?*
  Lead-free tableware contains NO lead.

  Lead-safe tableware contains some lead, but the amount of lead that can get into food does not exceed the California Proposition 65 standards. Either there is very little lead in the tableware, or very little of the lead actually passes into food with use.

A great resource for information:

Tamara Rubin became a strong advocate for lead testing after her sons became exposed and poisoned during renovations. She now tests numerous products and maintains an excellent website with information on lead and many heavy metals. Please check out her website and her documentary: MisLEAD

https://tamararubin.com/about/

Where Lead is Found:

1. Old exposure sources: ceramics (watch those antiques!), water pipes, old paint and paint dust, old venetian blinds, old leaded glass crystal, old mechanical equipment, old toys.
2. New exposure sources: still found in many independently tested ceramics.
3. Chocolate! Coco powder! This was big surprise. So, what's the low down on this?
    a. It's not clear where lead is getting into the chocolate processing. Some may come from the soil where it is grown. Some may come from air contamination due to the continued use of leaded gasoline in many countries. Some may come from old machinery with lead parts used in grinding. Other causes are being explored.
    b. The darker the chocolate the more likely it's higher in lead due to more concentrated chocolate liquor or coco powder.
    c. **So how much lead is in your chocolate?** As You Sow, an environmental advocacy group has been testing chocolate, and has an excellent easy to use online reference. Under "Toxic Chocolate." This group is working to pressure the chocolate industry to identify and fix sources of lead contamination in chocolate. Many of the chocolates tested have between 0.2 – 0.6 ug of lead per serving. So, if the item has 0.5 ug/ serving and your kid eats 6 servings in a day (a

whole chocolate Easter bunny?) then they are getting the upper limit of 3 ug/day that the FDA and CDC find to still be safe. If you're an adult eating that much then you're fine. Check the list for your favorite chocolates. Some have had much higher lead levels.

    d. My take is adults can still eat chocolate, but for kids you might want to check the chart to pick the best kinds.

5. Crayola crayons: levels are low if used as a toy, but too high if your kid eats them! https://tamararubin.com/2018/08/do-crayola-crayons-have-lead-2018/

6. Old Pyrex, pre 1971

7. Old Tupperware, pre 1971

8. Old Fiestaware, pre 1971

9. Many decorative plates and serving ware from US, Europe, China, Mexico.

10. Possibly in some Balsamic vinegars: see separate section below for details.

From the California Dept. of Public Health:

- Traditional glazed terra cotta ware made in some Latin American countries, such as Mexican bean pots. They are often quite rustic and usually have a transparent glaze. Unless they are specifically labeled as lead-free or sin plomo (Spanish), use of these pots for cooking is especially hazardous and should be stopped at once. Per her website: Tamara Rubin has found Mexican pottery labeled "lead free," which in fact tested very high for lead and was a likely source of a child's lead poisoning.

- Highly decorated traditional dishes used in some Asian communities.

- Home-made or hand-crafted tableware, either from the U.S. or a foreign country, unless you are sure the maker uses a lead-free glaze.

- Bright colors or decorations on the inside dish surfaces that touch the food or drink. This includes the upper rim of a cup or bowl.
- Decorations on top of the glaze instead of beneath it. If the decorations are rough or raised, if you can feel the decoration when you rub your finger over the dish, or if you can see brush strokes above the glazed surface, the decoration is probably on top of the glaze. If the decoration has begun to wear away, there may be an even greater lead hazard.
- Antique tableware handed down in families, or found in antique stores, flea markets and garage sales. These dishes were made before lead in tableware was regulated.
- Corroded glaze, or a dusty or chalky grey residue on the glaze after the piece has been washed. Tableware in this condition may represent a serious lead hazard and should not be used.

What to Do About Lead:

1. In order to avoid both lead and heavy metals, I relied on Tamara Rubin's information.
2. Lead is rarely found in plain white dishes. Lead-containing glazes or decorations on the outside of dishes or non-food surfaces are generally not a problem. I picked one of the white dish products that she tested and found safe, white Corelle.
3. You could also pick U.S. made enamel ware. (too expensive for me) Don't use enamel ware made in China because of the risk of both lead and other heavy metals. This covers virtually all the inexpensive enamel ware.
4. Stainless steel sippy cups with silicone lids and straws are now easy to find online.
5. Stainless steel plates are a good non-breakable options for kids, pools, camping. The ones I found are pretty plain. Hopefully, someone will come out with a decorative stamped version before too long.
6. Relegate antiques and family items to display only. This includes inherited china and crystal.

7. Research lead abatement before you allow any contractor to work on lead painted surfaces in your home. Supervise work to ensure compliance with precautions. Protect your children during abatement and clean up.

8. Older schools have been found to be significant sources of lead exposure in multiple cities in the U.S. and Canada. Lead leached from old pipes, paint dust, and other sources in schools can be a real concern. Consider getting samples from your child's school and having them tested.

9. If you have any concerns about exposure, get your kids tested right away.

10. Look up your kid's favorite chocolates on AsYouSow.com.

11. You can purchase simple lead sample swabs on line or from hardware stores. These will *not* tell you if there is lead *deeper* within an object, but will tell you if there is currently lead on the *surface* of a plate, window sill, venetian blind.

MERCURY

What to Know About Mercury:

Mercury is an elemental heavy metal. It occurs in many forms with various other atoms attached. All forms cause neurotoxicity and can be potentially lethal in higher doses. It can cross the placenta and blood brain barrier putting a fetus at special risk of neurologic damage. These are well documented and known risks. Since the Industrial Revolution, the mobilization of naturally occurring mercury by human action has resulted in very large increases in human exposure as compared to the past. Some primary sources are the burning of coal, other fossil fuels, and use of lime in cement production. These activities release mercury into the air in a form that can spread globally through air currents that settle and contaminate water and soil. Thus, Chinese coal sourced power plants can become a major source of mercury on U.S. waters and land. Furthermore, the past use of coal in the U.S. has led to extensive mobilization of mercury across the Atlantic and throughout Europe.

Where is Mercury Found:

Mercury bioaccumulates in animals that consume contaminated water, soils, or smaller fish.

1. Large fish that are high on the food chain have higher levels of mercury.
2. From Greenfacts.org: "large predatory fish, such as king mackerel, pike, shark, swordfish, walleye, barracuda, large tuna (as opposed to the small tuna usually used for chunk white canned tuna), scabbard and marlin, as well as seals and toothed whales, contain the highest concentrations.
3. In addition, bottom dwelling detritus eaters (crabs, shrimp) and filter feeders (clams, mussels, scallops) *may* be contaminated *if* local underwater soils are contaminated with mercury from current or previous industrial waste dumping.
4. Albacore and blue fin tunas (very large fish) have higher levels than the smaller tunas that are used for "chunk light" canned tuna.
5. Some older dental amalgams can release mercury gas during *placement or removal.*
6. Some non-traditional medicines may have mercury in them.

What to Do About Mercury:

1. Per the FDA: Do not eat shark, swordfish, king mackerel, or tilefish because they contain high levels of mercury.
2. Avoid albacore in pregnant women and young kids. Chunk light tuna in small servings 1 to 2 times per month are believed to be okay. See links below for safe fish types and serving sizes.
3. Know the source of any bottom dwelling or filter feeding seafood you eat. Make local inquires before harvesting and eating these

types of animals as they may have higher mercury levels if local contamination of water and soil is high.

4. Women who wish to get pregnant should avoid high mercury seafood. It can take a year to eliminate mercury from your body. High levels cause permanent neurotoxic damage to a fetus.

5. Per the FDA: Five of the most commonly eaten fish that are **low** in mercury are shrimp, canned light tuna, salmon, pollock, and catfish.

6. Fish sticks and frozen fish fillets are commonly made with low mercury fish and are considered safe.

7. For children under 50 lbs., I found varying recommendations on safe fish consumption.

8. The reference below from the FDA and EPA provides a great printable summary and list of safer and less safe fish.
   - *Advice About Eating Fish: For Women Who Are Or Might Become Pregnant, Breastfeeding Mothers, And Young Children.* FDA and EPA, 2015-2020 guidelines. https://www.fda.gov/downloads/Food/ResourcesForYou/Consumers/UCM536321.pdf

Author's note:

Please notice that the FDA "Good Choice" list contains multiple bottom dwelling and filter feeding organisms. It is important to know the source location of these animals. If they are fished from a location that is near a former industrial site, then there is potential for significant contamination. It's unfortunate, but this kind of information can be hard to find.

Some additional sources of information:
- *FDA/EPA 2004 Advice on What You Need to Know About Mercury in Fish and Shellfish,* July 2019. https://www.fda.gov/food/metals/what-you-need-know-about-mercury-fish-and-shellfish

- *Too Much Tuna Means Too Much Mercury for Kids*, Daniel Denoon, WebMD, Sept. 2012. https://www.webmd.com/children/news/20120919/too-much-tuna-too-much-mercury-kids#1

ARSENIC

What to Know About Arsenic:

First, some terminology for clarity. Arsenic occurs *naturally* in both its inorganic, and its organic forms. In this case, we are using the word "organic" in the "organic chemistry" sense of the word. So, organic arsenic has a carbon atom attached to the arsenic and inorganic arsenic does not have a carbon atom. We are not talking about natural or "organic" *farming* practices we're talking about *chemical structures.*

Organic Arsenic (with a carbon atom) is *naturally* found in fish and shellfish. It is benign and not a health concern.

Inorganic Arsenic (without a carbon atom) is found *naturally* in many soils around the world with varying concentrations. It was also previously used in pesticides, paints, wood sealants, paper products, and other industrial uses, but is now prohibited. Inorganic arsenic is highly water soluble. This means that ground water and plants that grow in water can be contaminated with inorganic arsenic both naturally and from old contamination of the soil. Established safe levels in drinking water are quite strict. We know from other parts of the world where contamination is high that the consequences of inorganic arsenic accumulation in people is very severe. Currently, there are no established safe standards for arsenic in food. The problem of accumulative dosing from *foods* had not been recognized until recently. However, inorganic arsenic is now found in a wide variety of foods partly due to the use of rice in multiple forms. This is especially concerning for infants and young children whose small bodies are at risk of greater impact.

Where is Inorganic Arsenic Found:

1. Rice and rice products are a potential source of inorganic arsenic in the U.S.
2. Rice based infant formula (!)
3. Infant rice cereal.
4. Some jarred baby food that contains rice or rice syrup.
5. Both white and brown rice even if it is "organically *grown*."
6. Contaminated ground or well water in the U.S. Some areas of the world have very high inorganic arsenic contamination of drinking water, and subsequent disease. Check before you drink!
7. Cereal bars with rice
8. Many "gluten free" products that use rice flour in place of wheat
9. Rice based pasta
10. Rice drinks
11. Athletic energy gels using rice syrup.
12. Because arsenic is water soluble that also means it can leach into water sources. Ground water or well water around the country can be contaminated with arsenic.

Recent studies have shown that for some people the cumulative intake of inorganic arsenic from foods can exceed the safe levels determined for water.

What to Do About Inorganic Arsenic:

1. Basmati rice from California, Pakistan, and India has the lowest arsenic levels. Sushi rice grown in California is also lower, as is Jasmine rice from Thailand. Rice labeled U.S.A., Texas, Louisiana, or Arkansas have the highest levels of inorganic arsenic. Brown rice has higher levels than white rice. The arsenic is absorbed from the soil and water. It is not related to whether the rice is "grown organically" or not.

2. Arsenic is water soluble so *rinsing the rice can reduce the arsenic by 30%*. Or you can cook with extra water and wash it away. Even without these steps, the levels are low for adults. Mostly take caution in pregnant women, babies, children, and those on a gluten free diet, who may eat more rice than others.

3. You can use water filters to remove arsenic. See the EWG water filter review link at the end of this section.

4. Organic Oatmeal Cereal may be a good first food choice for infants as opposed to rice cereal. Remember: any oatmeal based product that does not say "organic" may well have glyphosate (Round-up) in it! Glyphosate is used to "desiccate" or dry up and kill a grain crop just before harvesting. This makes plants drier and harvesting easier. Your grain, even non-GMO grain, is now freshly coated with glyphosate! Oh, how yummy! Just what I want to feed in concentrated form to my small child! Sigh. So, look for "organic oatmeal cereal" for your baby.

5. Avoid rice syrup based infant formulas unless told otherwise by your doctor.

6. Read baby food jar labels and avoid products that contain rice or rice syrup.

7. If you are pregnant and gluten intolerant, be careful of excessive rice based products.

8. Sports gels are often made with rice syrup.

The link below reviews **current testing of rice and rice products** with a very useful comparative list at the bottom of the article:

- *How Much Arsenic Is In Your Rice? Consumer Reports' New Data And Guidelines Are Important For Everyone But Especially For Gluten Avoiders*, November 2014. https://www.consumerreports.org/cro/magazine/2015/01/how-much-arsenic-is-in-your-rice/index.htm

Here's the link to the Environmental Working Group's water filter guide:

- https://www.ewg.org/tapwater/water-filter-guide.php#findfilter

Here's a statement from the National Institute of Environmental Health Sciences about accumulation of arsenic from food sources:

- *Studies Find Arsenic In Food Adds US,* Angela Spivey, Environmental Factor, NIEHS, March 2012. https://factor. niehs.nih.gov/2012/3/science-arsenic/index.htm

From the World Health Organization on arsenic:

- https://www.who.int/news-room/fact-sheets/detail/arsenic

From the Center for Disease Control on arsenic:

- https://www.cdc.gov/biomonitoring/pdf/arsenic_factsheet.pdf

From the FDA on arsenic:

- *Statement by Dr. Susan Mayne on FDA efforts to reduce consumer exposure to arsenic in rice.* FDA, April 2018. https:// www.fda.gov/NewsEvents/Newsroom/PressAnnouncements/ ucm604807.htm

From the New York Times on arsenic:

- *Should You Be Worried About the Arsenic in Your Baby Food?* Roni Caryn Rabin, New York Times, Dec. 2017. https:// www.nytimes.com/2017/12/07/well/eat/should-you-be-worrie d-about-the-arsenic-in-your-baby-food.html

BALSAMIC VINEGAR AND LEAD

What to Know About Balsamic Vinegar and Lead:

The question of whether balsamic vinegar is safe or not remains very unclear. Small amounts of lead have been found in balsamic, and red wine vinegars especially aged balsamic from Italy. The amounts are small, but lead is very toxic. It's not clear where the lead is coming from. It could be from the barrels it is aged in or from the soil where the grapes are grown. The amount of lead in vinegars varies enormously from one bottle to another even within the same brand. In some samples, the levels are truly extremely low. In others there could be concern if it was a regular diet item for children. (like in a spaghetti sauce) It's controversial as to whether the amount is significant.

Where Do You Find Lead in Balsamic Vinegar?

1. Balsamic vinegar, especially aged
2. Red wine vinegars

What to Do About Possible Lead in Balsamic Vinegar:

1. There is no lead in white, rice, fig, or raspberry vinegars, and some California balsamic vinegars are tested and labeled lead free. If you go to the article below it contains a long list of vinegars that tested safe in 2009.
2. On the very safe side, I'd keep the kids away from regular consumption of balsamic vinegar. I'd be more comfortable with a tested California vinegar or just use one of the many potential substitutes. For adults, I doubt it's an issue.
3. *Special Report: Some Vinegars - Often Expensive, Aged Balsamic - Contain A Big Dose Of Lead. Consumers Want To Know If Vinegars Are Safe, But There Are No Easy Answers,* Jane Kay, Environmental Health News, Nov 2009.
   https://www.ehn.org/special-report-some-vinegars-often-expensive-aged-balsamics-contain-a-big-dose-of-lead-2649749136.html

FIRE RETARDANTS - PBDEs aka polybrominated diphenyl ethers

What to Know About PBDEs:

PBDEs are flame retardant chemicals that are cousins of PCBs, which were banned in 1977. Nevertheless, they persist in the environment even today.

These are carcinogens. We have more and more evidence that fire retardants are bad players that don't really help with burn prevention. Many states are now changing laws to allow products to be made without fire retardants, however, sales people commonly remain unaware of the issues. Europe is working to remove these chemicals from most products. Electronics are a common source and remain only partially improved. While these chemicals are really impossible to fully avoid, you can reduce your child's exposure.

In California, a furniture tag must now indicate whether it was treated with fire retardant or not. It is now much easier to find upholstered furniture that is not *surface* treated with chemicals.

Where Are Fire Retardant Chemicals Found?

1. Cushions: polyurethane foam with its many fire retardant additives will break down over time. It becomes a dust in the home and ultimately gets on hands and is eaten. Vacuuming frequently and washing hands before eating can help. If you change out the old foam from the cushions, do it outside and wash the covers to reduce the contaminated dust in your home. When buying new furniture try to invest in cushion filling without polyurethane foam if you can.
2. Mattresses: old crib mattresses are probably loaded with fire retardants.
3. Some children's pajamas and sleep wear.
4. Electronics: remote controls, TV's, computers, phones, wires, and cables are loaded with an assortment of fire retardant chemicals.

What to Do About Fire Retardant Chemicals:

1. Pick the right crib mattress. A quick online hunt will provide you with multiple options for both crib and twin mattresses that do not have fire retardants. Your kids will spend huge amounts of time over the years on these mattresses, and your careful choice can really help limit their exposure to these chemicals. When

they outgrow the crib you can move the mattress to the floor for continued use.

2. Use a latex twin bed when they are older. If you can't afford a full latex mattress, try a cotton futon with a latex mattress topper for extra squish. Look for a non-vinyl, non-toxic mattress or topper cover.
3. Tight cotton PJ's have no retardant on them because they are tight.
4. Loose or tight polyester PJ's are naturally flame resistant, and therefore no retardant is applied.
5. Microfiber PJ's are highly flammable, make toxic gases when burned, often have fire retardant. Stay away.
6. Electronics: Don't let your babies or kids use electronic car keys or remotes for teething.

PHTHALATES

What to Know About Phthalates:

These chemicals are endocrine disruptors. They act like synthetic hormones and can affect estrogen, testosterone, and thyroid hormones.

Where are Phthalates Found?

They are commonly found in cosmetics and anything with a scent or fragrance. Unless the product says phthalate free, then assume they are in your soaps, shampoos, lotions, air fresheners, laundry detergents, etc. They are also used in plastics.

What to Do About Phthalates:

1. Avoid products that list "fragrance" as an ingredient.
2. Be very leery of air fresheners, scented candles, shampoos and lotions, etc. unless it says, "Phthalate free."

3. Stick to organic and Phthalate-free body care products for your kids
4. Avoid plastic.

LAVENDER AND TEA TREE ESSENTIAL OILS!

What to Know About Lavender and Tea Tree Oils:

I have to admit this one surprised me. Apparently, both of these oils contain some very estrogen-like compounds. We now have some case studies in which they were found to cause gynecomastia in boys. This is a condition in which hormone stimulation leads to enlargement of male breast tissue. There's also a case in which topically applied lavender products caused premature breast development in a female toddler. Both the male and female exposures came from topically applied products. In one study, boys had been using a lavender based cologne and the female toddler was exposed to lotions, wipes, and shampoos with lavender oils. In both the gynecomastia and the premature breast development cases, the breasts of the children returned to normal size once their exposure to the oils was stopped. Furthermore, the estrogenic compounds found in lavender and tea tree oil may also be found in other essential oils. We just don't have comprehensive testing yet. As of this writing, I haven't found any data on the use of aerosolized essential oils. The above concern is based on topical applications to skin. This is a very, very new concern and has not yet become widely known. See the articles and statements from the Endocrine Society from 2019. Link is below.

Bummer! I like smelly stuff! But between phthalates and now essential oils?!

Where are Lavender and Tea Tree Oils Found:

1. A wide variety of organic and non-organic body care products including many marketed for infants.

What to Do About Essential Oils:

1. Look for organic and "unscented" baby care products until further testing has been done on essential oils.
2. If you are going through fertility treatment or have a hormone based cancer, consider avoiding essential oils.

More info:
- *Essential Oils*, National Institutes of Environmental Services, Nov 2020. (note links at bottom of page for more info) https://www.niehs.nih.gov/health/topics/agents/essential-oils/index.cfm
- *Prepubertal Gynecomastia Linked To Lavender And Tea Tree Oils*, Henley et al, New England Journal of Medicine, NIH, Feb 2007. https://www.ncbi.nlm.nih.gov/pubmed/17267908
- *Premature Thelarche In The Setting Of High Lavender Oil Exposure*, Linklater, MD; Hewitt, MD, Journal of Pediatrics and Child Health, 2015. https://onlinelibrary.wiley.com/doi/pdf/10.1111/jpc.12837

Here's a press release from the Endocrine Society, 2018.
- *Chemicals In Lavender And Tea Tree Oil Appear To Be Hormone Disruptors, 2018.* https://www.endocrine.org/news-room/2018/chemicals-in-lavender-and-tea-tree-oil-appear-to-be-hormone-disruptors

TALC AND TALCUM POWDER

What to Know About Talc:

Talc is a clay mineral mined from the earth. The problem is that asbestos is often found in the same locations and contaminates the talc. Some talc has more asbestos than other talc. This is not regulated nor tested as the products are considered cosmetic or body care products. Inhaled asbestos has long been known to cause a lung cancer called mesothelioma. In addition, regular use of talcum powder on a woman's vulva is known to increase the risk of ovarian cancer.

Where is Talc Found?

1. Baby powder: some is talc based. Others are cornstarch based.
2. Cosmetics: many powder based products have talc.
3. Powders or powder-based sprays, such as products used for athlete's foot or foot odor, may contain talc.
4. Some antiperspirant sticks.

What to Do About Talc Exposure:

1. Read labels and don't use products with talc.
2. If using baby powder, look for ones with cornstarch. Be aware that inhaling any fine particle should be avoid, if possible.
3. Look for talc-free cosmetics and antiperspirants.
4. Look under "inactive or inert" ingredients and pick sprays that don't contain talc. If possible, switch to creams. Teach your kids not to accidentally inhale these foot care products.

FILTERING YOUR WATER

Environmental Working Group produces an excellent guide to water filters and what they filter.

- https://www.ewg.org/tapwater/water-filter-guide.php#findfilter

Well now, if you've made it to the end of this segment you may find yourself shaking in your shoes. It surely shakes me up every time I read it! There are just so many of these vague, but truly concerning, chemical threats. What's a parent supposed to do?

The truth is you can't protect your child from all of this all of the time. However, with a little info under your belt, you can cut back on your family's chemical exposure. If you manage that, you are rockin' it! If you're still shaking in your shoes, take a deep breath. Remember, we can't control everything. We just can't. The seat belt and car seat are probably more important to your child's safety and well-being. Do what you can, then get on with living.

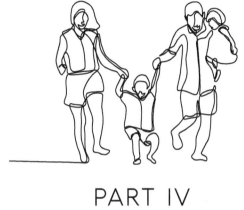

PART IV

THE BIG PICTURE

28

IT TAKES A FAMILY

THE VALUE OF FAMILY

AS WE MOVE THROUGH OUR busy life, there is much we take for granted. Some things feel normal or simply "the way it has always been." Yet, when we visit other countries we may find completely different "normals." Here are a few books that offer outside perspective on what we consider normative in family life:

1. *Parenting without Borders: Surprising Lessons Parents Around the World Can Teach Us*, by Christine Gross-Loh.
2. *The Danish Way of Parenting: What the Happiest People in the World Know About Raising Confident, Capable Kids*, by Jessica Joelle Alexander and Iben Sandahl.
3. *The Nordic Way of Everything: In Search of a Better Life*, by Anu Partanen.
4. *Bringing Up Bebe*, by Pamela Druckerman.

All of these books opened my eyes to the ways in which U.S. families are expected to manage with remarkably little family, community, or institutional support. In many parts of our world, this is *not* the norm. Another book that helped me look at parenthood with fresh insight was *All Joy and No Fun: the Paradox of Modern Parenthood* by Jennifer Senior. Many of us are so busy trying to get through our day that we forget to ask if it really has to be this way.

It is my belief that in this country, we as a society, fail our children from birth onward. We fail our families. I believe these failings will hold this country back more than any other force. Mothers and fathers want to have a family life. They want their kids to be well cared for and happy. And they want to work, use their brains, make money, and produce.

Yet, many American corporate environments, businesses, factories, law makers, and our working world in general act as if children and family life simply don't exist. They create environments in which it is nearly impossible to juggle family needs with a work life. In addition, there is little in the way of institutional governmental support for families. The result is parents who pull back at work so they can "lean in" at home. If you think of parenthood as a privilege for those who can afford children, then it seems unreasonable to expect governments to help families. But, if you see parenthood as a service that creates our culture's members, workers, and inventors, then we can recognize it as something that offers great value to our society. It becomes clear that it is the responsibility of the community to support the raising of our country's next generation.

If we want our work force to thrive, then we need to help parents. When the structure of our culture provides the support, time, and space that families need to maintain a happy family life, then and only then, will parents be able to truly focus on their life's industry.

WORDS FOR THE WORKING PARENT

Try really, really hard to put your foot down at work and leave on time. Just do it. On your way home take five minutes in the car before you go in the house to breathe. Just breathe, and let go of work. Get ready for family. The minute you hit the door you're going to be "on duty" and a stay-at-home-parent may well be fried and in need of a "baby break."

I've done it both ways. Stay-at-home mom and working mom. When I was working, I might have been tired and stressed by the end of work, but I was also "baby fresh." Sometimes I had to dig deep to find the energy for the kids, but the patience and the willingness was there. However, as a SAHM I am truly "kid fried" by the end of the day. Patience is gone. Gone. Gone. I usually make it through dinner and then I'm done. Done in. Done. By morning I'll be renewed, patient, and attentive all over again. But, after dinner I need that working and kid-fresh parent to step up and start shouldering most of the load.

I think my husband rather likes this time. He gets to take charge of the kids and do things *his* way. And if the "peanut gallery commentator" is soaking in a hot bath, then she can't gripe about too much dessert, extra TV, using the wrong shampoo, or pre-bedtime rough housing instigated by a "so called" adult. Once he's put the kids to bed, however, *he* thinks we should be done. He's hit *his* end of the day limit! Fortunately, I'm just enough revived by then to find some last little, bitty, bit of patience to handle the usual bedtime shenanigans.

Don't be surprised if you feel guilty about not being home enough. It seems to be a part of parenthood that no matter how good a parent we are being, we always find something to feel guilty about. Commit to making time for your family. No one's going to give it to you. You're going to have to fight for that time. Remember you are in this for the long haul. You will be loving, caring for, guiding, influencing, and present for your children day in and day out for a long, long time. They will need different things at different times, and you'll be there. Take pride in your contribution to the family and take the long view.

But do take that five minutes to breathe and shift gears before you walk in the door after work. Everyone inside is tired, fried, hungry, yet happy to see you! The coming home hour is an emotionally intense time of day and will always be prone to both joyous greetings and sudden meltdowns...within the same five minutes! It's okay. This is normal.

LET SPOUSE DO IT THEIR WAY

There is no doubt that a stay-at-home-parent knows how to do *everything* better than a working parent. Okay, maybe there is *some* doubt. Maybe they *occasionally* bring some fresh perspective to things. Harrumph. Regardless of the fact that "they don't know how to do *anything*," you *still* need to let them do things their own way. Sigh. It can be so hard to let go of the reins when you've only just gotten the beasties running in the right direction. Still. *Still.* You are an imperfect being. *You* might actually learn something from your partner. And they too are parents. Your partner gets to develop their own parenting style. Yikes!

You'll need to reach some agreement on the basics. How much TV time and when? How much junk food and when? Rigid nap times or flexible ones. Then expect, no really *expect*, that your partner will break all the rules. Now, here's the most important relationship secret for parents. When your partner breaks all the rules, just ignore it. Really, let it go. It's not that important in the larger scheme of things. Your kids will continue to grow and thrive. The earth will still move around the sun. The days will come and go. And perhaps you'll learn to be a bit less rigid and a bit less in control.

Remember how I told you that becoming a parent involves developing a whole new skill set? You're going to be running around mastering all these new parenting skills so you can gain some little bit of control over your life. And now you have to let go!? So, some *doofus*, okay a really nice, sweet, hard-working *doofus*, can do it *their* way! Aaargh! Yes, now that you have control, you have to let it go. It can be a very irritating life lesson. But, it's also freeing and good for your partnership.

MAKING IT WORK FOR PARENTS

This next bit is important, and hard to do in our culture. You will find yourself making decisions about what you feel your kids need as time goes along. What you will forget to do is ask yourself what *you* need?

What does your *partner* need? What does your *relationship* need? And, frankly, these are really, really important questions to consider. Your kids are programmed to grow up. They will do so in any of a variety of life and home situations. Set things up so they work for you, your partner, and your relationship. You can weave the kids' needs into almost anything. And the most, most important thing you can give them is happy stable parents.

If daycare is going great for your kids, but both parents are overwhelmed with the frantic daily juggle of drop-off and pick-up, then it's not working for *the family*. It will strain all the relationships. Don't be afraid to consider a nanny, or a different daycare location, or a pick-up / drop-off driver, or a mother's helper, or letting grandma live with you for a year.

Unfortunately, this is not as easy as it may sound. Despite the American love of "family values," we make it really, really hard to have a family in this country. Maybe the best thing for your family is for someone to stay home with the kids, but you can't afford it. Maybe Dad makes the most money, but Mom has the health insurance. Maybe both parents feel they'd be happier and more balanced if they worked, but childcare is not affordable. Maybe you have a child with special needs, and our country's failure to help leaves you without options. You'll find you need to make many decisions within the context of the limitations of *your* reality. All you can do is try to remember to include the needs of parents and relationships in the choices you make for your kids and family.

I offer one more tip that comes with the perspective of time. These first years of intensive childcare do ease up considerably as your kids get older. By first grade, you will probably be able to take your kids to early drop off at school, and pick them up from the after-school program. You'll still have to pay for it, of course. And you'll still have to handle sick days. And you'll struggle to figure out how to get everyone out of the house on time. (Hint: start teaching life skills and independence now!) Yes, there will be a new set of big kid parenting challenges. But your kids will put Nutella and peanut butter on their own Kashi waffles for breakfast (huge mess!) and pack their own school stuff (they will forget a lot of things, but that's okay!) and walk to the car under their own power.

So, if your relationship with your partner is feeling stretched by the strain of these early years…if *you* are feeling stretched by the strain of it all…it does ease up. Provided, of course, you don't get the baby bug again and have more rug rats!

GIVING THANKS

Families divide up parental duties in all kinds of ways. I suspect in the future more men will take time at home with kids, and more women will get back to work. Eventually, we'll have more negotiation between partners regarding the division of family work. However, regardless of whether parental roles take on a traditional form or a more modern one, it is very important to acknowledge the work and worries of your partner.

If you have a stay-at-home-parent, who shoulders most of the daily parenting challenges, cares for the family's emotional and physical well-being, manages the dinners and diets, researches the schools, then that person needs to know the other parent respects and values this work.

If you have a working parent, who shoulders most of the financial burdens, maintains the house and the car, balances the cash flow, and makes the family money, then that person needs to know that the other parent appreciates the hard work and worrisome burden they carry. Primary bread winners can often feel the burden of financial responsibility very deeply. Primary child care givers can often feel unappreciated for their work and sacrifices. Remember to say "thank you" to your partner. It is hugely important.

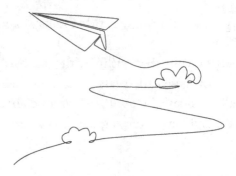

29

WHAT EXACTLY ARE WE TRYING TO ACCOMPLISH?

PARENTING GOALS: MY TWO CENTS WORTH

WHAT'S THE POINT OF ALL of this parental energy, hope, and angst? What are we hoping to accomplish with all the years invested in raising the little beasties? What do *you* want for that adult-in-training?

In our grandparent's time, we might have been aiming to raise adults who were "fine, moral, upstanding members of the community." We would hope to raise, "a good provider, a good homemaker, an asset to the family who would care for aging parents." I suspect, however, these ideas were not the first thoughts that popped into *your* head! Our parents, and many of our generation, might think more in terms of hoping to raise children who are "happy and healthy, self-fulfilled, financially successful, upwardly mobile, and doing personally rewarding work."

It's interesting that the goals of the past were often about instilling a sense of duty to others, while they neglected the needs of the individual. More recent goals are often about following a duty to ourselves, but they tend to neglect our duty to others. And mixed in there is this questionable new idea about *endless* upward mobility, and each generation doing "better" than the previous one.

I would argue that an emotionally healthy set of goals to guide our parenting thoughts is one that incorporates teaching a duty to both others and self. There are problems when we raise our kids to seek their "calling" in life. It suggests there is some special "thing" that will fulfill them and make them "happy" if only they can "find" it. If we spend too much time trying to figure out what makes us "happy," we risk getting lost in a meaningless pursuit of an ephemeral myth. It also implies that everything should revolve around us and our own needs. Yet, the world does not revolve around us. Furthermore, life often takes us on a different path than the one we'd planned to follow. That is not necessarily a bad thing. Nor is it necessarily a good thing. It is reality. Truth is "life is what *happens*, while you're making other plans."[9] So, we don't want to teach our kids that a good life lies in achieving some specific goal or path that will somehow fulfill them. They may wind up in an entirely different place, and a very different life. Instead, we can guide our children to "use *their* skills and interests to make the world a better place." Whether it's painting the community center a happy color or installing composting toilets in India, when we give to our community, we connect to our reason for being. And it is this connection that can offer real contentment with life.

I think we should teach our children that caring for others is a duty and an honor because providing food, and comfort, and a home for our family or for a stranger has great value. And, when we care for the needs of others, we connect to our reason for being. It is this connection that can offer real contentment with life.

I think we should aim to raise an adult who views the world through open minded compassion. Who judges not by superficial appearances but by deeper truths carefully sought. Who seeks to make the world a better place through actions big or small, because when we make the world a better place, we connect with our reason for being. And it is this connection that can offer real contentment with life.

---

[9] Allen Saunders.

I think we should teach our children to embrace their life's industry for the gifts it brings to the world as this will connect them to their reason for being and bring them joy.

KIDS ARE LIKE A BOX OF CHOCOLATES

You never know what you're gonna' get! Very, very true. Sweet, sticky, and often nutty, kids will surprise you every day. But I'm not just talking about the goofy things that kids will say and do. In the U.S., we have an overwhelming, almost fanatical, belief in the ability to control our own destiny. And that often extends to the idea that we can shape and develop our children into who we feel they should be, which is complete, utter, unequivocal, nonsense! Okay, okay, yes, you are their mother, their father, but that just means you get the *honor* of watching them grow into *themselves*. You don't get to decide who that self *IS*. They already *are* who they are from day one. And if you're not sure about that, ask any parent of twins. Different from day one. Individuals from day one. As my kid's pre-school teacher liked to say about treats, "You get what you get, and you don't have a fit!" So, if you were a tomboy who played tackle tag with the boys and hated pink (me), and you have a 5-year-old daughter who will only wear pink or princess dresses (true), then you love her for who she *IS*. And you do a bit of your own growing up when you make the effort to learn about something new for someone you love. There are many things in life we can't control. Who your children are is one of those things. Sometimes you just gotta go with the flow. And that "letting go" can be one of the great liberating life lessons of parenthood.

PRACTICING COMPASSION IN EVERYDAY LIFE

I'm not a religious person. I'm not even very "spiritual." Still, I've found wisdom in all kinds of places. One day, many years ago, I picked up a book by the Dalai Lama. What I remember from the book was the encouragement to, well, "practice compassion in everyday life." I find over the years that this comes back to me again and again. It is a powerful tool in life and in parenting. Practice compassion in everyday life. Practice compassion towards your children, and their struggles as they journey through this world and grow towards adulthood. Practice compassion for your spouse. For family members. For yourself. For other parents. Practice compassion for strangers in this community of our world. Practice it. In everyday life.

For more on that thought:
The Compassion Gap, by Nicholas Kristoff.
https://www.nytimes.com/2014/03/02/opinion/
sunday/kristof-the-compassion-gap.html

APPENDIX A

GOOD BOOKS FOR PARENTS

There are more good books in the bibliography but these are my favorites.

Earliest days:
1. *The Sleep Easy Solution*, Jennifer Waldberger and Jill Spivack
2. *Happiest Baby On The Block*, Harvey Karp, MD
3. *Baby-Proofing Your Marriage: How To Laugh More And Argue Less As Your Family Grows*. Stacie Cockrell, Cathy Oneill, Julia Stone
4. *Child Of Mine, Feeding With Love And Good Sense*, Ellyn Satter

General Parenting:
1. *Happiest Toddler On The Block*, Harvey Karp, MD
2. *The Kazdin Method For Parenting The Defiant Child*, Alan E Kazdin, Ph.D
3. *Duct Tape Parenting*, Vicki Hoefle
4. *Hunt, Gather, Parent: What Ancient Cultures Can Teach Us About The Lost Art Of Raising Happy Helpful Humans*, Michaeleen Doucleff, PhD
5. *The No-Cry Separation Anxiety Solution*, Elizabeth Pantley
6. *The Danish Way Of Parenting: What The Happiest People In The World Know About Raising Confident Capable Kids*. Jessica Joelle Alexander and Iben Sandahl

Feeding Kids and Families:
1. *Child Of Mine, Feeding With Love And Good Sense*, Ellyn Satter

2. *Secrets Of Feeding A Healthy Family: How To Eat, How To Raise Good Eaters, How To Cook,* Ellyn Satter.
3. *Getting To Yum*, Karen Le Billon
4. *Sicker, Poorer, Fatter: The Urgent Threat Of Hormone-Disrupting Chemicals To Our Health And Future… And What We Can Do About It.* Leonardo Trasande, MD, MPP.

Twin Specific Issues:
1. *Emotionally Healthy Twins*, Joan Friedman, Ph.D

The Parenthood Experience:
1. *Parenting Without Borders: Surprising Lessons Parents Around The World Can Teach Us*, Christine Gross-Loh
2. *The Danish Way of Parenting: What the Happiest People in the World Know About Raising Confident, Capable Kids*, Jessica Joelle Alexandra and Iben Sandahl
3. *The Nordic Way of Everything: In Search of a Better Life*, Anu Partanen
4. *All Joy, No Fun: The Paradox Of Modern Parenthood*, Jennifer Senior
5. *Bringing Up Bebe*, Pamela Druckerman

Boys and Boyhood:
1. *Raising Cain: Protecting The Emotional Life Of Boys*, Dan Kindlon, Ph.D. and Michael Thompson, Ph.D
2. *Boys Adrift: The Five Factors Driving The Growing Epidemic Of Unmotivated Boys And Underachieving Young Men*, Leonard Sax, MD, Ph.D
3. *The Way Of Boys*, Anthony Rao

Girls and Girlhood:
1. *Girls On The Edge: The Four Factors Driving The New Crisis For Girls*, Leonard Sax, MD, Ph.D

2. *Cinderella Ate My Daughter: Dispatches From The Front Lines Of The New Girlie-Girl Culture*, Peggy Orenstein

Potty Training and Bowel Issues:
   1. *Stress-Free Potty Training: A Commonsense Guide To Finding The Right Approach For Your Child*, Sara Au and Peter Stavinoha, Ph.D.,
   2. *The Ins And Outs Of Poop*, Thomas R Duhamel, Ph.D

Educating Kids:
   1. *Free To Learn: Why Unleashing The Instinct To Play Will Make Our Children Happier, More Self-Reliant, And Better Students For Life*, Peter Gray
   2. *Beyond Measure: Rescuing An Overscheduled, Overtested, Underestimated Generation*, Vickie Abeles with Grace Rubenstein
   3. *The Importance Of Being Little: What Young Children Really Need From Grown Ups*, Erika Christakis
   4. *What If Everybody Understood Child Development*, Rae Pica.
   5. *Bright Kids Who Can't Keep Up: Help Your Child Overcome Slow Processing Speed And Succeed In A Fast-Paced World,.* Ellen Braaten and Brian Willoughby
   6. *Range: Why Generalists Triumph In A Specialized World*, David Epstein

Emotional Support and Wisdom:
   1. *The Infertility Survival Guide: Everything You Need To Know To Cope With The Challenges While Maintaining Your Sanity, Dignity, And Relationships.* Judith Daniluk, Ph.D
   2. *Strong As A Mother: How To Stay Happy, Healthy, And Most Importantly Sane From Pregnancy To Parenthood*, Kate Rope.

Cultural Issues Affecting Parenthood:
   1. *America The Anxious,* Ruth Whippman.

2. *The Nordic Theory of Everything: In Search of a Better Life*, Ana Partanen.
3. *The Year Of Living Danishly: Uncovering The Secrets Of The Worlds Happiest People.* Helen Russel
4. *Women's Work: A Reckoning With Home And Help*, Megan Stack.
5. *Doughnut Economics: 7 Ways to Think Like a 21st Century Economist.* Kate Rayworth

Relationship Issues and Parenthood:
1. *How Not To Hate Your Husband After Kids*, Jancee Dunn
2. *The 5 love languages: the Secret to Love That Last,* Gary Chapman.
3. *The Dance of Anger*, Harriet Lerner.
4. *Babyproofing Your Marriage: How to Laugh More and Argue Less as Your Family Grows*, Stacie Cockrell, Cathey O'Neill, and Julia Stone

General Wisdom:
1. *Ethics for the New Millennium,* the Dalai Lama.
2. *The Compassion Gap*, Nicholas Kristoff, 3/2/2014, New York Times.

APPENDIX B

GOOD BOOKS FOR KIDS

1. *The Going To Bed Book,* Sandra Boynton (All her books are great!)
2. *Happy Hippo, Angry Duck!* Sandra Boynton
3. *Horns To Toes And In Between,* Sandra Boynton
4. *Pajama Time,* Sandra Boynton
5. *Snuggle Puppy,* Sandra Boynton
6. *Everyone Poops,* Taro Gomi
7. *Softy the Poop: Helping Families Talk About Poop,* Thomas DuHamel, PhD. and Kevin Brockschmidt
8. *I Love You All Day Long,* Frances Rusackas and Priscilla Burris
9. *The Kissing Hand,* Audrey Penn and Ruth Harper
10. *Llama, Llama Misses Mama,* Anna Dewdney
11. *The Run Away Bunny,* Margaret Wise Brown and Clement Hurd
12. *Oh My Baby, Little One,* Kathi Appelt and Jane Dyer
13. *Wherever You Are, My Love Will Find You,* Nancy Tillman
14. *How Full is Your Bucket…for Kids,* Tom Rath and Mary Reckmeyer
15. *Steam Train, Dream Train,* Sherri Dusky Rinker and Tom Lichtenheld.
16. *Goodnight, Goodnight, Construction Site,* Sherri Dusky Rinker and Tom Lichetenheld.
17. *Ladybug Girl,* David Soman and Jack Davis.
18. *Mike Mulligan and His Steam Shovel,* Virginia Lee Burton
19. *Katie and the Big Snow,* Virginia Lee Burton
20. *Kami and the Yaks,* Andrea Stenn Stryer and Bert Dodson.
21. *Two Cool Coyotes,* Jillian Lund.

22. *How to Babysit a Grandma/pa*, Jean Reagan and Lee Wildish.
23. *It's Hard to Be Five*, Jamie Lee Curtis and Laura Cornell
24. *I'm Gonna Like Me*, and others by Jamie Lee Curtis and Laura Cornell
25. *The Paper Bag Princess*, Robert Munsch and Micheal Martchencko
26. *Giraffes Can't Dance*, Giles Andreas and Guy Parker Rees
27. *Prince Cinders*, Babette Cole
28. *Princess Smarty Pants*, Babette Cole
29. *The Tale of Custard the Dragon*, Ogden Nash and Lynn Munsinger
30. *Rosie's Magic Horse*, Russell Hoban
31. *A Balloon for Isabel*, Deborah Underwood and Laura Rankin

For starting school:
1. *Miss Bindergarten Gets Ready for Kindergarten*, Joseph Slate, Joseph and Ashley Wolff
2. *T'was the Night Before Kindergarten*, Natasha Wing and Julie Durell (a series)

APPENDIX C

USEFUL WEBSITES

1. Multiples of America http://www.multiplesofamerica.org
2. Regarding hunter-gatherer education
   https://link.springer.com/article/10.1007/s13164-017-0347-2
3. Regarding *Free to Learn*, Dr Peter Gray- hunter-gatherer children
   https://www.naturalchild.org/peter_gray/hunter-gatherers.html
4. RESOLVE National infertility support group.
   https://resolve.org
5. CDC Fertility Clinic info. Assisted Reproductive Technology
   Success Rates by clinic
   http://www.cdc.gov/art/NationalSummary_SuccessRates.htm
6. Growth Charts https://www.cnn.com/2018/04/04/health/
   growth-chart-parenting-strauss/index.html
7. Constipation based encopresis help
   https://dulwichcentre.com.au/beating-sneaky-poo-1.pdf
8. Perinatal Mood Disorders
   a. Postpartum Depression Fact Sheet from NIH
      https://www.nimh.nih.gov/health/publications/
      postpartum-depression-facts/index.shtml
   b. About Postpartum Anxiety
      https://www.parents.com/parenting/moms/healthy-mom/
      the-other-postpartum-problem-anxiety/
11. National Suicide Prevention Lifeline, dial 988 anywhere in
    the U.S. This 24-hour suicide prevention helpline specializes
    in handling situations related to suicide and emotional
    distress.
12. Depression, Psych Central, list of depression hotlines and chat lines.
    https://psychcentral.com/lib/depression-hotline-numbers/

13. Environmental Working Group, EWG
14. National Institute of Environmental Health Sciences
https://www.niehs.nih.gov/health/topics/agents/index.cfm

APPENDIX D

TOYS AND GIFTS BY AGE

Age 9-12 months: everything will go in their mouth!
1. entertainment center
2. soft balls
3. blocks
4. rattles
5. board books
6. fabric in different textures- stuff them in an empty tissue box or wipes container
7. cardboard boxes- big and small

Age 18 months + : everything will *still* go in their mouth!
1. wooden trains and tracks
2. toy cell phones / car keys
3. Melissa and Doug toys- pizza, cupcakes
4. empty spray bottle and wash cloth
5. cardboard boxes
6. water table
7. board books
8. stuffed animals

Age 2 years old + :(many kids will still explore with their mouth...sigh)
1. sit and scoot toys- best with built in storage trunk under the seat
2. electronic alphabet device
3. Hot Wheels cars and track
4. toy vacuum or other home appliance

5. water/ sand table for outdoor play.
6. small, hand held dust pan and brush
7. pots, pans, cups

Age 3+

1. costumes- imaginary play explodes at this age
2. doctor kits
3. Magformers
4. Battat take apart vehicles
5. scoot bikes
6. Kumon tracing / letters/ numbers books
7. zoo/museum memberships
8. Melissa and Doug toys: costumes, coloring books, imaginary play
9. craft kit- magic markers, paper, glue, hole punch, tape, pencil w/ sharpener, erasers, safety scissors, googly eyes, pom poms, etc. (careful of choking hazards!)
10. play kitchen or store
11. play food
12. play cook ware
13. shopping cart
14. card board boxes- all sizes!

Age 4+

1. Legos
2. 3 wheel scooter w/ <u>helmet</u>
3. larger balls
4. dinosaur figures- some will love, some will find scary
5. simple remote control vehicles- start with the cheap ones from the drug store!
6. costumes and imaginary play toys
7. mask and snorkel

Age 5+

1. bicycle with training wheels
2. more books
3. 2 wheel scooter
4. paint sets with good brushes
5. clay
6. craft kits age specific- jewelry, needle point, etc.
7. science kits- crystals, robots, chemistry
8. more complex remote control vehicles
9. a simple drone
10. costumes are still cool!
11. At this point many kids will start to have expressible preferences that can help guide you.
12. Nerf weapons
13. water guns

Age 6+

1. costumes are still cool!
2. bike, trike, or things that go
3. building kits
4. ant farms, lady bug kits, praying mantis egg cases (from your nursery)
5. microscope
6. good pair of binoculars
7. camper's head lamp
8. drone with camera

A FEW CHAPTER NOTES

Chapter 2: Growing Pains for Grown Ups
1. *Miscarriage*, GrowbyWebMD. https://www.webmd.com/baby/guide/pregnancy-miscarriage#1

Chapter 4: The New Fatherhood
1. *Sweden Is Apparently Full Of 'Latte Dads' Carrying Toddlers — And It's A Sign Of Critical Social Change.* Libby Kane, Insider, Apr 4, 2018.

Chapter 19: Fear Based Childhood Education
1. *How Hunter-Gatherers Maintained Their Egalitarian Ways.* Peter Gray PhD., Psychology Today, May 16, 2011.
2. https://www.psychologytoday.com/us/blog/freedom-learn/201105/how-hunter-gatherers-maintained-their-egalitarian-ways
3. *How The First Farmers Changed History.* Carl Zimmer, New York Times, Oct. 17, 2016. https://www.nytimes.com/2016/10/18/science/ancient-farmers-archaeology-dna.html
4. *Free to Learn*, Peter Gray, Basic Books, 2015.
5. *Pioneers In Our Field: Freidrich Froebel, Founder Of The First Kindergarten.* Early Childhood Today Editorial Staff, Scholastic Inc., 2021.
6. *History of Head Start.* US Dept. of Health and Human Resources, Office of Head Start. https://www.acf.hhs.gov/ohs/about/history-of-head-start
7. *Don't Dismiss that 30 Million Word Gap Quite So Fast*, Robert Pondiscio. EducationNext, 6/6/2019.
8. *The Neuroscience of 20-Somethings*, Ferris Jabr. Scientific American, 8/29/12.

9. *Reading Instruction In Kindergarten: Little Gain And Much To Lose*, Nancy Carlsson-Paige, Geralyn Bywater McLaughlin, and Joan Wolfsheimer Almon, Alliance for Childhood.

10. *Early Academic Training Produces Long-Term Harm Research Reveals Potential Risks Of Academic Preschools And Kindergartens.* Peter Gray, Psychology Today, May 5, 2015

11. *Reading Instruction In Kindergarten: Little Gain And Much To Lose*, Nancy Carlsson-Paige, Geralyn Bywater McLaughlin, & Joan Wolfsheimer Almon, Alliance for Childhood.

Chapter 21: The Pathless Journey

1. *Parenting Without Borders: Surprising Lessons Parents Around the World Can Teach Us*, Christine Gross-Loh, PhD.

2. *Bringing Up Bebe*, Pamela Druckerman

3. *Rise and Shine: What Kids Eat Around the World,* M. Wollan, and H. Whitaker, New York Times, 2014.

Chapter 22: The Truth About American Motherhood

1. *The Feminine Mystique*, Betty Friedan, 1963, WW Norton Publishing.

2. Women's Unpaid Work Must Be Included In GDP Calculations: Lessons From History. Luke Messac, MD, Ph.D. The Conversation, June 20, 2018.

3. *Sweden Is Apparently Full Of 'Latte Dads' Carrying Toddlers-And It's A Sign Of Critical Social Change*, Libby Kane, Insider, Apr 4, 2018.

4. *What The U.S. Can Learn From Finland, Where School Starts At Age 7,* Claudio Sanchez, National Public Radio, March 8, 2014

5. *The Way We Measure Economies Is Inherently Sexist,* Diane Coyle, World Economic Forum, 4/2016. https://www.weforum.org/agenda/2016/04/why-economic-policy-overlooks-women/

6. *19th Amendment to the US Constitution: Women's Right to Vote.* https://www.ourdocuments.gov/doc.
7. *Married Women's Property Acts in the United States.* https://en.wikipedia.org
8. *Conjugal Bonds And Wage Labor: Rights Of Contract In The Age Of Emancipation.* Amy Dru Stanley, Journal of American History, 9/1988.
9. *Domestic Violence in the United States.* Wikipedia.org
10. *A Brief History Of Birth Control In The US.*, Carrie Baker, Christen Thompson and others, Our Bodies Ourselves, July 2020. https://www.ourbodiesourselves.org/book-excerpts/health-article/a-brief-history-of-birth-control/
11. *Women and Law*, President and Fellows of Harvard Law, Women, Enterprise, and Society, pub. of Harvard Business School, 2010. https://www.library.hbs.edu/hc/wes/collections/women_law/
12. *7 Shocking Things Women Weren't Allowed to Do Until Fairly Recently*, Beth Dreher, 8/13/2016, Woman's Day.

Chapter 23: Common Issues of the Early Years of Parenting
Soothing…

1. *Chemicals in Lavender and Tea Tree Oils Appear to be Hormone Disrupters,* March 19, 2018, Endocrine Society. https://www.endocrine.org/news-and-advocacy/news-room/2018/chemicals-in-lavender-and-tea-tree-oil-appear-to-be-hormone-disruptors

Breast vs. Bottle

1. *Beneficial Effects Of Breastfeeding In Women With Gestational Diabetes Mellitus.* Daniela Much et al., Molecular Metabolism, June 2014.

Chapter 24: Parenting Issues of the Later Early Years

Reading Anxiety
1. *Learning to Read: What Age is the "Right" Age?* Susan
    Goldberg, Today's Parent, May 7, 2016. https://www.
    todaysparent.com/family/activities/right-age-to-read/

Multi-aged Play Groups
1. Gray, Peter PhD. Free to Learn: Why Unleashing the Instinct
    to Play will Make Our Children Happier, More Self-reliant,
    and Better Students for Life. Basic Books, 2013.

Learning Differences
1. *The Dyslexic Advantage: Unlocking the Hidden Potential of the
    Dyslexic.* Plume, July 31, 2012.
2. *Two States. Eight Text Books. Two American Stories.* Dana
    Goldstein, New York Times, Jan. 2020. https://www.nytimes.
    com/interactive/2020/01/
    12/us/texas-vs-california-history-textbooks.html?action=
    click&module=Well&pgtype=Homepage&section=Education
3. *How Much Do You Know About Dyslexia?* Richard Branson,
    The Virgin Foundation, 2017. https://www.virgin.com/
    richard-branson/how-much-do-you-know-about-dyslexia
4. *Dyslexia in the Prison Population*, Kathryn Currier
    Moody, Ph.D, Education Up-date, 2000. http://www.
    educationupdate.com/archives/2008/DEC/html/spec--
    dyslexia.html
5. *The Dyslexic Advantage*, Fernette Eide, MD and Brock Eide
    ,MD, MA., Plume, reprinted 2012.
6. The Understood Team. https://www.understood.org/en/
    learning-thinking-differences/child-learning-disabilities/
    executive-functioning-issues/what-is-executive-function

Kindergarten Readiness
1. *Early Childhood Education in Finland*, Becky Searls. Medium, May 2017. https://mapmates.org/early-childhood-education-i n-finland-21dd0cb728fb

Chapter 26: Let's Talk Serious Safety

Car Seats
1. California Highway Patrol, Child Safety Seats. https://www. chp.ca.gov/programs-services/programs/child-safety-seats

Chapter 27: Toxins, Fear and Evaluating Relative Risk
1. *Your Receipts Could Be Making You Sick.* Jacob Passey, Market Watch, Jan. 2018. https://www.marketwatch.com/story/ your-receipts-could-be-making-you-sick-2018-01-17
2. *Why Is Glyphosate Sprayed On Crops Right Before Harvest?* Ken Roseboro, EcoWatch, March 2016. https://www.ecowatch. com/roundup-cancer-1882187755.html
3. *Lead In Food, Foodwares, And Dietary Supplements.* FDA, Feb. 2020. https://www.fda.gov/food/metals-and-your-food/ lead-food-foodwares-and-dietary-supplements
4. GreenFacts.org https://www.greenfacts.org/en/mercury/l-3/ mercury-4.htm#0p0
5. *Contaminants in Orcas*, Port Townsend Marine Science Center. https://ptmsc.org/programs/investigate/citizen-science/ completed-projects/orca-project/contaminants-in-orcas

BIBLIOGRAPHY

BOOKS:

1. Abeles, Vicki and Rubenstein, Grace. *Beyond Measure: Rescuing an Overscheduled, Overtested, Underestimated Generation.* Simon and Schuster, 2015.
2. Alexandra, Jessica Joelle and Sandahl, Iben. *The Danish Way Of Parenting: What The Happiest People In The World Know About Raising Confident Capable Kids.* Tachere Peigie, 2016.
3. Armstrong, Thomas PhD. *The Myth Of The ADHD Child: 101 Ways To Improve Your Child's Behavior And Attention Span Without Drugs, Labels, Or Coercion.* Penguin Random House, 2017.
4. Au, Sara and Stavinoha PhD, Peter. *Stress-free Potty Training: a Commonsense Guide to Finding the Right Approach for Your Child.* AMACOM American Management Association, 2008.
5. Braaten, Ellen and Willoughby, Brian. *Bright Kids Who Can't Keep Up: Help Your Child Overcome Slow Processing Speed And Succeed In A Fast-Paced World.* Guilford Press, 2014.
6. Brooks, Kim. *Small Animals: Parenthood In The Age Of Fear.* Flatiron Books, 2018.
7. Chapman, Gary. *The 5 Love Languages: the Secret to Love That Lasts.* Northfield Pub., 2015.
8. Christakis, Erika. *The Importance of Being Little: What Young Children Really Need from Grown Ups.* Penguin Books, 2017.
9. Cockrell, Stacie and O'Neill, Cathy and Stone, Julia. *Babyproofing Your Marriage: How to Laugh More and Argue Less as Your Family Grows.* Harper Collins, 2007.
10. Cox PhD., Adam J. *Cracking the Boy Code: How to Understand and Talk with Boys.* Canada, New Society Publishers, 2018.

11. Dalai Lama and Vreeland, Nicholas. *An Open Heart: Practicing Compassion in Everyday Life.* Bay Back Books, 2004.

12. Daniluck PhD., Judith C. *The Infertility Survival Guide: Everything You need to know to Cope with the Challenges While Maintaining Your Sanity, Dignity, and Relationships.* New Harbinger Publications, 2001.

13. Doucleff, PhD., Michaeleen. *Hunt, Gather, Parent: What Ancient Cultures Can Teach Us About The Lost Art Of Raising Happy Helpful Humans*, Avid Reader Press, 2021.

14. Druckerman, Pamela. *Bringing Up Bebe.* Penguin Press, 2012.

15. Duhamel PhD., Thomas R. *The Ins and Outs of Poop.* Maret Publishing, 2012.

16. Dunn, Jancee. *How Not To Hate Your Husband After Kids.* Little Brown and Comp., 2018.

17. Eide, Brock and Fernett MDs. *The Dyslexic Advantage: Unlocking the Hidden Potential of the Dyslexic.* Plume, 2012.

18. Epstein, David. *Range: Why Generalists Triumph In A Specialized World.* Riverhead Books, 2019.

19. Flink, David. *Thinking Differently: An Inspiring Guide For Parents Of Children With Learning Disabilities.* Harper Collins, 2014.

20. Friedan, Betty, *The Feminine Mystique.* WW Norton Publishing, 1963.

21. Friedman, PhD., Joan. *Emotionally Healthy Twins: A New Philosophy for Parenting Two Unique Children.* Da Capo Press, 2008.

22. Galinsky, Ellen. *The Six Stages Of Parenthood.* Da Capo Press, 1981.

23. Gray, Peter PhD. *Free to Learn: Why Unleashing the Instinct to Play will Make Our Children Happier, More Self-reliant, and Better Students for Life.* Basic Books, 2013.

24. Gross-Loh, Christine. *Parenting Without Borders: Surprising Lessons Parents Around the World Can Teach Us.* The Penguin Group, 2013.

25. Heitner, Devorah PhD. *Screenwise: Helping Kids Thrive And Survive In Their Digital World.* Bibliomotion, 2016.
26. Hoefle, Vicki. *Duct Tape Parenting.* Bibliomotion inc., 2012.
27. Karp, Harvey MD. *The Happiest Baby on the Block.* Bantam Revised, 2015.
28. Karp, Harvey MD. *The Happiest Toddler on the Block.* Bantam Revised, 2008.
29. Kazdin, PhD, Alan E. *The Kazdin Method for Parenting the Defiant Child.* First Mariner Books, 2009.
30. Kindlon, PhD., Dan, and Thompson, PhD. Michael, *Raising Cain: Protecting the Emotional Life of Boys.* Ballantine Books, 2000.
31. Lareau, Annette. *Unequal Childhoods: Class, Race, and Family Life.* University of CA Press, 2011.
32. Le Billon, Karen. *Getting to Yum: the Seven Secrets of Raising Eager Eaters.* Harper Collins Publishers, 2014.
33. Lerner, Harriet. *The Dance of Anger.* Harper Collins, 1985.
34. McCraith, Sheila. *Yell Less, Love More: How The Orange Rhino Mom Stopped Yelling At Her Kids And How You Can Too!* Fair Winds Press, 2014.
35. Meeker MD, Meg. *Boys Should Be Boys: 7 Secrets to Healthy Sons.* Ballantine Books, 2008.
36. Millwood, Molly PhD. *To Have And To Hold: Motherhood, Marriage, And The Modern Dilemma.* Harper Collins, 2019.
37. Orenstein, Peggy. *Cinderella Ate My Daughter: Dispatches from the Front Lines of the New Girlie-girl Culture.* Harper, 2011.
38. Pantley, Elizabeth. *The No-Cry Separation Anxiety Solution.* McGraw Hill, 2010.
39. Partanen, Anu. *The Nordic Theory Of Everything.* Harper Paperbacks, 2019.
40. Pica, Rae. *What if Everybody Understood Child Development.* Corwin, 2015.
41. Rayworth, Kate. *Doughnut Economics: 7 Ways to Think Like a 21ˢᵗ Century Economist.* Chelsea Green Pub., 2018.

42. Rope, Kate. *Strong As A Mother: How To Stay Healthy, Happy, And Most Importantly Sane From Pregnancy To Parenthood*. St. Martin's Griffin, 2018.

43. Russel, Helen. *The Year Of Living Danishly: Uncovering The Secrets Of The Worlds Happiest People*. Icon Books, 2016.

44. Satter, Ellyn. *Child of Mine: Feeding with Love and Good Sense*. Bull Publishing, 2000.

45. Satter, Ellyn MS. *Secrets Of Feeding A Healthy Family: How To Eat, How To Raise Good Eaters, How To Cook*. Kelcy Press, 2008.

46. Sax MD PhD, Leonard. *Boys Adrift: The Five Factors Driving the Growing Epidemic of Unmotivated Boys and Underachieving Young Men*. Basic Books, 2007.

47. Sax MD PhD, Leonard. *Girls On the Edge: the Four Factors Driving the New Crisis for Girls*, Basic Books, 2020.

48. Schumaker, Heather. *It's OK To Go Up The Slide: Renegade Rules For Raising Confident And Creative Kids*. Tarcher Penguin, 2016.

49. Senior, Jennifer. *All Joy, No Fun: the Paradox of Modern Parenthood*. Ecco, 2015.

50. Spencer, Paula. *Momfidence! An Oreo Never Killed Anybody and Other Secrets of Happy Parenting*. Three Rivers Press, 2006.

51. Sole-Smith, Virginia. *The Eating Instinct: Food Culture, Body Image, And Guilt In America*. Henry Holt and Co., 2018.

52. Stack, Megan. *Women's Work: A Reckoning With Home And Help*. DoubleDay, 2019.

53. Traig, Jennifer. *Act Natural: A Cultural History Of Misadventures In Parenting*, Ecco, 2019.

54. Trasande, Leonardo MD, MPP. *Sicker, Poorer, Fatter: The Urgent Threat Of Hormone-Disrupting Chemicals To Our Health And Future…And What We Can Do About It*. Houghton, Mifflin, Harcourt, 2019.

55. Waldburger LCSW, Jennifer and Jill Spivack, LCSW. *The Sleep Easy Solution*. Health Communications Inc., 2007.

56. Whippman, Ruth. *America The Anxious*. Griffin, 2017.

ARTICLES:

1. *The Relentlessness of Modern Parenting*, Claire Cain Miller, New York Times, 12/25/2018.
2. *The Special Misogyny Reserved For Mothers*, Hilary Frank, New York Times, 12/31/2018.
3. *Raising Kids Isn't Easy. Parenting Advice Often Makes It Harder*, Jennifer Sazali, New York Times, 1/2/2019.
4. How Millennials Became The Burnout Generation, Anne Helen Petersen, Buzzfeed News, 1/5/2019.
5. *The Particular Horror Of Long Commutes For Young Families*, Marsha Rommer, New York Times, 10/31/2018.
6. *Why Sports Parents Sometimes Behave So Badly*, Emilie Le Beau Lucchesi, New York Times, 11/2018.
7. *Why You Should Stop Yelling At Your Kids*, Stephen Marche, New York Times, 9/2018.
8. *In The Country Of Motherhood, Finding My Own Path*, Olga Mecking, New York Times, 1/18/19.
9. *Why Girls Beat Boys At School And Lose To Them At The Office: Hard Work And Discipline Help Girls Outperform Boys In Class, But That Advantage Disappears In The Work Force. Is School The Problem?* Lisa Damour, New York Times, 1/7/2019.
10. *Day Care For All: The Progressive To-Do List Is Missing A Very Important Idea.* Katha Pollitt, New York Times, 2/9/19.
11. *The Perpetual Panic Of American Parenthood*, Pamela Druckerman, New York Times, 10/13/2016.
12. *The Real Mommy War Is Against The State: Stop Blaming Yourselves. Blame The Total Lack Of Social Supports.* Caitlyn Collins, New York Times, 2/9/2019.
13. *Americans Are Having Fewer Babies They Told Us Why*, Claire Cain Miller, New York Times, 4/5/2018.
14. *Millennials Are Putting Off Having Kids. We Already Have Two: Becoming A Parent Before Your Friends Have Even*

Considered It Comes With A Unique Set Of Challenges, Ivan Caveny, New York Times, 3/12/19.

15. *Rick Steves Wants To Set You Free*, Sam Anderson, New York Times, 3/2019.

16. *How to Minimize Exposure to Hormone Disrupters*, Perry Klass, MD, New York Times, 4/1/19.

17. *Chemicals in Food May Harm Children Pediatrician's Group Says*, Roni Rabin, New York Times, 7/23/18.

18. *Food Additives and Child Health*, American Academy of Pediatrics, 8/2018.

19. *BPA In Cans And Bottles Linked To Rapid Rise In BP*, New York Times, Anahad O'Connor, 12/8/2014.

20. *How To Avoid The Sneakiest Sources Of BPA*, Jennifer Grayson, Huffington Post, 2/9/2010.

21. *The Burden Of Parent Homework*, Karen Barrow, New York Times, 3/27/19.

22. *How to Raise Vegetable Eaters*, Rachel Cernansky, New York Times, 4/3/19.

23. *The Data All Guilt-Ridden Parents Need: What Science Tells Us About Breast-Feeding, Sleep Training And All The Agonizing Decisions Of Parenthood*, Emily Oster, New York Times, 4/19/2019.

24. *Giving Birth Landed Me in the Psych Ward*, Lisa Abramson, New York Times, 9/27/19.

25. *Early Motherhood Has Always Been Miserable: "I declare if I tho't I was to be thus occupied for the rest of my life," one new mom wrote in 1828, "I would lie down & die."* Jessica Grosse, New York Times, 11/9/2019.

26. *The Truth About Pregnancy Over 40: More Than 100,000 Americans Give Birth In Their 40s Each Year, But What Does That Mean For The Health Of Their Pregnancies And Their Babies?* Reyhad Harmanci, New York Times, 11/12/2019.

27. *The Unbearable Sensation Of Being: Some Kids Find Everyday Stimuli Excruciating. Scientist Are Finally Figuring Out Why.* Claire Conway, UCSF Magazine, summer 2018.

28. *Sugar Is Not The Enemy. Myths About Hyperactivity And Sugar In Children Persist, Despite Evidence That Debunks The Connection.* Virginia Sole-Smith, New York Times, 3/17/2020.

29. *Sweden Is Apparently Full Of 'Latte Dads' Carrying Toddlers — And It's A Sign Of Critical Social Change.* Libby Kane, Insider, 4/4/2018

30. *Post-Partum Anxiety: The Other Baby Blues We Need To Talk About. Parents*, Stacy Colino and Nicole Fabian-Weber, 2/10/2020.

31. *Pioneers In Our Field: Freidrich Froebel, Founder Of The First Kindergarten.* Early Childhood Today Editorial Staff, Scholastic Inc., 2021.

32. *A Brief History of kindergarten.* Angèle Sancho Passe. Published by Redleaf Press, p. 42, 2010.

33. *Don't Dismiss that 30 Million Word Gap Quite So Fast*, Robert Pondiscio. EducationNext, 6/6/2019.

34. *The Neuroscience of 20-Somethings*, Ferris Jabr. Scientific American, 8/29/12.

35. *Does Early Reading Instruction Help Reading In The Long-Term? A Review Of Empirical Evidence.* Sebastian Paul Suggate, Rosejourn, 7/2013.

36. *Early Educational Milestones As Predictors Of Lifelong Academic Achievement, Midlife Adjustment, And Longevity*, Margaret L. Kern and Howard S. Friedman, J Appl Dev Psychol. 2008.

37. *The Sooner, The Better: Early Reading To Children*, Frank Niklas, Caroline Cohrssen, Collette Tayler, Sage, 10/1/2016.

38. *How Do Kids Learn To Read? What The Science Says.* Sarah Schwartz & Sarah D. Sparks, Education Week, 10/2/2019.

39. *Independent Reading And The 'Social Turn': How Adolescent Reading Habits And Motivation Relate To Cultivating Social Relationships.* Matthew Knoester, Networks, Spring 2010.

40. *Early Academic Training Produces Long-Term Harm Research Reveals Potential Risks Of Academic Preschools And Kindergartens.* Peter Gray, Psychology Today, 5/5/2015.
41. *Reading Instruction In Kindergarten: Little Gain And Much To Lose.* Nancy Carlsson-Paige, Geralyn Bywater McLaughlin, & Joan Wolfsheimer Almon, Alliance for Childhood.
42. Women's Unpaid Work Must Be Included In GDP Calculations: Lessons From History .Luke Messac, MD, PhD. The Conversation, 6/20/2018.
43. *The Way We Measure Economies Is Inherently Sexist.* Diane Coyle, World Economic Forum, 4/2016.
44. *What The U.S. Can Learn From Finland, Where School Starts At Age 7.* Claudio Sanchez, National Public Radio, 3/8/2014.
45. *Conjugal Bonds And Wage Labor: Rights Of Contract In The Age Of Emancipation.* Amy Dru Stanley, Journal of American History, 9/1988.
46. *Lead Poisoning: A Historical Perspective*, Jack Lewis, EPA Archive, updated 9/16/2016.
47. *The Rage Mothers Don't Talk About: Mothers are supposed to be patient martyrs, so our rage festers beneath our shame.* Minna Dubin, 4/14/2020, New York Times.
48. *State of the States: Teacher Preparation Policy.* National Council on Teacher Quality, nctq.org, 3/2021. https://www.nctq.org/publications/State-of-the-States-2021:-Teacher-Preparation-Policy

ACKNOWLEDGEMENTS

This is a self-published book. I make no apologies for that. Our current publishing system is so antiquated that non-fiction authors have no hope of being considered unless they are famous or heavily credentialed. It is thanks to the many new self-publishing programs, that we continue to have the opportunity to hear the voices of the lowly masses. This is no small thing. So, thank you to the developers of these programs. Without your work, my voice and many others, would likely go unheard.

I am also deeply indebted to the many parents who have shared their wisdom and support as I transformed from parenting newbie to opinionated pontificator. You saved my life again and again, and I thank you!

Thank you, also, to all the women down the ages who have done all the silent caring, all the unpaid woman's work. To the keepers of half our culture even when unseen and unheard. Thank you to the women who have had the courage to wrest themselves free of society's constraints and to reach for something truer to themselves.

Thank you to the men who are struggling to find and be their whole self. Those who have found in fatherhood an opportunity for connection so valuable that it's worth all the hardship and challenges.

Thank you to my husband who encouraged me to write. Who continued to encourage me even when it took a long loooooong time to birth a book while learning to parent.

Many thanks to my wonderful editor, Gloria Beverage. You made this book so much better, and your inspiration propelled me through the final work.

Thank you to my parents for…well, for so so much.

ABOUT THE AUTHOR

Kathleen Cawley is a 57-year-old a physician assistant who practiced pediatric and adult medicine for 18 years. She is the mother of 12-year-old boy-girl twins, and a writer who grew up with a bunch of nerdy intellectuals.

At 39, Kathleen married a man with extraordinary energy who could match her pun for pun. Better still, an opinionated woman just made him smile.

A few years ago, Kathleen and her family moved from the cool, crowded, chaos of the San Francisco Bay Area to the unrelenting heat of the Sacramento summer sun. Currently, a fulltime at-home-mom *and* a fulltime writer, Kathleen is working on books about the politics of parenthood, parenting in the elementary school years, the new shape of fatherhood, and other issues that get her fired up. She is a regular guest columnist for the Auburn Journal where she writes about parenting. You can also find her wildly fun children's book, "Grandma Becky's Blue Tongue."

When she's not researching, writing, or herding cats, she likes to travel, paint, kayak, swim, watch re-runs of nature documentaries, and kvetch with her mom friends.

CPSIA information can be obtained
at www.ICGtesting.com
Printed in the USA
JSHW011027151222
34886JS00009B/16

9 798987 106808